Adult Attachment Patterns in a Treatment Context

Attachment theory posits that the need for attachment is a life-long phenomenon that becomes especially relevant in times of crisis or trauma. When adults experience illness, accidents, assaults, psychological difficulties, or losses, their attachment-behavioural systems are activated, motivating them to seek help and support from family and friends and/or from helping professionals. However, the resulting request for help is affected and shaped by earlier experiences regarding the support and trustworthiness of attachment figures. Can others be trusted? Is it safe to show vulnerability? How should one behave to increase the likelihood of receiving the help needed?

Adult Attachment Patterns in a Treatment Context provides an integrated introduction to the subject of adult attachment. Research into adult attachment patterns offers professional helpers a theoretically sound insight into the dynamics underlying a range of client behaviours, including some of the more puzzling and frustrating behaviours such as denying obvious pain or continually pushing the professional for more personal involvement. Sarah Daniel shows how applying knowledge of attachment patterns to treatment settings will improve the way in which professionals engage with clients and the organization of treatments. This book will be relevant to a range of helping professionals such as psychotherapists, psychologists and social workers, both in practice and in training.

Sarah I. F. Daniel is a clinical psychologist and she is currently employed as an associate professor in the Department of Psychology, University of Copenhagen.

Adult Attachment Patterns in a Treatment Context

Relationship and narrative

Sarah I. F. Daniel

Routledge
Taylor & Francis Group

LONDON AND NEW YORK

First published 2015
by Routledge
27 Church Road, Hove, East Sussex BN3 2FA

and by Routledge
711 Third Avenue, New York, NY 10017

Routledge is an imprint of the Taylor & Francis Group, an informa business

British Library Cataloguing-in-Publication Data
A catalogue record for this book is available from the British Library

Library of Congress Cataloging-in-Publication Data
A catalog record for this title has been requested

ISBN: 978-0-415-71873-8 (hbk)
ISBN: 978-0-415-71874-5 (pbk)
ISBN: 978-1-315-75393-5 (ebk)

Typeset in Times
by Cenveo Publisher Services

Contents

Illustrations

Figures

Tables

Acknowledgments

This book was translated from the Danish version *Relation og fortælling. Tilknytningsmønstre i en behandlingskontekst* (2012, Copenhagen: Samfundslitteratur) by Elizabeth Xiao-an Li and further edited and adapted by Sarah I. F. Daniel.

Figure 1.1 is based on Bartholomew, K. (1990). Avoidance of intimacy: An attachment perspective. *Journal of Social and Personal Relationships*, 7(2), 147–178, and reprinted with permission from Sage Publications Ltd.

Figure 2.1 is based on Mikulincer, M. & Shaver, P. R. (2007). *Attachment in adulthood: Structure, dynamics, and change*, New York: Guilford Publications, and reprinted with permission from Guilford Publications.

A detailed overview of the Patient Attachment Coding System is included in Table A.1 with permission from Alessandro Talia and Madeleine Miller-Bottome.

Introduction

When working as a psychologist, doctor, social worker, nurse, or in other professional caregiving roles, one meets people who, to different extents, feel weak, vulnerable, or in a crisis, and who are in need of support and care. Most people in caregiving and treatment professions choose this field of work because of a sincere desire to help others. Because of this desire to help, treatment providers may find it hard to understand or accept when clients are unwilling to receive help or to cooperate in the way proposed. However, professional caregivers commonly come across clients who are sceptical and wary, clients who are unable to express their problems, clients where cooperation proves difficult, and clients who demand more than the caregiver can offer.

Treatment providers share the challenge of avoiding frustration and finding a way to help clients who, for some reason or other, appear 'difficult' to work with. In these cases, understanding the underlying causes of a client's behaviour in treatment can prove crucial, for example, understanding the cause of the client's scepticism or understanding why some clients struggle to express and describe their problems. This book shows how current research in *attachment theory* can give insight into the background of the relational challenges encountered with some clients, and how treatment providers can manage these challenges in their work with adult clients.

The book is primarily aimed at treatment providers and counsellors in the social and health sectors, as well as students working towards a career in these professions. The book especially focuses on the treatment of individual adult clients. Although it may prove of interest to people working with couples and families, the book contains only limited discussion of the particular challenges of couples and family therapy. The aim of the book is to provide a broad introduction to the theory of and research into *adult attachment patterns*, and to show attachment patterns' relevance to different treatment forms and settings. This book therefore does not serve as an exhaustive 'manual' or instruction for psychotherapy, milieu therapy, or other treatment forms, but rather provides a theoretical perspective that can inform and be integrated into a wide range of treatment practices.

Attachment theory is relevant to the understanding of helping relationships, as it is fundamentally about relationships where one party seeks support and help from another party who, in the specific context, is stronger and/or more knowledgeable. Since the British psychiatrist John Bowlby established attachment theory in the mid-twentieth century, the majority of the published literature has been about the relationship between children and parents. It is now commonly known that children's psychological development depends on their opportunity to form attachments to one or more stable caregivers. Attachment varies in quality from secure attachment to different forms of insecure attachment depending on the caregivers' sensitivity and behaviour. Detailed knowledge exists of the correlation between the individual attachment patterns children form in relation to their central caregivers and the children's future well-being and social competences (Thompson, 2008).

Throughout the past 25 years, intensive research has been carried out into the question of how attachment patterns are developed and continued in adulthood, where the most important attachment figures are no longer parents but partners and close friends (Feeney, 2008, Mikulincer and Shaver, 2007). In attachment theory, it is a central assumption that the *attachment system* – the inborn behavioural system which motivates children to form attachments to caregivers – is active throughout life and continues to play an important role in adulthood. Thus attachment is just as relevant to adults, but naturally manifests itself differently in adults than in children.

If children fall and hurt their knees, their attachment systems are activated and they will turn to their caregivers for comfort and support. As adults we do not necessarily need to be comforted if we scrape our knee, but our attachment system still becomes activated when we are scared, sick, or feel vulnerable. When the attachment system is activated, the immediate impulse will be to seek support and comfort from the people closest to us, or (if these persons are unavailable or inadequate) perhaps from professional caregivers. However, the way in which a person approaches potential helpers will be influenced by the person's previous experience of how people have reacted to his or her desire for support and care.

For this reason, even when people seek help for a concrete problem – for example, physical illness – there is always more at stake in their relationship to the helper. Is it wise to put one's trust in another person? Is it better to be brave and suppress the pain? Or is it better to be 'on one's toes' and clearly express any problems to secure the caregivers' attention? Adult attachment patterns consist in such *expectation structures* and *action strategies* in relation to other people. These are not necessarily conscious, but are a result of one's accumulated experience in attachment relationships (Main, 1995, Mikulincer et al., 2003).

In psychotherapy, attachment patterns may be part of what one works at changing; for example, a client may wish to improve his or her ability to openly express vulnerability and need for proximity in relation to a spouse. In other situations, attachment patterns are simply conditions that influence treatment. For example, some clients have a fear of being let down or forgotten and will therefore be especially persistent in ensuring that the helper understands how much they are troubled by their back pain, or whatever the problem may be. In both cases, having knowledge of attachment and attachment patterns can be important – in the first case, to better collaborate with the client on changing the pattern; and in the second case, to better tolerate the client's personal 'style' and find the most constructive approach to treating the client.

The subtitle of this book, 'Relationship and Narrative', refers to two different 'channels' through which adults' attachment patterns are expressed, which can both affect and inform treatment. Attachment patterns are partly expressed in an *interpersonal* dimension as different forms of relational dispositions; for example, being trusting, open, dismissive, vigilant, anxious, or demanding. The interpersonal dimension of attachment patterns is relevant to all forms of treatment where the helper interacts personally with the person seeking help.

Furthermore, attachment patterns are expressed in a *narrative* dimension in the form of different patterns in the clients' narratives of themselves and their problems. These narratives can be coherent, contradictory, unemotional, confusing, unorganized, or abstract. The narrative dimension of attachment patterns is especially relevant to psychotherapy and other treatment forms involving prolonged conversations between treatment provider and client. However, some elements of the narrative dimension – for example, the inclination to either exaggerate or downplay problems – is relevant to all treatment providers.

The first part of the book provides a general introduction to adult attachment patterns and their relevance to treatment. Chapter 1 briefly describes attachment theory and the current research-based knowledge of adult attachment patterns. In Chapter 2, attachment theory's general implications for treating adult clients are outlined.

The second part of the book examines the four prototypical attachment patterns. Chapter 3 describes *secure* attachment; Chapter 4, *avoidant* attachment; Chapter 5, *ambivalent* attachment; and Chapter 6, *disorganized* attachment. All of these four chapters start by describing how the particular attachment pattern affects the interpersonal interaction between treatment provider and client, and subsequently how it is reflected in the client's narrative.

The book's third part summarizes the implications of attachment theory for the treatment of adult clients. Chapter 7 describes how to distinguish between different attachment patterns in practice and discusses the fruitfulness of classifying people according to these patterns. Chapter 8 describes how to adapt treatment style to the client's attachment pattern. Finally, Chapter 9 considers whether and how clients' attachment patterns can be changed through psychotherapeutic treatment.

Because of the broad aims of this book, it has been necessary to select a cohesive terminology, which in some cases cannot avoid being contrary to terms used in specific fields of practice. Thus the term 'treatment provider' is used throughout for the professional who enters into some form of helping relationship with one or more persons, while the service this professional supplies is termed 'treatment'. In this book, 'treatment' should therefore be understood in the broadest possible sense, covering medical treatment, psychotherapy, nursing, counselling, coaching, etc. The person seeking and/or receiving treatment is termed 'client'.

Attachment theory is related to many other psychological theories, and some readers will recognize descriptions or theoretical accounts from other contexts. Several of the central points of attachment theory are also formulated in other theories, often with slightly different concepts. Thus, not everything attachment theory has to offer is necessarily 'new' and original. In this context, the great strength of attachment theory is that it offers a cohesive terminology and draws on a large and continually increasing base of empirical research that underpins its theoretical points.

References

Fenney, J. A. 2008. Adult romantic attachment: Developments in the study of couple relationships. In Cassidy, J. & Shaver, P. (eds) *Handbook of attachment: Theory, research, and clinical applications*, 2nd ed. New York: Guilford Press.

Main, M. 1995. Recent studies in attachment: Overview, with selected implications for clinical work. In Goldberg, S. & Muir, R. (eds) *Attachment theory: Social, developmental, and clinical perspectives*. Hillsdale, NJ: Analytic Press.

Mikulincer, M. & Shaver, P. R. 2007. *Attachment in adulthood: Structure, dynamics, and change*, New York: Guilford Press.

Mikulincer, M., Shaver, P. R. & Pereg, D. 2003. Attachment theory and affect regulation: The dynamics, development, and cognitive consequences of attachment-related strategies. *Motivation and Emotion*, 27, 77–102.

Thompson, R. A. 2008. Early attachment and later development: Familar questions, new answers. In Cassidy, J. & Shaver, P. (eds) *Handbook of attachment: Theory, research, and clinical applications*, 2nd ed. New York: Guilford Press.

Part I

Adult attachment patterns and treatment relationships

Chapter 1

Adult attachment patterns

Attachment theory is a psychological theory originating in the work of British psychiatrist John Bowlby in the mid-twentieth century. In his central three-volume work, *Attachment and Loss*, he considered what proximity to consistent caregivers means to a child's development, as well as the psychological effects of loss or separation from caregivers (Bowlby, 1969, 1973, 1980). Bowlby's theory has since been extended and elaborated by a number of researchers throughout the world and attachment theory continues to be a field of rapid growth.

The aim of this chapter is to provide a general introduction to attachment theory and more specifically to adult attachment patterns. The chapter will not provide an exhaustive account of attachment theory and the connected research, and the description of research in children's attachment will be kept to a general level. The purpose of the chapter is to provide an account of attachment and adult attachment patterns detailed enough to form the background knowledge necessary for the book's second and third parts, in which specific attachment patterns are discussed in a treatment context. A number of the properties of adult attachment patterns introduced in this chapter will be discussed in greater depth in the book's second part, where each pattern is described individually.

Theoretical and historical roots: attachment in childhood

In the wake of the Second World War, many children had lost their parents or been separated from them for longer periods of time. The World Health Organization therefore asked the child psychiatrist Bowlby to draw up a report of the implications that separation and loss had for children's mental health. Attachment theory emerged from Bowlby's efforts to gain a theoretical understanding of the powerful reactions he and his colleagues observed in children separated from their parents for prolonged periods of time – for example, in connection with hospitalization.

The children underwent a sequence of different reactions, first protesting violently and restlessly searching for their absent parents. Usually a phase of despair and despondent whimpering followed, which then eventually gave way to an emotional 'disconnection', where the children appeared to give up recovering the relationship with their parents. At this point the children no longer reacted with joy when reunited with their parents, but reacted instead with seemingly 'flat' indifference (Bowlby, 1973, Kobak and Madsen, 2008).

The evolutionary basis of attachment

In order to understand the significance of children's emotional ties to their parents, Bowlby turned to evolutionary psychology. Evolutionary psychology is concerned with the roots of different psychological phenomena in the evolutionary history of humans. In contrast to the dominant view at the time – that children become attached to their parents because they provide them with food – Bowlby claimed (1969) that the impulse to attach to caregivers is an expression of a *primary inborn motivational system*, which is directly related to the survival of mankind. Children thus enter the world with an instinctive drive to attach to caregivers; a need which is just as powerful as the need for food or sleep.

Compared to most baby animals, the human child is extremely helpless and depends on long-term protection and care from adults in order to survive. The inborn behavioural and motivational system – the *attachment system* – serves to ensure that infants stay in continual physical proximity to adults who will take care of them. The need for attachment is so basic that a child will also become attached to 'caregivers' who are not caring at all, but are on the contrary rejecting or even violent, as long as these are the dominant adults in the child's life.

According to Bowlby (1969) the attachment system functions as a 'cybernetic', that is, a goal-oriented system similar to a thermostat. The goal of the system is the security provided by physical closeness to the caregiver. In safe situations, when the child is lively and in good form, the attachment system is on standby, and the child is busy exploring the world. However, if there are signs of danger – for example, if surroundings are unfamiliar, if strangers are present, or if the child is unwell or has been hurt – the attachment system is activated and the child will draw closer to the caregiver or start crying to summon the caregiver. Once the child has had sufficient contact with the caregiver and no longer feels threatened or insecure, the attachment behaviour is interrupted and the child calms down. All parents will recognize this small 'drama', which is repeated every day and innumerable times throughout the life of a small child; it is not damaging to the child, but an inevitable part of any childhood.

However, something that is damaging to small children is prolonged periods of time without regular contact with one or more consistent caregivers. Children who grow up in institutions where staff constantly changes may thus develop serious mental and emotional problems even if they never experience lack of food or physical care (Rutter, 2008). Loss or prolonged separation from caregivers similarly has significant psychological consequences and, for example, increases the risk of depression later in life (Kobak and Madsen, 2008). Presently, we are seeing a rapid expansion of our knowledge about the significance of attachment relationships for the early development of children's brains, and about how experiences in attachment relationships can affect future development, also on a neurobiological level (Polan and Hofer, 2008).

Ainsworth's Strange Situation and individual differences

Although Bowlby's ideas about the significance of attachment for psychological development were based on his experiences from clinical work and observation, he was very much a theorist. Today attachment theory is strongly associated with an empirical research tradition due to Bowlby's fruitful collaboration with the Canadian-American psychologist Mary Ainsworth. Ainsworth set out to study how attachment between children and parents took place in practice and she conducted thorough observational studies of infants and mothers in both Uganda and USA.

To observe the attachment system in action in a controlled environment, she invented the so-called Strange Situation, which is the most important method for examining attachment patterns between children of the age of 1 and their caregivers (Ainsworth et al., 1978). The Strange Situation is conducted in a laboratory room, which is fitted out with different exciting toys, and involves two short separations and reunions between child and caregiver. During the first separation, the child is alone in the room with a stranger, and during the second separation the child is completely alone (Solomon and George, 2008).

In her studies, Ainsworth focused on the attachment relationship between child and mother. On the basis of attachment theory as it was formulated at that time, she expected that all children not subjected to long-term separation from their mothers would behave in the same way in the Strange Situation: they would become anxious due to the unfamiliar situation and stranger, but be soothed by their mother. They would protest when their mother left, but calm down once she returned. However, it turned out that the children reacted to the separation from, and reunion with, their mothers in markedly different ways (Ainsworth et al., 1978).

More than half of the children reacted as Ainsworth expected them to. Another group was not visibly worried by the situation, did not protest when the mother left and ignored her when she returned. Finally, one group was greatly agitated even while the mother was still in the room, protested violently when she left, and reacted ambivalently, alternating between clinging to her and angrily rejecting her when she returned. These ways of reacting were considered expressions of three different patterns of attachment, one of which was secure and two of which constituted different types of insecurity. As already mentioned, the first pattern made up more than half of the children Ainsworth observed, and was termed *secure* attachment. The second pattern was termed *avoidant* attachment, and the third pattern was termed *ambivalent* attachment. Ainsworth's work thus constituted the starting point for the extensive research since carried out in attachment patterns or individual differences in the quality of attachment.

Attachment patterns and caregiving environment

Based on her detailed home observations of children and their mothers, Ainsworth was able to relate the children's reactions in the Strange Situation to specific patterns in the children's everyday interaction with their mothers (Ainsworth et al., 1978). The securely attached children's mothers were attentive to their signals and were quick to react with comfort and care when the children displayed a need for this. The mothers of avoidant children emphasized independence and were dismissive when their children sought comfort. The ambivalent children's mothers were more unpredictable: at times they were warm and caring; at other times, absent or preoccupied with their own concerns.

The correlation between sensitive response to children's attachment behaviour and secure attachment in children has later been confirmed by a large number of studies (Belsky and Fearon, 2008, De Wolff and van Ijzendoorn, 1997). Furthermore, studies following children who were observed in the Strange Situation study at the age of 1 have indicated that secure attachment is related to a number of positive emotional and social competences later in life, while inse-cure attachment involves a risk of developing problems later on (Thompson, 2008). However, it is important to bear in mind that insecure attachment is not 'abnormal' or pathological. Up to half of all children in middle-class families without any particular problems are insecurely attached. Nor is insecure attach-ment synonymous with what is termed 'attachment disorders' in child psychiatry diagnostics, which is a much more rare and serious phenomenon (DeKlyen and Greenberg, 2008).

According to attachment theory, secure, avoidant, and ambivalent attachment in children are all the result of a relevant adjustment to the family environment into which children are born. To express and regulate attachment needs, children 'select' the strategy that provides the greatest possible degree of security and support in relation to their particular caregivers (Main, 1995, Weinfield et al., 2008). If caregivers are available and responsive to attachment signals, it is most appropriate for children to express attachment needs clearly and straightforwardly. If caregivers emphasize independence and reject children when they cry and desire proximity, the children learn to suppress tears and turn attention away from attachment needs. In this way, the children are better able to maintain proximity to their caregivers and thus gain a certain degree of security. If caregivers are available and responsive at times, but at other times are not, children become hypervigilant of signs indicating the caregivers' state of mind and learn to exag-gerate the expression of attachment needs to ensure their attention.

Although insecure attachment patterns may be considered as children's appropri-ate adjustment to their social environment, these patterns do, however, involve a number of costs for these children compared to children with secure attachment patterns. In the child's first year, and later, there is a close relationship between the attachment system and the *exploration system*, which is the inborn behavioural system that prompts the child to explore surroundings and learn new things. The child is only capable of exploring surroundings if he or she feels safe – that is, if the child's attachment system is not activated (Ainsworth et al., 1978).

The attachment system of the ambivalently attached child, who is constantly in doubt as to whether the caregiver is available for comfort if needed, is overactive. This means that the child struggles to find peace to play and learn. In contrast, the avoidantly attached child strives to deactivate the attachment system. However, this can only be done by turning attention away from one's own feelings and the interpersonal interaction with the caregiver. The avoidant strategy results in a reduced capacity to identify and describe feelings and in not learning to rely on other people when experiencing hard times. Although the avoidant child is more free to explore the surroundings than the ambivalent child, keeping the attachment system 'at bay' requires great effort, and is done at the expense of attention to feelings and relationships (Main, 1995).

Organized and disorganized attachment

Common to all three attachment patterns mentioned so far is the fact that they form an organized and coherent 'strategy' for managing the attachment system. Whereas secure attachment represents the most flexible regulation of the attachment system, avoidant attachment is connected with a systematic *deactivation* of the attachment system, while ambivalent attachment is connected with a systematic *hyperactivation* of the attachment system.

However, by closely studying video recordings of the Strange Situation, one of Ainsworth's students, the American psychologist Mary Main, noticed that one group of children could not be clearly classified according to the three organized patterns (Main and Solomon, 1986). These children exhibited changing or contradictory strategies or a complete collapse of strategies when facing the Strange Situation. For example, some approached the caregiver when reunited, but would simultaneously turn their heads away. Others would simply sit rocking back and forth or remain completely motionless. Main and her colleagues described these types of behaviours as an expression of a fourth attachment pattern, *disorganized* attachment, which is especially frequent among children who have been subjected to abuse or serious neglect.

Later research has shown that children with disorganized attachment patterns often find their caregivers frightening, either because their behaviour towards the child is hostile or inappropriate, or because the caregivers themselves were traumatized and therefore become overwhelmed and incapable of supporting the child when needed (Lyons-Ruth and Jacobvitz, 2008). This creates an unsolvable dilemma for the child. The child's attachment system urges the child to seek comfort from caregivers when scared. However, if the caregiver is simultaneously the source of fear, the child experiences irreconcilable impulses to simultaneously approach and withdraw from the caregiver.

Like the 'organized' insecure attachment patterns, disorganized attachment is not in itself a sign of mental illness in a child. However, out of the four attachment patterns it is the pattern most systematically connected to mental problems in the long term (Dozier et al., 2008, Greenberg, 1999).

Infant attachment patterns are relationship-specific

The majority of research in child attachment has focused on children's relationship with their mothers. This may partly be for cultural reasons and because it can be easier to recruit mothers than fathers for research projects of long duration. However, this does not mean that children do not become attached to fathers or other consistent caregivers, such as grandparents or older siblings. Most children have more than one attachment figure and will prefer different attachment figures in different situations; for example, preferring their father when in unfamiliar surroundings and preferring their mother when ill.

An important point regarding attachment patterns in early childhood is that they are *relationship-specific*. Thus, studies in which the same child has been observed in the Strange Situation with both mother and father show that the child's attachment to each parent can vary. For example, the child may be securely attached to his father and avoidantly attached to his mother (Steele et al., 1996). At this time in childhood, attachment patterns are a feature of a *relationship* rather than a feature of the child.

The relationship-specific nature of attachment patterns is one of the most important arguments against the claim that attachment patterns have nothing to do with the quality of parents' care, but are rather linked to inborn traits such as temperament. Existing research – for example, twin studies – indicate that attachment patterns are not inborn, genetically determined features, but rather a product of children's interaction with their environments (Fraley et al., 2013, Vaughn et al., 2008).

Thus, the tendency for attachment patterns to be passed down through generations does not mean that these patterns are a genetically inherited trait, but rather indicates a 'psychological' inheritance, in which ways of managing the attachment system are passed on to children through patterns in the way they are cared for (Bretherton, 1990, van Ijzendoorn and Bakermans-Kranenburg, 1997). A parent who has learned to hold back tears and 'be brave' may, for instance, struggle to endure his child's tears, because they represent something the parent attempts to avoid contact with. For this reason, avoidant parents may directly or indirectly encourage their child to suppress signs of vulnerability.

Although a child's attachment pattern initially only 'exists' in the relationship in which it has arisen, with time it will become part of the child's general psychological makeup, and the child will carry this into other relationships. In the early exchanges with attachment figures, children learn basic aspects of security and care that will be significant for the children's later psychological development and ultimately when becoming parents themselves.

Further development of childhood attachment patterns

Bowlby was a psychoanalytically trained psychiatrist, and one of his most important reasons for working with attachment and attachment relationships was the significance of these for long-term mental health and well-being. The majority of research in attachment theory has centred on the relationship between young children and their caregivers, and the theory's greatest impact has been related to the care of infants and toddlers. Nevertheless, attachment theory is a theory about lifelong development (Ainsworth, 1989), and there has been a gradual increase in research into attachment in later childhood, adolescence and adulthood. Thus, we can begin to observe how attachment experiences in early childhood are consolidated and extended in adulthood (Mikulincer and Shaver, 2007).

Internal working models

A central concept in attachment theory's account of the development and continuation of attachment patterns throughout life is the concept 'internal working model' (Bowlby, 1969, Bretherton and Munholland, 2008). The internal working model is established during early interaction with caregivers and constitutes the child's inner 'representation' or 'knowledge base' of attachment. This working model gradually becomes more complex, partly as a result of the child's biological maturation and partly as a direct result of the child's relational experiences.

In the first years of life, the child forms representations of relationships on a *procedural* level, as non-verbal knowledge of how to behave when interacting with others. With language acquisition the child also becomes capable of representing relationships on a *semantic* level as linguistic generalizations, and later also on an *episodic* level as a conscious recollection of concrete, experienced events (Bretherton, 1990, Crittenden, 1990). The verbal interplay with caregivers plays an important role, as the child's first semantic generalizations concerning relationships are mainly drawn from here, just as caregivers participate in 'rehearsing' the child's first conscious recollections through dialogue about experienced events (Harley and Reese, 1999).

The function of the internal working model is to provide predictability in the child's attachment interactions, so the child can act in the most suitable way when interacting with caregivers (Bowlby, 1969). Long before acquiring language, the child will already have acquired knowledge about the special 'rules' that apply in interaction with caregivers – rules of what experiences to expect when the attachment system is activated, and how best to approach caregivers. Naturally, none of this is the result of conscious deliberation or 'strategizing' on the child's part, but rather practice-based, procedural learning. On a physical, procedural level, parts of this learning will continue into adulthood and may be expressed through varying comfort zones for physical contact or different ways of establishing or avoiding eye contact.

As the child begins to master language, the child will also begin to make use of semantic generalizations, which are initially appropriated from caregivers, for example, "Brave boys don't cry." However, children will quickly start making their own verbal generalizations. Such attitudes or generalizations relating to attachment and attachment relationships constitute a hierarchy of knowledge ranging from generalizations of 'local' validity, such as, "Daddy won't listen to me, when I'm upset", to more comprehensive, general views of self or views of life; for example, "No one will ever love me if I show weakness."

Such personal 'truths' about attachment may be a product of generalizations based on concrete attachment experiences. The view that no one will love you if you show weakness may be a personal conclusion drawn on the basis of a large number of episodes where a caregiver has been rejecting. Some of these views and attitudes to attachment will be consciously accessible, while others will largely affect a person's actions outside of conscious awareness. People with avoidant attachment patterns are not necessarily conscious of the fact that they expect others to be dismissive, yet this expectation will still mark their interpersonal interaction.

In this way, the internal working model constitutes the 'medium' through which earlier experiences from attachment relationships are carried forward and affect new relationships later in life (Berlin et al., 2008). Adults' working models consist of a complex network of different types of knowledge, with roots in different attachment relationships and different periods of the person's development (Collins et al., 2004). Because adults' working models are complex entities, the models' different components can be disconnected or in conflict.

According to Bowlby (1988), one of the characteristics of insecure attachment patterns is that certain parts of the attachment-related information are separated from other parts, perhaps even from consciousness, as part of a psychological defence. Thus, concrete episodic recollections of interaction with caregivers, who have been rejecting of expressions of attachment needs, may be in conflict with generalized semantic convictions that have been appropriated from these caregivers. A mother may assure her son that she loves him and will always take care of him, yet 'brush him off' when he is upset by saying, "Come on, give me a smile." To avoid the pain related to the experienced rejection and to maintain the idea of himself as loved and his mother as caring, the son may trivialize or 'rewrite' the significance of the rejection or simply 'forget' it. As an adult, this person will have a semantic view of his mother as loving and caring, but at the same time hold a set of episodic recollections that do not support or directly contradict this view.

Stability and change

Internal working models are dynamic in the sense that they are open to new information and change (Bretherton and Munholland, 2008). For instance, a child may have a caring and attentive mother; the child's internal working model will therefore contain an expectation that expressions of attachment needs will be met with warmth and comfort, an experience of the mother as caring, and of himself as someone who 'deserves' comfort and care. If the mother then loses her job, becomes depressed, and starts drinking, the child will gain a new set of qualitatively different experiences with a psychologically absent and irritable mother. These experiences will gradually lead to a 'revision' of the internal working model. The child will no longer have a well-founded expectation of comfort and support and will begin to experience the mother as dismissive and himself as unloved and unworthy of receiving care. If the quality of interaction with the caregiver changes radically, a secure attachment can thus be transformed into an insecure attachment or vice versa (Waters et al., 2000). This will typically relate to events such as divorce, new marriage, mental illness, changed financial circumstances, or other things that change the caregiver's conditions for functioning as a parent (Fraley et al., 2013).

However, while internal working models are open to change, they also contain an inbuilt 'resistance' to change because they influence the interpretation of relational reality. If the child with the caring mother does not experience long-term change in her emotional availability, but only a single episode in which the mother yells and rejects the child due to excessive stress, this will not result in a complete shift of the internal working model. The child will still experience the mother as fundamentally caring. Similarly, a child ambivalently attached to his father will continue to be hypervigilant to the father's availability, even if the father reacts promptly with comfort and support on a few occasions. Likewise, in later interaction with other people, the child may interpret these people's actions in light of experiences with the unreliable father: "My football coach supports me, but I know I can't count on that, and any moment he may become preoccupied by something else and forget about me." The subjective experience of other people's actions will be 'coloured' by the established working model (Collins et al., 2004).

Furthermore, internal working models are not just linked to thoughts and feelings about close relationships, but also to a set of action strategies that may turn these into self-fulfilling prophecies. People with a secure attachment pattern approach others with an immediate trust and faith that they are well-meaning, and this may generate a positive reaction from others. On the other hand, a person with an ambivalent attachment pattern, who is constantly afraid of being let down, and therefore keeps a watchful eye on other people and constantly insists on contact, can become so overwhelming for other people that they actually do abandon her and thus confirm the expectation that other people cannot be trusted. Similarly, the avoidant person, who never dares approach others for support and care because she expects to be rejected, will never get the opportunity to experience that people might be supportive and caring if she showed vulnerability.

From relationship-specific action strategies to generalized knowledge

Whereas attachment patterns in young children are relationship-specific, adult attachment patterns are generally considered more trait-like due to an *internalization* and *generalization* of the experience-based knowledge acquired from a person's attachment relationships so far (Bowlby, 1988). Just as cognitive development commonly proceeds from acquiring knowledge rooted in local situations towards obtaining more general and abstract understandings of phenomena, throughout childhood and adolescence a set of increasingly generalized views of what to expect from caregivers and other attachment figures is formed and consolidated. The internal working model ends up holding generalized views of self and other across specific attachment situations.

If a person has had qualitatively different experiences in different attachment relationships – for example, a very caring mother and a very dismissive father – this person's approach to relationships in adulthood will usually be dominated by one of these sets of expectations and strategies (Berlin et al., 2008, Fraley et al., 2011). The person will thus have a fundamental 'attitude' which is either secure or avoidant, but will likely have access to the alternate attitude or 'model' in some situations as well.

An area that still remains to be thoroughly explored by attachment-related research is the question of which factors determine the dominant model for people with 'mixed' attachment experiences (Howes and Spieker, 2008). Although for most people one can identify one way of regulating the attachment system as their primary pattern or strategy, it is important to note that most people's childhood experiences are multifaceted. Many will thus have potential access to both secure, avoidant, and ambivalent strategies, even though, for instance, an ambivalent hyperactivation of the attachment system is their primary mode of operation. The idea of attachment patterns as 'composites' will be elaborated in Chapter 7.

The two following sections will present two different methods for assessing adult attachment patterns. These two methods are both designed to measure 'generalized' attitudes and action strategies related to attachment. These attachment measures – the Adult Attachment Interview and adult attachment self-report measures – also represent the most important research traditions within the study of adult attachment patterns. These methods are especially relevant to the aim of this book because they tap into a person's general state of mind with respect to attachment, which he or she carries forward into other relationships, including treatment relationships.

The Adult Attachment Interview

The Adult Attachment Interview (AAI) is an important tool for assessing adult attachment patterns (Hesse, 2008, Main et al., 2008). The interview was developed in the mid-1980s by the previously mentioned American psychologist Mary Main and her colleagues in the context of a research project in which a group of children and their mothers were followed for several years. The children were examined in the Strange Situation at the age of 1, and were seen again at the age of 6. At this time their mothers were also interviewed about their experiences in attachment relationships.

Content and structure of the interview

The interview, which has later been expanded, consists of 20 questions with fixed rules for further probing depending on the interviewee's answers (George et al., 1996). In other words, it is a highly structured interview that does not leave room for 'individual variation' on the part of interviewers. Depending on how detailed the interviewee's answers are, the interview can last from about one to three hours. If the interview is conducted as part of a research project, it must be transcribed verbatim according to detailed guidelines.

The interviewer first asks for a brief overview of the interviewee's family situation in childhood and a general description of the childhood relationship to parents or other primary caregivers. Subsequently, the interviewee is asked to provide five adjectives describing the relationship to each childhood caregiver. Once such a list has been provided, the interviewer requests specific childhood memories to illustrate the chosen adjectives. The interview proceeds with a detailed unfolding of attachment-relevant situations in childhood such as separations from parents, being ill, or experiences of rejection. Losses and potential traumatic experiences in relation to attachment are carefully explored. Additionally, the interviewee is asked to reflect on childhood experience – for instance, by stating who they felt closest to and why, why they think their parents behaved as they did, and how they think that they have been affected by childhood experiences.

The interview is characterized by the interviewee being asked a large number of interconnected questions concerning childhood attachment experiences within a short period of time (Hesse, 2008). Some questions request general descriptions and assessments on an abstract, *semantic level*; for example, adjectives describing the relationship to parents. Other questions inquire at an *episodic level* about specific recollections of situations with the parents. In this way, inquiry is made into several 'layers' of the internal working model, and divergent parts as well as possible contradictions are revealed.

The interview also requires interviewees to reflect on childhood attachment experiences and their emotional consequences. Because of the content of the questions, the interviewee's attachment system will inevitably be activated. Thus, the interview shows the extent to which a person is able to remain focused and communicate a coherent and comprehensible narrative while emotions and thoughts related to childhood attachment are activated.

Narrative characteristics of attachment patterns

When Main and her colleagues conducted the AAI with mothers whose children had already been observed in the Strange Situation, they discovered common *narrative* features in interviews from mothers with children in the same attachment category (Main et al., 2005, 2008). The mothers were thus similar, not in terms of the contents of their narrative – their concrete childhood experiences – but in terms of the way in which they 'organized' their narrative. Today, the special narrative characteristics discovered by Main and her colleagues form the basis for the way in which the AAI is analysed or 'coded', and the relation between the AAI and Strange Situation classification has since been confirmed by a large number of independent studies (van Ijzendoorn, 1995).

In the AAI, mothers of securely attached children talked about their childhood in an open, credible, coherent, nuanced, and sufficiently detailed way. These kinds of interviews are termed *secure/autonomous* in the AAI coding system. Mothers of avoidant children were likely to list positive adjectives that they were unable to substantiate with concrete memories; to be brief, struggle to remember episodes, and downplay possible negative experiences. These interviews are termed *dismissing*. Mothers of ambivalent children recounted their childhood in a disorganized, lengthy and confusing manner, with many irrelevant details, often confusing persons and times, and they were inclined to get carried away by their emotions, for example, talking angrily and lengthily about current problems with their parents although asked about their past. These interviews are termed *preoccupied*. Later it has been discovered that mothers of children with disorganized attachment are likely to exhibit particular lapses in their narrative or signs of magical reasoning when discussing loss or traumatic experiences related to caregivers. These interviews are termed *unresolved with respect to loss or trauma.*

On the basis of the analyses relating children's attachment to narrative characteristics of the parents' AAI, a detailed manual for coding the interview has gradually been developed (Main et al., 2002). The coder reads through the interview transcription several times and assesses it on a number of different scales, especially focusing on the way the interviewee organizes the narrative of his or her attachment experiences: whether it is coherent, comprehensible, and credible. In the end, the interview is characterized as a whole as exhibiting one of the four patterns, *secure, dismissing, preoccupied*, or *unresolved*. Interviews that are unresolved with respect to loss or trauma are also assigned an alternative category that best characterizes the interview's remaining passages not concerned with loss and/or trauma. Finally, a special category is used for interviews that cannot be classified because they are characterized by a more serious lack of inner coherence or contain conflicting elements of both dismissing and preoccupied attachment. These interviews are termed *cannot classify.*

Learning to code the AAI correctly requires 18 months of special training. This ensures consistency in the way the interview is evaluated in different research groups. However, this also makes the AAI a resource-demanding tool. The different attachment categories measured with the AAI are relatively stable over time – 78–90 per cent fall into the same category when interviewed again after a period of up to 18 months – and the AAI categories are independent of the concrete interviewer. Furthermore, research has shown that AAI classifications are independent of general intelligence, language proficiency, inclination to depict oneself in a socially acceptable way, and of general memory skills (Bakermans-Kranenburg and van Ijzendoorn, 1993, Benoit and Parker, 1994, Crowell et al., 1996, Hesse, 2008, Sagi et al., 1994). In other words, it is not the case that people categorized as secure because they present a coherent narrative of their childhood are generally more intelligent or articulate. Furthermore, people categorized as dismissing because they struggle to remember concrete episodes from their childhood with which to substantiate their positive semantic generalizations do not have a poorer memory than others. Research indicates that the narrative phenomena seen in the AAI are specifically related to the study of attachment.

What does the AAI measure?

According to Main, Kaplan and Cassidy (1985), the AAI measures what they call 'states of mind with respect to attachment', which refers to different ways of relating to attachment. However, it is only to a limited extent a question of conscious 'attitudes'; rather, it is about special ways of regulating attention and emotions in relation to attachment, and these are to a large extent automatic and unconscious processes. Parallel to the avoidant child's effort to deactivate the attachment system, the dismissing interview is marked by a tendency to downplay the importance of attachment and unpleasant experiences with attachment figures and an aversion to turning attention to attachment and attachment-related emotions. This is, for example, seen in the insistence on inability to remember concrete episodes from childhood interaction with caregivers. In the preoccupied interview, a hyper-activation of the attachment system is reflected in chaotic and confusing accounts, where the interviewees get 'carried away' by their attachment-related emotions and are thus unable to create a common thread. In this way, the narrative features observed in the coding system are assumed to reflect the same differences in the regulation of the attachment system as those observed in children in the Strange Situation, but which in adults are also expressed on a linguistic level (Main, 1995).

Although people who narrate their childhood experiences coherently and comprehensibly often describe loving and caring relationships with parents, this is not always the case. In the AAI, some interviewees recount extremely difficult experiences with caregivers without downplaying these difficulties or being carried away to such an extent that their narrative becomes incoherent or incomprehensible. Such interviews are categorized as secure, and parents who are able to reflect on a troubled childhood in this way are disposed to form secure attachment relationships to their own children (Phelps et al., 1998).

Secure interviews are often characterized by a high degree of 'reflective functioning' or 'mentalization'. These two concepts describe the same phenomenon, which has increasingly gained attention in attachment literature (Fonagy and Target, 1997, Fonagy et al., 2002). 'Mentalization' refers to the ability to see and describe oneself and others as thinking and feeling beings, whose actions reflect intentions and plans, rather than solely focusing on external behaviour. Well-functioning mentalization, which is developmentally connected to secure attachment relationships, is also characterized by modesty regarding the possibility of being able to completely 'decipher' one's own and others' mental states. Thus, mentalization entails consideration of the feelings and thoughts that underlie one's own and others' actions, while being aware of the possibility of being wrong and deceiving oneself. Insecure interviews often display limited mentalization. Dismissing interviews for example lack consideration of one's own and others' thoughts and feelings, while preoccupied interviews usually take these into account, however, often expressing them with bombastic certainty, as if the interviewee is capable of reading his or her caregivers' thoughts.

It is important to note that the AAI coding system was developed in the context of developmental psychological research, which is primarily focused on the passing on of attachment patterns from parents to their children. Thus the AAI primarily has *predictive* validity, that is, a parent's attachment category in the AAI will likely predict the attachment pattern that his or her child exhibits in the Strange Situation (van Ijzendoorn, 1995). In contrast, the few studies that followed people assessed in the Strange Situation as children up until adulthood, where they were assessed with the AAI, indicate a significantly weaker connection between people's own category in the Strange Situation and their later AAI category (Fraley, 2002, Grossman et al., 2005, Pinquart et al., 2013, Waters et al., 2000). Therefore, the AAI cannot be considered a 'gauge' of a person's own childhood attachment, although there is a certain degree of stability, especially with regard to secure attachment in safe and stable environments.

Just as insecure attachment patterns in the Strange Situation are not indicative of psychopathology, insecurity in the AAI is not an expression of mental disorder either. Up to half of a normal population is categorized as insecure (van Ijzendoorn and Bakermans-Kranenburg, 1996). However, in groups diagnosed with mental disorders, insecure attachment as measured by the AAI is greatly overrepresented (Dozier et al., 2008, van Ijzendoorn and Bakermans-Kranenburg, 2008), which is often interpreted as a sign that insecure attachment forms part of the background for the development of mental disorders. However, most studies carried out in the area are cross-sectional, that is, studies in which the presence of mental disorders and attachment patterns are evaluated simultaneously. Therefore, it is not possible to infer a causal relationship in the context. It may just as well be that having a mental disorder affects one's attachment pattern towards insecurity, and it is likely that both mechanisms are at play, perhaps to different extents in different diagnostic groups. The question can only be resolved through more longitudinal studies that follow people over a length of time and where attachment patterns are measured before mental illness appears. The current knowledge in the area will be further discussed in Chapter 9.

Adult attachment questionnaires

While Main and her colleagues developed the AAI for measuring adult attachment patterns in developmental psychology, researchers in personality and social psychology became interested in the significance of attachment for adult romantic relationships. The American psychologists Cindy Hazan and Philip Shaver argued that adult romantic relationships have many important features in common with childhood attachment relationships, and that individual differences corresponding to the individual differences Ainsworth identified in children can be found in adults' ways of approaching romantic relationships (Hazan and Shaver, 1987, Zeifman and Hazan, 2008).

The early self-report measures

Hazan and Shaver (1987) created a simple questionnaire describing three different attachment patterns: *secure, avoidant* and *anxious*, corresponding to secure, avoidant, and ambivalent attachment in children. In this test, people were asked to read three short descriptions of thoughts and emotions related to romantic relationships and select the one that best described themselves. Those who endorsed descriptions of themselves as finding it easy to get close to others, being comfortable with depending on others, and not worrying about being abandoned were considered secure. People who were uncomfortable with closeness and depending on others, and who agreed to feeling nervous when others wanted more intimacy, were considered avoidant. And, finally, people who endorsed descriptions of themselves as often wanting more closeness than others and as worrying that their partners do not love them or might leave them were considered anxious.

Hazan and Shaver (1987) discovered that people's answers to this test were meaningfully connected to a number of features of their romantic relationships and recollections of experiences with their parents. Furthermore, the distribution of the three categories corresponded reasonably to the distribution normally seen in the corresponding Strange Situation categories. However, unlike the AAI, no actual longitudinal studies have been carried out in which people observed in the Strange Situation as children were followed and given the questionnaire as adults. Therefore, there is no direct documentation for the similar distribution of patterns in the Strange Situation and in Hazan and Shaver's measure actually being caused by developmental continuity.

Although many, including Hazan and Shaver, considered this early questionnaire too simple, it constituted the starting signal for a flood of research in the area. Since then, a large number of different questionnaires have been developed to measure adult attachment patterns, which in this research tradition are usually termed *attachment styles*. These questionnaires include among others, Adult Attachment Questionnaire (Simpson et al., 1996), Adult Attachment Scale (Collins, 1996), Attachment Style Questionnaire (Feeney et al., 1994) and Relationship Style Questionnaire (Griffin and Bartholomew, 1994).

Similar to Hazan and Shaver's instrument, some of these questionnaires operate with three different attachment patterns. Others divide the avoidant pattern in two, where one is characterized by *dismissing avoidance* and the other by *fearful avoidance* (Bartholomew and Horowitz, 1991). Finally a number of these questionnaires can be scored in terms of two or more continuous scales rather than as separate categories.

Global dimensions in self-reported attachment styles

Brennan, Clark and Shaver (1998) combined the questions of all existing question-naires and subjected them to a so-called factor analysis – a statistical method used to draw out the global 'factors' or dimensions, under which different questions in a questionnaire can be summarized. They discovered that the questions in the questionnaires could be accounted for by two independent dimensions: *attachment avoidance* and *attachment anxiety*. In other words, a person's attachment style as measured with these questionnaires can be characterized by one score on a scale for attachment avoidance and another score on a scale for attachment anxiety (see Figure 1.1).

The *secure* attachment style is characterized by low avoidance and low anxi-ety. The *dismissing* attachment style is characterized by high avoidance and low anxiety, and the *preoccupied* attachment style by low avoidance and high anxiety. Finally, the *fearful* style is characterized by high avoidance and high anxiety. However, there are gradual transitions between these styles, and therefore a person's response to the questionnaires can be placed anywhere within the two-dimensional coordinate system made up of the avoidance and anxiety axes.

According to Mikulincer and Shaver (2007), the scale of attachment avoidance corresponds conceptually to the deactivation dimension. The effort to deactivate the attachment system is linked to reluctance to opening up to or allowing oneself to depend on other people. The scale of attachment anxiety corresponds concep-tually to the hyperactivation dimension. Hyperactivation of the attachment system is linked to fear of being abandoned, uncertainty about a partner's love, and general worry about close relationships.

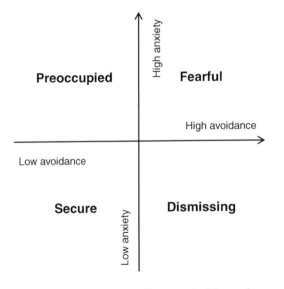

Figure 1.1 Dimensions in self-reported adult attachment patterns.

On the basis of an integrative analysis of the existing questionnaires, Brennan, Clark and Shaver developed a new questionnaire with the 36 existing questions they found best measured the two attachment dimensions. Today the Experiences in Close Relationship Scales (ECR) (Brennan et al., 1998), later revised by Fraley, Waller and Brennan (2000), is the most used questionnaire in personality and social psychological attachment research. In this questionnaire, the person is asked to evaluate 36 statements about the way he or she generally experiences close relationships (for example, with partners, close friends or relatives) on a scale from 1 to 7, where 1 corresponds to 'strongly disagree' and 7 corresponds to 'strongly agree'.

Based on a person's answers, a score for avoidance and a score for anxiety can be calculated. The answers can also be evaluated categorically to describe the person as secure, dismissing, preoccupied, or fearful. However, it is commonly agreed that attachment patterns, as they are measured by these questionnaires, can best be described as 'dimensional' phenomena with gradual transitions rather than absolute distinctions between different categories (Crowell et al., 2008).

Important theoretical and empirical distinctions

In recent years, attachment theory has gained immense popularity, which makes it important to clearly delimit its area of validity. Attachment theory is not, and does not intend to be, a 'complete' developmental psychological theory in the sense that it seeks to comprise all the dimensions of the psychological development of human beings. It emphasizes the centrality of attachment and attachment relationships in psychological development, but not necessarily at the expense of other dimensions of human life.

Thus, the attachment system is considered one of a number of inborn motivational systems. These also include the exploration system, the sociability system and the sexual/reproductive system (Cassidy, 2008), which all play a crucial role in the life of human beings, but are not the focus of attachment theory. Nor is attachment theory a theory about all interpersonal relationships or all aspects of the relationship to attachment figures, just as it is not an exhaustive personality theory.

Attachment relationships and other relationships

According to Bowlby (1969), attachment can be defined as an emotional bond to another person who cannot simply be replaced by someone else. The attachment relationship is characterized by a need to maintain proximity, distress at separation, joy at reunion, and grief at loss. Furthermore, attachment relationships are especially characterized by attachment figures functioning as a secure base for exploring the world and as a safe haven in which to seek refuge in times of adversity and anxiety (Ainsworth, 1989).

The secure base and safe haven function can literally be seen in young children, who, taking their caregiver's lap as their starting point, will venture into the world occasionally glancing back to ensure that the caregiver is still there, and if becoming startled will immediately rush back to the safe haven of their caregiver's arms. However, it is seen more subtly in the teenager, who is busy with social activities with friends yet constantly relies on his parents' support if problems arise, and it can also be seen in the woman who returns home to her partner for comfort and support after a gruelling day at work.

The concept 'attachment' is only used to refer to the party in a relationship who leans on and seeks security from the other party. Thus children are usually attached to their parents, whereas parents are not attached to their children in an attachment-theoretical sense (Broberg et al., 2008). In adult romantic relationships, both parties are attached to each other as well as being each other's attachment figure, since who seeks support and comfort and who provides it will vary from situation to situation (Feeney, 2008).

Attachment relationships are the relationships that provide us with our basic feeling of security, and they are not built from one day to the next (Marvin and Britner, 2008). There are many relationships in which it is safe to assume that attachment and attachment patterns play a limited role, for example, relationships with work colleagues. Although with time some treatment relationships can come to resemble an attachment relationship for the client, far from all treatment relationships are attachment relationships. However, this does not mean that the attachment system is not in play in the interaction between client and treatment provider. The distinction between actual attachment relationships and relationships in which attachment is brought into play will be elaborated in Chapter 2, which deals with attachment patterns' general relevance to treatment relationships.

Finally, the relationship to attachment figures contains a number of elements that have nothing in particular to do with attachment. Parent–child relationships, for example, also involve limit-setting and communication of practical skills, while adult romantic relationships also involve sexuality and social prestige. Attachment patterns tell us something about the way people behave in situations of danger, insecurity, or crisis. However, they do not necessarily tell us anything about parents' abilities to help their child with homework or how well a married couple cooperate when dealing with their finances.

Childhood attachment and adult attachment patterns

At times, the literature presents a highly deterministic interpretation of attachment theory, according to which early interaction between mother and child results in a given attachment pattern which hereafter is forever 'engraved' in the child and determines future psychological development. First of all, this does not correspond to Bowlby's ideas. Although isolated quotations from his works may be interpreted in this way, he was crucially aware of the potential for change in human beings' psychological development. Second, it does not correspond to the existing research-based knowledge in the area. One of the strengths of attachment theory is its commitment to empirical research. Even if Bowlby had been deterministically minded, it would be wrong and against his spirit to maintain this as theoretical 'dogma' when research points in a different direction.

As previously described, attachment patterns are not necessarily stable throughout childhood. Nor are they stable as the child moves from childhood into adulthood. A number of longitudinal studies following people over time from the first attachment in childhood and into early adulthood have been carried out with mixed results (Fraley, 2002, Grossman et al., 2005, Pinquart et al., 2013, Waters et al., 2000). Some studies point to moderate stability, especially with regard to the distinction between secure and insecure attachment, while others found low stability. Stability appears to be highest in groups without any special psychosocial problems, while it is lower in high-risk groups. Finally it seems that instability – that is, a shift from secure to insecure attachment or vice versa – is often meaningfully linked to intervening life events, such as the loss of a parent. Attachment relationships are changeable, as are attachment patterns.

In the discussion of whether attachment patterns are stable from childhood to adulthood, it is worth noting that the concept 'attachment pattern' signifies something different when measured at different points in development. All existing longitudinal studies have measured attachment in childhood using the Strange Situation, which measures a relationship-specific phenomenon (most often in relation to the mother) at a behavioural level, and in adulthood using the AAI, which measures a generalized phenomenon at a verbal-narrative level. 'Generalized' attachment in early childhood cannot be measured, but in reality the Strange Situation should be conducted using all the child's attachment figures if a comprehensive – and more complex – picture of the child's attachment pattern is to be drawn.

Similarly it is possible to measure adults' attachment patterns in a more relationship-specific way; for example, by using one of the customary questionnaires, but asking the person to focus on a specific relationship. An interview similar to the AAI exists, which focuses on the relationship to a current partner rather than the relationship to parents (Crowell and Owens, 1996). Studies examining both general and relationship-specific attachment patterns in adults have found that they do not always correlate. This is no surprise, as there are always two parties influencing the quality of attachment in a romantic relationship (Owens et al., 1995, Treboux et al., 2004). When evaluating the correlation between attachment in childhood and adult attachment, it is therefore important to specify the focus accurately.

The interview tradition and the self-report tradition

In the literature on attachment patterns, the terminology used is tremendously diverse and varying. Each of the different tools for measuring both child and adult attachment patterns has its own terminology. Sometimes two different concepts are used for the same phenomenon, while the same concept is at times used about two entirely different phenomena. Whereas results from different questionnaires filled out by the same people correlate to a certain extent, there is limited correspondence between attachment patterns measured with AAI and attachment patterns measured with questionnaires (Roisman et al., 2007). It is therefore possible for a person to appear avoidant/dismissing in interviews and secure in self-report tests.

The discrepancy between the interview and self-report methods are really not that surprising. They focus on different relational domains – the relation to parents in the case of the AAI, and the relation to partners in the case of most questionnaires – and they are scored and evaluated in very different ways. Although it is obvious that the two methods do not measure 'the same thing', there are still a number of areas where the same questions have been examined with both methods with similar results (Mikulincer and Shaver, 2007).

Both methods draw on the same theory, and their theoretical understanding of attachment patterns is largely similar, especially with regard to the three original patterns – secure, avoidant/dismissing, and ambivalent/preoccupied – while the AAI's special category for unresolved loss or trauma diverges more from the fearful pattern described in the self-report literature. Hopefully, in the future, more research will make use of both methods, so we can come to know more about how they are connected and which factors explain when they deviate.

The rest of this book will use the terminology of the Strange Situation – *secure, avoidant, ambivalent,* and *disorganized* – as an integrative and transverse denomination of adult attachment patterns. This terminology has been selected because it is familiar to many in the field of child psychology and is adequately descriptive, as well as to underline the fact that this book is not narrowly based on a single method. The descriptions of the four adult attachment patterns, which form the main content of the book's second part, will draw on both the interview method and the questionnaire method as both have been used in research which may prove inspiring and relevant to practitioners in treatment contexts. The concept 'attachment pattern' is therefore used in a relatively broad and 'non-technical' sense, making it suitable for practical contexts, but which is not specific enough in a research context. However, when research results are reviewed, the specific methods applied will be noted.

References

Ainsworth, M. S. 1989. Attachments beyond infancy. *American Psychologist*, 44, 709–716.

Ainsworth, M. S., Blehar, M. C., Waters, E. & Wall, S. 1978. *Patterns of attachment: A psychological study of the strange situation*. Hillsdale, NJ: Lawrence Erlbaum.

Bakermans-Kranenburg, M. J. & van Ijzendoorn, M. H. 1993. A psychometric study of the Adult Attachment Interview: Reliability and discriminant validity. *Developmental Psychology*, 29, 870–879.

Bartholomez, K. & Horowitz, L. M. 1991. Attachment styles among young adults: A test of a four-category model. *Journal of Personality and Social Psychology*, 61, 226–244.

Belsky, J. & Fearon, P. 2008. Precursors of attachment security. In Cassidy, J. & Shaver, P. (eds) *Handbook of attachment: Theory, research, and clinical applications*, 2nd ed. New York: Guilford Press.

Benoit, D. & Parker, K. C. H. 1994. Stability and transmission of attachment across three generations. *Child Development*, 65, 1444–1456.

Berlin, L. J., Cassidy, J. & Appleyard, K. 2008. The influence of early attachments on other relationships. In Cassidy, J. & Shaver, P. (eds) *Handbook of attachment: Theory, research, and clinical applications*, 2nd ed. New York: Guilford Press.

Bowlby, J. 1969. *Attachment and Loss: Vol. 1. Attachment*. London: Pimlico.

Bowlby, J. 1973. *Attachment and Loss: Vol. 2. Separation*. London: Pimlico.

Bowlby, J. 1980. *Attachment and Loss: Vol. 3. Loss*. London: Pimlico.

Bowlby, J. 1988. *A secure base: Clinical applications of attachment theory*. London: Routledge.

Brennan, K. A., Clark, C. L. & Shaver, P. R. 1998. Self-report measurement of adult attachment: An integrative overview. In Simpson, J. A. & Rholes, W. S. (eds) *Attachment theory and close relationships*. New York: Guilford Press.

Bretherton, I. 1990. Communication patterns, internal working models, and the intergenerational transmission of attachment relationships. *Infant Mental Health Journal*, 11, 237–252.

Bretherton, I. & Munholland, K. A. 2008. Internal working models in attachment relationships: Elaborating a central construct in attachment theory. In Cassidy, J. & Shaver, P. (eds) *Handbook of attachment: Theory, research, and clinical applications*, 2nd ed. New York: Guilford Press.

Broberg, A. G., Granqvist, P., Ivarsson, T. & Mothander, P. R. 2008. *Tilknytningsteori. Betydningen af nære følelsesmæssige relationer*. København: Hans Reitzel.

Cassidy, J. 2008. The nature of the child's ties. In Cassidy, J. & Shaver, P. (eds) *Handbook of attachment: Theory, research, and clinical applications*, 2nd ed. New York: Guilford Press.

Collins, N. L. 1996. Working models of attachment: Implications for explanation, emotion, and behavior. *Journal of Personality and Social Psychology*, 71, 810–832.

Collins, N. L., Guichard, A. C., Ford, M. B. & Feeney, B. C. 2004. Working models of attachment: New developments and emerging themes. In Rholes, W. S. & Simpson, J. A. (eds) *Adult attachment: Theory, research, and clinical implications*. New York: Guilford Publications.

Crittenden, P. M. 1990. Internal representational models of attachment relationships. *Infant Mental Health Journal*, 11, 259–277.

Crowell, J. A., Fraley, R. C. & Shaver, P. 2008. Measurement of individual differences in adolescent and adult attachment. In Cassidy, J. & Shaver, P. (eds) *Handbook of attachment: Theory, research, and clinical applications*, 2nd ed. New York: Guilford Press.

Crowell, J. A. & Owens, G. 1996. Current Relationship Interview and scoring system. Unpublished manuscript, State University of New York, Stony Brook.

Crowell, J. A., Waters, E., Treboux, D., O'Connor, E., Colon-Downs, C. & Feider, O. 1996. Discriminant validity of the Adult Attachment Interview. *Child Development*, 67, 2584–2599.

De Wolff, M. & van Ijzendoorn, M. 1997. Sensitivity and attachment: A meta-analysis on parental antecedents of infant attachment. *Child Development*, 68, 571–591.

DeKlyen, M. & Greenberg, M. T. 2008. Attachment and psychopathology in childhood. In Cassidy, J. & Shaver, P. (eds) *Handbook of attachment: Theory, research, and clinical applications*, 2nd ed. New York: Guilford Press.

Dozier, M., Stovall-McCough, C. & Albus, K. E. 2008. Attachment and psychopathology in adulthood. In Cassidy, J. & Shaver, P. (eds) *Handbook of attachment: Theory, research, and clinical applications*, 2nd ed. New York: Guilford Press.

..

Feeney, J. A. 2008. Adult romantic attachment: Developments in the study of couple relation-ships. In Cassidy, J. & Shaver, P. (eds) *Handbook of attachment: Theory, research, and clinical applications*, 2nd ed. New York: Guilford Press.

Feeney, J. A., Noller, P. & Hanrahan, M. 1994. Assessing adult attachment. In Sperling, M. B. & Berman, W. H. (eds) *Attachment in adults: Clinical and developmental pesrpectives*. New York: Guilford Press.

Fonagy, P., Gergely, G., Jurist, E. L. & Target, M. 2002. *Affect regulation, mentalization, and the development of the self*. New York: Other Press.

Fonagy, P. & Target, M. 1997. Attachment and reflective function: Their role in self-organization. *Development and Psychopathology*, 9, 679–700.

Fraley, R. C. 2002. Attachment stability from infancy to adulthood: Meta-analysis and dynamic modeling of developmental mechanisms. *Personality & Social Psychology Review*, 6, 123–151.

Fraley, R. C., Roisman, G. I., Booth-Laforce, C., Owen, M. T. & Holland, A. S. 2013. Interpersonal and genetic origins of adult attachment styles: A longitudinal study from infancy to early adulthood. *Journal of Personality and Social Psychology*, 104, 817–838.

Fraley, R. C., Vicary, A. M., Brumbaugh, C. C. & Roisman, G. I. 2011. Patterns of stability in adult attachment: An empirical test of two models of continuity and change. *Journal of Personality and Social Psychology*, 101, 974–992.

Fraley, R. C., Waller, N. G. & Brennan, K. A. 2000. An item response theory analysis of self-report measures of adult attachment. *Journal of Personality and Social Psychology*, 78.

George, C., Kaplan, N. & Main, M. 1996. Adult Attachment Interview, 3rd edition. Unpublished manuscript, Department of Psychology, University of California at Berkeley.

Greenberg, M. T. 1999. Attachment and psychopathology in childhood. In Cassidy, J. & Shaver, P. R. (eds) *Handbook of attachment: Theory, research, and clinical applications*. New York: Guilford Press.

Griffin, D. & Bartholomew, K. 1994. Models of the self and other: Fundamental dimensions underlying measures of adult attachment. *Journal of Personality and Social Psychology*, 67, 430–445.

Grossman, K. E., Grossman, K. & Waters, E. (eds) 2005. *Attachment from Infancy to Adulthood: The Major Longitudinal Studies*. New York: Guilford Press.

Harley, K. & Reese, E. 1999. Origins of autobiographical memory. *Developmental Psychology*, 35, 1338–1348.

Hazan, C. & Shaver, P. 1987. Romantic love conceptualized as an attachment process. *Journal of Personality and Social Psychology*, 52, 511–524.

Hesse, E. 2008. The Adult Attachment Interview: Protocol, method of analysis, and empir-ical studies. In Cassidy, J. & Shaver, P. (eds) *Handbook of attachment: Theory, research, and clinical applications*, 2nd ed. New York: Guilford Press.

Howes, C. & Spieker, S. J. 2008. Attachment relationships in the context of multiple care-givers. In Cassidy, J. & Shaver, P. (eds) *Handbook of attachment: Theory, research, and clinical applications*, 2nd ed. New York: Guilford Press.

Kobak, R. R. & Madsen, S. D. 2008. Disruptions in attachment bonds: Implications for theory, research, and clinical intervention. In Cassidy, J. & Shaver, P. (eds) *Handbook of attach-ment: Theory, research, and clinical applications*, 2nd ed. New York: Guilford Press.

Lyons-Ruth, K. & Jacobvitz, D. 2008. Attachment disorganization: Genetic factors, parent-ing contexts, and developmental transformation from infancy to adulthood. In Cassidy, J. & Shaver, P. (eds) *Handbook of attachment: Theory, research, and clinical applications*, 2nd ed. New York: Guilford Press.

Main, M. 1995. Recent studies in attachment: Overview, with selected implications for clinical work. In Goldberg, S. & Muir, R. (eds) *Attachment theory: Social, developmental, and clinical perspectives*. Hillsdale, NJ: Analytic Press.

Main, M., Goldwyn, R. & Hesse, E. 2002. Adult Attachment Scoring and Classification Systems. Version 7.1. Department of Psychology, University of California at Berkeley.

Main, M., Hesse, E. & Goldwyn, R. 2008. Studying differences in language usage in recounting attachment history: An introduction to the AAI. In Steele, H. & Steele, M. (eds) *Clinical Applications of the Adult Attachment Interview*. New York: Guilford Press.

Main, M., Hesse, E. & Kaplan, N. 2005. Predictability of attachment behaviour and representational processes at 1, 6, and 19 years of age: The Berkeley longitudinal study. In Grossman, K. E., Grossman, K. & Waters, E. (eds) *Attachment from Infancy to Adulthood: The Major Longitudinal Studies*. New York: Guilford Press.

Main, M., Kaplan, N. & Cassidy, J. 1985. Security in infancy, childhood, and adulthood: A move to the level of representation. *Monographs of the Society for Research in Child Development*, 50, 66–104.

Main, M. & Solomon, J. 1986. Discovery of a new insecure-disorganized/disoriented attachment pattern. In Brazelton, T. B. & Yogman, M. W. (eds) *Affective development in infancy*. Norwood, NJ: Ablex.

Marvin, R. S. & Britner, P. A. 2008. Normative development: the ontogeny of attachment. In Cassidy, J. & Shaver, P. (eds) *Handbook of attachment: Theory, research, and clinical applications*, 2nd ed. New York: Guilford Press.

Mikulincer, M. & Shaver, P. R. 2007. *Attachment in adulthood: Structure, dynamics, and change*, New York: Guilford Press.

Owens, G., Crowell, J. A., Pan, H., Treboux, D., O'Connor, E. & Waters, E. 1995. The prototype hypothesis and the origins of attachment working models: Adult relationships with parents and romantic partners. *Monographs of the Society for Research in Child Development*, 60, 216–233.

Phelps, J. L., Belsky, J. & Crnic, K. 1998. Earned security, daily stress, and parenting: A comparison of five alternative models. *Development and Psychopathology*, 10, 21–38.

Pinquart, M., Fuessner, C. & Ahnert, L. 2013. Meta-analytic evidence for stability in attachments from infancy to early adulthood. *Attachment & Human Development*, 15, 189–218.

Polan, H. J. & Hofer, M. A. 2008. Psychobiological origins of infant attachment and its role in development. In Cassidy, J. & Shaver, P. (eds) *Handbook of attachment: Theory, research, and clinical applications*, 2nd ed. New York: Guilford Press.

Roisman, G. I., Holland, A., Fortuna, K., Fraley, R. C., Clausell, E. & Clarke, A. 2007. The Adult Attachment Interview and self-reports of attachment style: An empirical rapprochement. *Journal of Personality and Social Psychology*, 92, 678–697.

Rutter, M. 2008. Implications of attachment theory and research for child care policies. In Cassidy, J. & Shaver, P. (eds) *Handbook of attachment: Theory, research, and clinical applications*, 2nd ed. New York: Guilford Press.

Sagi, A., van Ijzendoorn, M. H., Scharf, M. & Koren-Karie, N. 1994. Stability and discriminant validity of the Adult Attachment Interview: A psychometric study in young Israeli adults. *Developmental Psychology*, 30, 771–777.

Simpson, J. A., Rholes, W. S. & Phillips, D. 1996. Conflict in close relationships: An attachment perspective. *Journal of Personality and Social Psychology*, 71, 899–914.

Solomon, J. & George, C. 2008. The measurement of attachment security and related constructs in infancy and early childhood. In Cassidy, J. & Shaver, P. (eds) *Handbook of attachment: Theory, research, and clinical applications*, 2nd ed. New York: Guilford Press.

Steele, H., Steele, M. & Fonagy, P. 1996. Associations among attachment classifications of mothers, fathers, and their infants. *Child Development*, 67, 541–555.

Thompson, R. A. 2008. Early attachment and later development: Familar questions, new answers. In Cassidy, J. & Shaver, P. (eds) *Handbook of attachment: Theory, research, and clinical applications*, 2nd ed. New York: Guilford Press.

Treboux, D., Crowell, J. A. & Waters, E. 2004. When "new" meets "old": Configurations of adult attachment representations and their implications for marital functioning. *Developmental Psychology*, 40, 295–314.

van Ijzendoorn, M. H. 1995. Adult attachment representations, parental responsiveness, and infant attachment: A meta-analysis on the predictive validity of the Adult Attachment Interview. *Psychological Bulletin*, 117, 387–403.

van Ijzendoorn, M. H. & Bakermans-Kranenburg, M. J. 1996. Attachment representations in mothers, fathers, adolescents, and clinical groups: A meta-analytic search for normative data. *Journal of Consulting and Clinical Psychology*, 64, 8–21.

van Ijzendoorn, M. H. & Bakermans-Kranenburg, M. J. 1997. Intergenerational transmission of attachment: A move to the contextual level. In Atkinson, L. & Zucker, K. J. (eds) *Attachment and psychopathology*. New York: Guilford Press.

van Ijzendoorn, M. H. & Bakermans-Kranenburg, M. J. 2008. The distribution of adult attachment representations in clinical groups: A meta-analytic search for patterns of attachment in 105 AAI studies. In Steele, H. & Steele, M. (eds) *Clinical Applications of the Adult Attachment Interview*. New York: Guilford Press.

Vaughn, B. E., Bost, K. K. & van Ijzendoorn, M. 2008. Attachment and temperament: Additive and interactive influences on behavior, affect, and cognition during infancy and childhood. In Cassidy, J. & Shaver, P. (eds) *Handbook of attachment: Theory, research, and clinical applications*, 2nd ed. New York: Guilford Press.

Waters, E., Hamilton, C. E. & Weinfield, N. S. 2000. The stability of attachment security from infancy to adolescence and early adulthood: General introduction. *Child Development*, 71, 678–683.

Weinfield, N. S., Sroufe, L. A., Egeland, B. & Carlson, E. A. 2008. Individual differences in infant–caregiver attachment: Conceptual and empirical aspects of security. In Cassidy, J. & Shaver, P. (eds) *Handbook of attachment: Theory, research, and clinical applications*, 2nd ed. New York: Guilford Press.

Zeifman, D. & Hazan, C. 2008. Pair bonds as attachments: Reevaluating the evidence. In Cassidy, J. & Shaver, P. (eds) *Handbook of attachment: Theory, research, and clinical applications*, 2nd ed. New York: Guilford Press.

Chapter 2

Attachment and treatment relationships

Attachment is fundamentally about security; knowing that someone stands by you and protects you from danger. Treatment providers often come across people whose basic security has been shaken. They are perhaps threatened by illness or adversity, life's regular course has been turned upside down by bereavement or divorce, or mental problems stand in the way of a sense of coherence and meaning in life. According to attachment theory, the insecurity experienced when facing illness, trauma, or threats of breakdown in life, leads to an unavoidable activation of the attachment system. This chapter will begin by accounting for the relevance of this knowledge for treatment: what does activation of the attachment system generally entail, and how does it affect people with different attachment patterns? This is followed by a discussion of the extent to which treatment providers can and should function as a 'secure base' and 'safe haven' for clients, and of how this function resembles and differs from regular attachment figures such as parents. Finally, the chapter will discuss how treatment providers are affected by their own attachment experiences and what this means for interaction with clients.

The attachment behavioural system in adulthood

In his description of the attachment system, Bowlby drew on the idea of inborn behavioural systems serving a species' survival, which was formulated in ethology, that is, the study of animals' behaviour in relation to their environment. In a human child, a number of species-specific triggers will generate a feeling of insecurity and thus activate the attachment system (Bowlby, 1969, Simpson and Belsky, 2008). There are obvious evolutionary advantages of children calling for their caregivers and keeping close to them in dangerous situations. It is also obvious that the *specific* behaviour expedient for small children in threatening situations is not as appropriate for older children or adults. The attachment system is a 'goal-directed' system, a so-called cybernetic control system, which entails inbuilt flexibility and development (Sroufe and Waters, 1977). It is not an instinctive system as seen in some animals, where a specific stimulus always triggers the same sequence of inborn behaviours – for example, special mating dances that are automatically triggered by the presence of specific sense impressions in some bird species. Instead, the attachment system is a behaviour-regulating system, which undergoes a significant development from birth to adulthood and is open to both general and individual environmental influence. The attachment systems of adult humans operate in other, more complex ways than children's attachment systems do, and there is significant individual variation in the way that adults relate to and respond to attachment system activation. However, the attachment system's goal is the same for everyone in all phases of life: gaining security and protection.

How does the attachment behavioural system operate?

From birth, human beings are equipped with a repertoire of behaviours activated in threatening situations. Infants have an inborn tendency to cry and cling to their caregivers if they feel insecure. Young children are completely dependent on their caregivers' help to regulate their emotional state and re-establish a basic feeling of security (Cassidy, 1994, Thompson et al., 1995). With development and experience, the repertoire of possible actions in threatening situations is significantly increased and there will be a greater difference in the way different children react. For example, in the Strange Situation, children at the age of 1 can already be observed to suppress the inclination to cry or seek physical intimacy when the caregiver leaves them, and instead appear unaffected by the situation. The avoidant child has experienced that the likelihood of security-inducing proximity to the caregiver is increased when refraining from expressing want and despair. Instead the child attempts to downregulate emotional discomfort by focusing attention on the toys in the laboratory room (Ainsworth et al., 1978, Solomon and George, 2008).

Naturally, adults possess an even more versatile arsenal of strategies for seeking security and comfort when they are fearful or upset. Some are constructive – for example, seeking support from a close friend – and some are less constructive – for example, turning to drink. Adults' self-reliance and larger arsenal of action strategies also entail a different *threshold* for activation of the attachment system (Marvin and Britner, 2008). Whereas the small child feels insecure when left alone in a room, this will usually not be the case for adults. However, there is always a relation between people's available coping resources and their threshold for attachment system activation. This, for instance, is why elderly people, who are weaker and have more difficulty taking care of themselves, often exhibit an increase in attachment behaviour and an increased need to lean on attachment figures, who will often be their own adult children (Ainsworth, 1989, Magai, 2008).

Based on theory and extensive experimental studies, Mikulincer and Shaver (2007) devised a detailed model of the way the attachment system operates in adults (see Figure 2.1). According to their model, the attachment system is activated if a person feels threatened or in danger. In adults, the threat that activates the attachment system can both be internal and external. This means, for instance, that the attachment system can be activated by an actual loss or break-up, but also by the *thought* of being abandoned. The moment a person feels threatened – whether

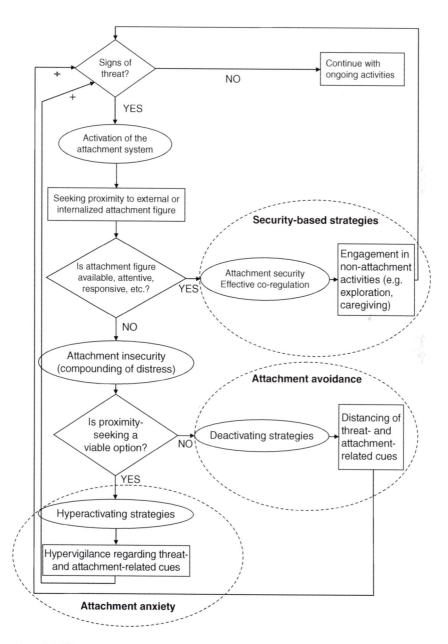

Figure 2.1 The activation and dynamics of the attachment system.

the threat is realistic or not – an automatic, unconscious activation of attachment-related information occurs, so that thoughts, feelings, and actions related to attachment become more accessible (Mikulincer et al., 2003, Shaver and Mikulincer, 2002). Thus, the experience of feeling threatened actualizes a person's entire attachment history. This is important for treatment providers to keep in mind, as they will often encounter people for whom thoughts and emotions regarding care, rejection, abandonment, etc. figure prominently.

Activation of a person's attachment experiences often means that he or she will be greatly sensitive to whether a treatment provider is reliable and supportive. Although treatment providers are commonly a fleeting presence in a client's life, they will often encounter people in vulnerable situations, where the question of security is 'brought to a head'. People who have experienced that attachment figures let them down at decisive moments will be especially wary of potentially being let down by their treatment provider. People whose attachment figures were unable to deal with their vulnerability will be acutely aware of signs that their expressions of weakness and vulnerability are making their treatment provider uncomfortable, too (Brumbaugh and Fraley, 2006, Lopez, 2009, Tolmacz, 2009, Wallin, 2007). When treatment providers are faced with reactions from a client that seem unreasonable or out of proportion, it may be helpful to understand how these reactions are tied to the client feeling threatened and in some clients to the activation of past attachment-related experiences of a strongly negative character.

Because attachment system activation is tied to a person's cognitive and emotional assessment of whether a given situation is insecure or threatening, the specific situations in which attachment activation occurs will vary from individual to individual (Mikulincer et al., 2009, Shaver and Mikulincer, 2009). These individual differences become especially important in 'grey zones' and ambiguous situations where the potential for individual interpretation is relatively large, while acute lethal danger will activate the attachment system in everyone. One set of attachment-related differences between adults is thus constituted by the range and types of situations or difficulties that lead to activation of the attachment system to begin with. For avoidant/deactivating people, it will usually require more for the attachment system to be activated, because they routinely turn attention away from situations, thoughts, or fantasies that awaken attachment needs. In contrast, people with ambivalent/hyperactivating attachment patterns will tend to have a lower threshold for attachment system activation, as they are disposed to hypervigilance and worry about potential abandonment or losses. Apart from differences related to the conditions for attachment system activation, another set of differences are constituted by the way people react when their attachment systems are activated, that is, differences in 'coping strategies'.

Attachment patterns and coping strategies

In psychology, 'coping strategies' or 'coping mechanisms' are terms for the set of behaviours a person makes use of when facing adversity (Lazarus and

Folkman, 1984). Adults' coping strategies are determined by more than just attachment patterns. However, in situations where the attachment system is activated, a person's attachment pattern affects the coping mechanisms he or she will typically employ. According to Mikulincer and Shaver (2008), in situations where the attachment system is activated, a person's coping strategy will primarily depend on two evaluations, which can be conscious, but most often take place at an unconscious, automatic level based on past experiences: 1) Is there an attachment figure who is available, attentive, and responsive? 2) Can anything good come from seeking proximity?

In attachment activating situations, an important difference between children and adults is that the small child will always be dependent on specific, present attachment figures, whereas the adult will often start by turning to 'attachment figures' on an internal, psychological level. People who have experienced constructive and secure attachment relationships throughout life will have formed internal representations of caring and protective others that function as an inner 'secure base' (Holmes, 2001, Mikulincer et al., 2003, Zimmermann, 1999). In situations where the attachment system is activated, people with secure representations are able to draw upon an inner voice telling them that everything will be fine, that they are loved, and that someone worries about them and takes care of them. In some situations, access to the inner secure base will be enough for a person to be calmed and regain a sense of security. In other situations, the person will turn to other people for help and support based on the belief and expectation that others will be available, attentive, and caring.

Similar to the evaluation of whether a given situation is threatening, the evaluation of whether attachment figures are available and responsive will depend on access to actual and potential attachment figures, as well as on the person's previous attachment experiences. For people with insecure attachment patterns, attachment system activation will also increase the likelihood of reconnecting with memories of support being unavailable from attachment figures and related expectations. This means that people with insecure attachment patterns are more disposed to notice signs that actual or potential attachment figures are unavailable or unresponsive (Collins et al., 2004, Mikulincer and Shaver, 2007). In encounters between clients and treatment providers, in which the client has no particular foreknowledge of whether the treatment provider is reliable or not, the client with negative attachment experiences will therefore have a tendency to approach the relationship with negative or mixed expectations. On the other hand, clients with predominantly positive attachment experiences will tend to have positive expectations regarding the treatment relationship, as their experience tells them that other people can provide help and support.

In the event that a person with an activated attachment system concludes that an actual or potential attachment figure is unavailable or unresponsive, the next evaluation according to Mikulincer and Shaver's (2007) model (see Figure 2.1) is whether seeking proximity is a good strategy. This evaluation marks the difference between the avoidant/deactivating and the ambivalent/hyperactivating attachment patterns. People whose experience in attachment relationships has led them to expect that expressions of vulnerability and help-seeking will be met with consistent rejection, thus further worsening the situation, will attempt to avoid relying on others in difficult situations. The more threatened they feel, the more inclined they will be to avoid contact with others, while at the same time attempting to deny their fear or distress (Cassidy, 1994, Mikulincer et al., 2009). However, people whose attachment experiences have led them to expect that attachment figures might provide help and support, although they cannot take it for granted, tend to make use of diametrically opposite coping strategies. Rather than deny their vulnerability or distress, they will focus on it and amplify the expression of it in an attempt to ensure attention and help from others (Cassidy, 1994, Cassidy and Berlin, 1994, Mikulincer et al., 2009).

People with a primarily avoidant/deactivating or an ambivalent/hyperactivating pattern each in their own way have trouble reacting constructively in situations where the attachment system is activated. Both ways of reacting, however, are indicative of a consistent 'strategy'. As discussed in Chapter 1, these patterns may be described as 'organized' as opposed to 'disorganized' patterns. Sometimes people have had attachment experiences where it proved impossible to decide whether seeking proximity was a good strategy, and where neither avoidant nor ambivalent strategies resulted in the coveted sense of security. People who have lived with unpredictable, perhaps even abusive, attachment figures, can at times have a strong simultaneous impulse towards both an avoidant and an ambivalent strategy (Cassidy and Mohr, 2001, Hesse and Main, 2000, Lyons-Ruth and Jacobvitz, 2008). People with this contradictory, disorganized pattern may withdraw from contact due to fear of rejection, while at the same time longing for this contact and feeling lost without it. Unlike people with a purely avoidant pattern, these people do not succeed in maintaining a feeling of not needing others, but are trapped between unbearable alternatives which leave them especially vulnerable to psychological problems (Dozier et al., 2008).

For treatment providers, it will often prove relevant to assess client coping strategies and take these into account. For some clients, the act of seeking treatment will in itself be part of their preferred way of dealing with difficulties. For securely attached people, it will make perfect sense to seek out crisis therapy if they have been assaulted, for example. They seek out treatment based on a positive expectation that help is possible (Lopez et al., 1998, Riggs et al., 2002). Ambivalently attached people may be inclined to seek out one treatment provider after another to deal with problems that may be unclearly delimited or formulated. They feel a strong need to seek others' help to tackle their problems, but may find it hard to use this help constructively and will be sensitive to potential letdowns (Lopez, 2009, Vogel and Wei, 2005). For other clients, treatment will be partly involuntary, and to some extent go against their preferred coping strategy. Avoidant clients will normally prefer to 'take care of themselves' rather than confide in other people and rely on their help (Dozier et al., 2001, Muller, 2010). Thus, treatment providers face fundamentally different tasks when trying to establish constructive treatment relationships to ambivalent or avoidant clients. The diverse challenges in establishing good contact with clients with different attachment patterns will be treated in more depth in Chapter 8.

The treatment provider as a secure base and safe haven

In many treatment situations, the contact between treatment provider and client is so fleeting or brief that there is no basis for forming a real relationship. However, in the literature about long-term psychotherapeutic treatment, discussion of the client–therapist relationship as an attachment relationship has become more widespread (Farber and Metzger, 2009, Mallinckrodt, 2010, Parish and Eagle, 2003). In the book *A Secure Base*, in which Bowlby (1988) considered the psychotherapeutic consequences of attachment theory, he described the client–therapist relationship as analogous to the relationship between mother and child, and he underlined the importance of the therapist 'acting' as a secure base and safe haven for the client. In all treatment relationships, treatment providers can draw inspiration from some of the features that attachment research has linked to the ability to establish secure attachment relationships. However, there are essential differences between treatment relationships and parent–child relationships. In the following, it will first be discussed how fitting the analogy between the parent–child relationship and the treatment provider–client relationship is, followed by a consideration of what it entails to serve as a secure base and safe haven for one's clients.

How appropriate is the analogy?

Because of the element of professionalism present in the relationship between clients and treatment providers, there is a significant difference between this relationship and clients' other attachment relationships. In the relationship to clients, the treatment provider serves primarily as a treatment provider and only secondarily as a person. Naturally, treatment roles differ widely in terms of personal involvement. For instance, a contact person in milieu therapy in psychiatric settings will be much more personally involved than a physiotherapist treating sports injuries. However, all treatment providers have a defined task to perform in relation to the client, and this takes place within a delimited institutional and temporal framework. This means that the level of availability and emotional support which children can find in a secure attachment relationship to a parent will not be found within the framework of a treatment relationship – not even in long-term psychotherapy.

Another important difference between parent–child relationships and treatment relationships consists in the differing degrees of emotional investment. Whereas parents usually have a strong emotional investment in their children, most treatment providers have numerous clients who necessarily play a much smaller role in the treatment provider's life – something clients' are aware of, although they may sometimes wish it were different (Lopez, 2009). Whereas parents most often are the all-important attachment figures for their children, treatment providers are not necessarily attachment figures for clients, and, even if they are, they will usually neither be their client's only nor primary attachment figure, as most clients also draw support from other intimate relationships. Whether treatment providers end up serving as attachment figures to their clients depends on the client, the client's life situation, the type of treatment, and the context of the relationship.

As mentioned in Chapter 1, actual attachment relationships are theoretically characterized by a number of features: the search for contact or proximity, discomfort or longing at separation, sorrow at loss, using the attachment figure as a secure base and safe haven, and seeing the attachment figure as 'stronger' and 'wiser' (Ainsworth, 1989, Cassidy, 2008). Attachment figures are thus people who constitute an important source of security in one's life, and who provide support in hard times. Furthermore, attachment figures are irreplaceable – not just any therapist or contact person will suffice if the relationship develops into an actual attachment relationship.

Common experience as well as empirical studies indicate that some long-term treatment relationships come to resemble attachment relationships in which the client seeks comfort and support from his or her treatment provider, thinks about the treatment provider in difficult situations, misses the treatment provider during prolonged separation – for example, in connection with holidays – and feels joy when seeing the treatment provider again (Farber and Metzger, 2009, Obegi, 2008, Parish and Eagle, 2003). The likelihood that the treatment provider will serve as an actual attachment figure is increased with the treatment's duration and frequency of contact. However, the client's attachment pattern also plays a part. Avoidant clients are less inclined to become attached to their treatment providers. Although no empirical studies have been carried out in the area, one would expect that it is more rare for clients to form attachment relationships to treatment providers who work with more delimited, physical problems, such as rehabilitation after a knee injury, than to treatment providers who are more involved in the client's mental health, such as a psychotherapist or a doctor involved in more thorough, long-term treatment.

Just as with all other attachment relationships between adults, treatment relationships differ from parent–child relationships because of the two parties' developmental equality. In the parent–child relationship the difference between adult and child in terms of development, knowledge, and ability establishes an inherent asymmetry. Contrary to this, attachment relationships between adults, such as romantic relationships, are usually symmetrical (Zeifman and Hazan, 2008), although in some romantic relationships it may primarily be one party that seeks security, while the other supplies it. Just like parent–child relationships, treatment relationships are asymmetrical in that only one party seeks help and support and the other serves as a 'resource person'. However, this does not necessarily mean that the treatment provider is generally 'stronger' or 'wiser' than the client. In some cases the treatment provider's competences are relatively limited, and the client will not feel inclined to depend on the treatment provider or consider him or her a general attachment figure.

In the treatment of adults, the distribution of roles and the degree of asymmetry will usually depend on the context and on 'negotiation' between the parties. There may be a difference in the degree to which the treatment provider is given the status of 'expert' and how much responsibility the treatment provider has and assumes for the client's well-being. In some cases, misunderstandings and 'mismatch' between client and treatment provider can be attributed to expectations regarding the distribution of roles between them, where one party may expect or desire a more asymmetrical relationship than the other, whether it be the treatment provider who expects to be awarded status as an especially knowledgeable and strong person, or perhaps the client who expects the treatment provider to take on more responsibility in 'taking care' of him or her.

What does serving as a secure base and safe haven entail?

Even in cases where treatment providers do not become actual attachment figures for clients, they may still find inspiration and guidance in attachment theory's observations of what serving as a 'secure base' and 'safe haven' entails. As mentioned, many clients will meet the treatment provider in a situation in which their attachment systems are to some degree activated. Therefore it may be relevant to consider which type of care and support is constructive and conducive under the given circumstances.

Attachment theory's conclusion about the specific functions of security-generating attachment figures have been elegantly summarized in the context of a parent–child intervention programme called the 'Circle of Security' (Marvin et al., 2002). Here, a child's interaction with a secure attachment figure is described as a circular process, where the caregiver alternately serves as a secure base and safe haven depending on whether the child's attachment system is activated. A central point is that children have different needs depending on the current attachment dynamic. When the child's attachment system is not activated, the caregiver's function is to form a secure base that the child can use as a starting point for exploring the world. When the child's attachment system becomes activated, the caregiver's function is to be a safe haven, in which the child can seek refuge. An important part of a secure attachment figure's function in relation to a child is being attentive to the child's current state and to respond accordingly. If this is applied to treatment relationships, it suggests that there are times where it is preferable for treatment providers to serve as a secure base, and times where it is better to act as a safe haven.

When the client is upset and distraught, a safe haven is required. This entails that the treatment provider supports the client and takes the lead in the situation (Mallinckrodt et al., 2009). It is important to 'meet' the client in the fear or vulnerability at play when the attachment system is activated. Even though few treatment relationships offer scope for extensive comfort, most treatment providers will have different opportunities for supporting the client's feeling of security in these situations. Above all, it is important that the treatment provider sees and acknowledges the client's feelings. If treatment providers find it difficult to witness and 'contain' the client's insecurity, they may end up pressing the client to 'pull himself together' or 'man up', which will only contribute to the client's acute sense of insecurity.

However, in many treatments there will also be phases where the client is not marked by current crisis or attachment system activation. In these phases, the treatment provider should serve as a secure base for the client. It is important not to retain the clients in an overly 'protected' position when they need support to wrestle with problems on their own (Mallinckrodt et al., 2009). If treatment providers are anxious that clients cannot 'take care of themselves', they may end up keeping clients in a dependent position and thus hinder them from using their own strengths and acting independently. In these cases, it is important to retire to the background, encouraging the client's own problem-solving efforts.

The client's position with respect to attachment system activation may change over the course of treatment, from meeting to meeting, or even within a single session. If treatment providers are to serve as a secure base or safe haven, a continual monitoring of the client's position and needs is necessary (Wallin, 2007). An important point in relation to this is that everyone – even the most secure of attachment figures – occasionally makes mistakes and meets the other person in a 'wrong' way. Secure attachment relationships are precisely characterized by attachment figures who constantly adjust their behaviour based on the child's response and 'correct' or 'repair' when it becomes clear that a crisis signal was overlooked at first or that they have been overprotective (Beebe et al., 2010, Belsky and Fearon, 2008, Lyons-Ruth, 1999). This continual repair is in itself an important element of secure attachment and contributes to establishing trust that mismatches and difficulties can be overcome. The idea of the treatment provider as a secure base and safe haven is therefore not a demand for a completely empathic and faultless response at all times – this is simply not within the realm of possibilities, neither is it what generally constitutes the makings of secure attachment relationships.

The attachment experiences of the treatment provider

It is not just clients who approach treatment relationships with attachment patterns based on previous relationships. The same is, of course, true of the treatment provider. The difference is that the treatment provider is not in a crisis – at least, this is not the focus of the relationship – nor does the treatment provider seek help from the client. As described in Chapter 1, a parent's own attachment experiences are significant for the parent's ability to care for his or her own child. Since the relationship between client and treatment provider resembles the parent–child relationship in that the treatment provider's task is to care for the client, treatment providers' attachment patterns can also be significant for their relationship to clients (Daniel, 2006, Dozier and Bates, 2004, Dozier et al., 1994). This section focuses on two possible consequences of this. First of all, the treatment providers' own attachment experiences may affect their work regardless of the client in treatment, partly because of the emotions that treatment generates in the treatment provider, and partly because of the treatment providers' 'blind spots', where their view of clients are influenced by their own attachment patterns. Second, the inter-action between the client's and treatment provider's attachment-related disposi-tions may entail that some 'matches' between specific clients and treatment providers are more appropriate and productive than others.

Countertransference and 'blind spots'

All treatment providers may find themselves in situations where elements of their own personality and background can impede optimal interaction with a client. In the psychodynamic tradition, special attention is paid to the treatment provider's 'countertransference', that is, his or her emotional reaction to the client, which may be more or less contingent on the treatment provider's own personality and background (Gabbard, 2001, Sandler et al., 1970). In many treatment professions, supervision is routinely employed and, among other things, serves to turn attention to such idiosyncratic reactions and compensate for them in treatment. Inappropriate countertransference or 'blind spots' can be rooted in many different things. However, in this context a central factor is the treatment provider's attachment pattern. Because treatment providers often face people whose attachment system is activated, their own attachment experience can easily be brought into play (Ligiero and Gelso, 2002, Slade, 2008, Wallin, 2007).

In parent–child relationships, secure parents are best able to respond attentively and appropriately to their child's needs when the child is upset or insecure. The more disposed parents are to deactivate their attachment system, the more inclined they are to reject or downplay the child's attachment behaviour. The more disposed parents are to hyperactivate their attachment system, the more likely they are to misinterpret the child and react out of step with the child's needs; for example, overdramatizing or becoming upset if the child seeks refuge in them (De Wolff and van Ijzendoorn, 1997, George and Solomon, 2008, Pederson et al., 1998). In treat-ment contexts, there is also reason to believe that securely attached treatment providers interact most constructively with clients. Securely attached treatment providers are less inclined to display inappropriate countertransference reactions such as rejecting or being critical of the client (Ligiero and Gelso, 2002).

Studies indicate that treatment providers with avoidant attachment patterns are less empathetic and more critical of clients, especially demanding and crisis-ridden clients (Mohr et al., 2005). Avoidant treatment providers are inclined to overlook vulnerability and pain in clients who do not clearly exhibit their distress and need for support, because they attempt to downplay such feelings in their own coping and emotion regulation. Thus, avoidant treatment providers' tendency to downregulate their own attachment system can result in a 'blind spot' with respect to clients' vulnerability and attachment needs (Dozier and Bates, 2004). They will be more comfortable if contact with their client is kept at a relatively impersonal and professional level, which can be problematic for some treatment forms and contribute to the client not feeling sufficiently 'seen' or 'heard' by the treatment provider.

Whereas avoidant treatment providers may lack empathy, ambivalent treatment providers are significantly more inclined to 'feel with' their clients, also to such a degree that it can become problematic for the treatment relationship. Ambivalent treatment providers are more inclined to respond to and be especially attentive to a client's feelings of vulnerability. However, they can also more easily be affected and thus magnify and sustain the client's vulnerability. Simultaneously, ambivalent treatment providers will be at risk of feeling rejected and shut out by the client if they are unable to relate to the client on a deeper, emotional level. This can result in inappropriate dynamics, especially with avoidant clients. Whereas avoidant treatment providers can be 'blind' to their client's vulnerability, ambivalent treatment providers' 'blind spot' consists in being blind to a client's strength and ability to cope on his or her own, just as ambivalent treatment providers may at times confuse the feelings that the client awakens in them with their client's feelings (Dozier and Bates, 2004, Dozier and Tyrrell, 1998, Mallinckrodt, 2000).

Although there is some empirical evidence of the quality of treatment relationships being affected by the treatment providers' attachment patterns, the results are not as unequivocal as those regarding the influence of clients' attachment patterns (Daniel, 2006). A possible explanation is that the treatment provider's personality is not necessarily brought into play as much as the client's. As described earlier, the treatment relationship differs from the parent–child relationship because treatment providers are not as emotionally invested in individual clients as parents usually are in their children. Treatment providers see clients at certain times and in delimited situations. If a treatment provider is disposed towards an avoidant attachment pattern and therefore feels a certain discomfort when witnessing a client's intense vulnerability, then by virtue of the relationship's limits it will be easier to take note of this inappropriate reaction and compensate for it in the contact with the client. The degree to which insecure attachment patterns in the treatment provider poses a problem will likely depend on the context.

The attachment-related 'match' between client and treatment provider

An interesting question in relation to the role of clients' and treatment providers' attachment patterns in treatment relationships is the question of interaction effects or 'matches' between the particular attachment tendencies of the two people in the relationship. Both theory and research indicate that the most constructive and unproblematic treatment relationships will be between treatment providers and clients with secure attachment patterns (Berant and Obegi, 2009, Slade, 2008), although there may of course be matches or 'mismatches' in a number of other dimensions, such as social background, outlook, etc. As already mentioned, it is also an advantage that treatment providers are securely attached regardless of the client's attachment pattern. However, even securely attached treatment providers may tend towards a more avoidant or ambivalent pattern. For example, one can be secure with a certain tendency to 'reserve' or secure with a certain tendency to worrying or dramatizing (Hesse, 2008). Here the question is whether treatment providers work best with clients with similar attachment tendencies, or whether having opposite attachment inclinations is in fact an advantage.

Unfortunately, very few studies have evaluated the interaction between clients' and treatment providers' attachment patterns. A single study indicates that it may prove advantageous for clients to work with a treatment provider who leans towards the opposite side of the deactivation/hyperactivation dimension, at least in so far as the treatment provider is predominantly secure. A group of 54 psychiatric patients and their case managers were all interviewed with the AAI; all case managers had secure attachment patterns, but varied between 'leaning towards' a more deactivating or hyperactivating style. It turned out that the more deactivating patients had better treatment alliances and functioned better if their case manager leaned towards a hyperactivating style, and vice versa (Tyrrell et al., 1999).

Even though this study stands alone and has yet to be supported by other studies, theoretically its results make sense based on the idea that the treatment provider helps to 'adjust' for clients' insecure attachment patterns (Bernier and Dozier, 2002, Mallinckrodt, 2010, Shane and Shane, 2001). Avoidant/deactivating as well as ambivalent/hyperactivating strategies all come at a cost for clients, who may either be cut off from an important part of their emotional reality, or contrastively be flooded by difficult emotions at the expense of overview and the ability to act. A moderately ambivalent treatment provider, who does not take an avoidant client's unaffectedness and self-reliance at face value, may be able to make room for expressing vulnerability, which in the end may contribute to better aiding the client with his or her problems. Conversely, a moderately avoidant treatment provider, who is not carried away by violent displays of emotions, may be able to help an ambivalent client create a greater distance to his or her own distress and feel more able to cope with the situation. Obviously, in both cases it is likely that this adjusting influence is constructive within a certain zone beyond which the difference between treatment provider and client becomes too great (Mallinckrodt, 2010). A treatment provider who is not just moderately, but very, hyperactivating may, for example, feel personally rejected by an avoidant client and push him or her for emotional involvement, which will likely lead to the client abandoning treatment.

The idea of matching client and treatment provider may seem of purely theoretical interest, since in practice it will seldom be possible to measure both clients' and treatment providers' attachment patterns and make matches based on this. However, regardless of which attachment pattern treatment providers have, they may draw inspiration from the idea of matching and thus strategically adjusting the treatment *relationship* to correspond with the client's attachment pattern. This question will be treated in more depth in Chapter 8 following a detailed account of the four primary attachment patterns.

References

Ainsworth, M. S. 1989. Attachments beyond infancy. *American Psychologist*, 44, 709–716.

Ainsworth, M. S., Blehar, M. C., Waters, E. & Wall, S. 1978. *Patterns of attachment: A psychological study of the strange situation.*, Hillsdale, NJ: Lawrence Erlbaum.

Beebe, B., Jaffe, J., Markese, S., Buck, K., Chen, H., Cohen, P., Bahrick, L., Andrews, H. & Feldstein, S. 2010. The origins of 12-month attachment: A microanalysis of 4-month mother–infant interaction. *Attachment & Human Development*, 12, 6–141.

Belsky, J. & Fearon, P. 2008. Precursors of attachment security. In Cassidy, J. & Shaver, P. (eds) *Handbook of attachment: Theory, research, and clinical applications*, 2nd ed. New York: Guilford Press.

Berant, E. & Obegi, J. H. 2009. Attachment-informed psychotherapy research with adults. In Obegi, J. H. & Berant, E. (eds) *Attachment theory and research in clinical work with adults*. New York: Guilford Press.

Bernier, A. & Dozier, M. 2002. The client–counselor match and the corrective emotional experience: Evidence from interpersonal and attachment research. *Psychotherapy: Theory, Research, Practice, Training*, 39, 32–43.

Bowlby, J. 1969. *Attachment and Loss: Vol. 1. Attachment*, London: Pimlico.

Bowlby, J. 1988. *A secure base: Clinical applications of attachment theory*, London: Routledge.

Brumbaugh, C. C. & Fraley, R. C. 2006. Transference and attachment: How do attachment patterns get carried forward from one relationship to the next? *Personality and Social Psychology Bulletin*, 32, 552–560.

Cassidy, J. 1994. Emotion regulation: Influences of attachment relationships. *Monographs of the Society for Research in Child Development*, 59, 228–283.

Cassidy, J. 2008. The nature of the child's ties. In Cassidy, J. & Shaver, P. (eds) *Handbook of attachment: Theory, research, and clinical applications*, 2nd ed. New York: Guilford Press.

Cassidy, J. & Berlin, L. J. 1994. The insecure/ambivalent pattern of attachment: Theory and research. *Child Development*, 65, 971–981.

Cassidy, J. & Mohr, J. J. 2001. Unsolvable fear, trauma, and psychopathology: Theory, research, and clinical considerations related to disorganized attachment across the life span. *Clinical Psychology: Science and Practice*, 8, 275–298.

Collins, N. L., Guichard, A. C., Ford, M. B. & Feeney, B. C. 2004. Working models of attachment: New developments and emerging themes. In Rholes, W. S. & Simpson, J. A. (eds) *Adult attachment: Theory, research, and clinical implications*. New York: Guilford Publications.

Daniel, S. I. F. 2006. Adult attachment patterns and individual psychotherapy: A review. *Clinical Psychology Review*, 26, 968–984.

De Wolff, M. & van Ijzendoorn, M. 1997. Sensitivity and attachment: A meta-analysis on parental antecedents of infant attachment. *Child Development*, 68, 571–591.

Dozier, M. & Bates, B. C. 2004. Attachment state of mind and the treatment relationship. In Atkinson, L. & Goldberg, S. (eds) *Attachment issues in psychopathology and intervention*. London: Lawrence Erlbaum.

Dozier, M., Cue, K. L. & Barnett, L. 1994. Clinicians as caregivers: Role of attachment organization in treatment. *Journal of Consulting and Clinical Psychology*, 62, 793–800.

Dozier, M., Lomax, L., Tyrrell, C. L. & Lee, S. W. 2001. The challenge of treatment for clients with dismissing states of mind. *Attachment & Human Development*, 3, 62–76.

Dozier, M., Stovall-McClough, C. & Albus, K. E. 2008. Attachment and psychopathology in adulthood. In Cassidy, J. & Shaver, P. (eds) *Handbook of attachment: Theory, research, and clinical applications*, 2nd ed. New York: Guilford Press.

Dozier, M. & Tyrrell, C. 1998. The role of attachment in therapeutic relationships. In Simpson, J. A. & Rholes, W. S. (eds) *Attachment theory and close relationships*. New York: Guilford Press.

Farber, B. A. & Metzger, J. A. 2009. The therapist as secure base. In Obegi, J. H. & Berant, E. (eds) *Attachment theory and research in clinical work with adults*. New York: Guilford Press.

Gabbard, G. O. 2001. A contemporary psychoanalytic model of countertransference. *Journal of Clinical Psychology*, 57, 983–991.

George, C. & Solomon, J. 2008. The caregiving system. A behavioral systems approach to parenting. In Cassidy, J. & Shaver, P. R. (eds) *Handbook of attachment: Theory, research, and clinical applications*, 2nd ed. New York: Guilford Press.

Hesse, E. 2008. The Adult Attachment Interview: Protocol, method of analysis, and empirical studies. In Cassidy, J. & Shaver, P. (eds) *Handbook of attachment: Theory, research, and clinical applications*, 2nd ed. New York: Guilford Press.

Hesse, E. & Main, M. 2000. Disorganized infant, child, and adult attachment: Collapse in behavioral and attentional strategies. *Journal of the American Psychoanalytic Association*, 48, 1097–1127.

Holmes, J. 2001. *The search for the secure base. Attachment theory and psychotherapy*. London: Brunner Routledge.

Lazarus, R. S. & Folkman, S. 1984. *Stress, appraisal, and coping*. New York: Springer Publishing Company.

Ligiero, D. P. & Gelso, C. J. 2002. Countertransference, attachment, and the working alliance: The therapist's contribution. *Psychotherapy: Theory, Research, Practice, Training*, 39, 3–11.

Lopez, F. G. 2009. Clinical correlates of adult attachment organization. In Obegi, J. H. & Berant, E. (eds) *Attachment theory and research in clinical work with adults*. New York: Guilford Press.

Lopez, F. G., Melendez, M. C., Sauer, E. M., Berger, E. & Wyssmann, J. 1998. Internal working models, self-reported problems, and help-seeking attitudes among college students. *Journal of Counseling Psychology*, 45, 79–83.

Lyons-Ruth, K. & Jacobvitz, D. 2008. Attachment disorganization: Genetic factors, parenting contexts, and developmental transformation from infancy to adulthood. In Cassidy, J. & Shaver, P. (eds) *Handbook of attachment: Theory, research, and clinical applications*, 2nd ed. New York: Guilford Press.

Lyons-Ruth, K. 1999. The two-person unconscious: Intersubjective dialogue, enactive relational representation, and the emergence of new forms of relational organization. *Psychoanalytic Inquiry*, 19, 576–617.

Magai, C. 2008. Attachment in middle and later life. In Cassidy, J. & Shaver, P. (eds) *Handbook of attachment: Theory, research, and clinical applications*, 2nd ed. New York: Guilford Press.

Mallinckrodt, B. 2000. Attachment, social competencies, social support, and interpersonal process in psychotherapy. *Psychotherapy Research*, 10, 239–266.

Mallinckrodt, B. 2010. The psychotherapy relationship as attachment: Evidence and implications. *Journal of Social and Personal Relationships*, 27, 262–270.

Mallinckrodt, B., Daly, K. & Wang, C.-C. D. 2009. An attachment approach to adult psychotherapy. In Obegi, J. H. & Berant, E. (eds) *Attachment theory and research in clinical work with adults*. New York: Guilford Press.

Marvin, R. S. & Britner, P. A. 2008. Normative development: The ontogeny of attachment. In Cassidy, J. & Shaver, P. (eds) *Handbook of attachment: Theory, research, and clinical applications*, 2nd ed. New York: Guilford Press.

Marvin, R. S., Cooper, G., Hoffman, K. & Powell, B. 2002. The Circle of Security project: Attachment-based intervention with caregiver–pre-school child dyads. *Attachment & Human Development*, 4, 107–124.

Mikulincer, M. & Shaver, P. 2008. Adult attachment and affect regulation. In Cassidy, J. & Shaver, P. (eds) *Handbook of attachment: Theory, research, and clinical applications*, 2nd ed. New York: Guilford Press.

Mikulincer, M. & Shaver, P. R. 2007. *Attachment in adulthood: Structure, dynamics, and change*. New York: Guilford Press.

Mikulincer, M., Shaver, P. R., Cassidy, J. & Berant, E. 2009. Attachment-related defensive processes. In Obegi, J. H. & Berant, E. (eds) *Attachment theory and research in clinical work with adults*. New York: Guilford Press.

Mikulincer, M., Shaver, P. R. & Pereg, D. 2003. Attachment theory and affect regulation: The dynamics, development, and cognitive consequences of attachment-related strategies. *Motivation and Emotion*, 27, 77–102.

Mohr, J. J., Gelso, C. J. & Hill, C. E. 2005. Client and counselor trainee attachment as predictors of session evaluation and countertransference behavior in first counseling sessions. *Journal of Counseling Psychology*, 52, 298–309.

Muller, R. T. 2010. *Trauma and the avoidant client. Attachment-based strategies for healing*. New York: W.W. Norton & Company.

Obegi, J. H. 2008. The development of the client–therapist bond through the lens of attachment theory. *Psychotherapy: Theory, Research, Practice, Training*, 45, 431–446.

Parish, M. & Eagle, M. N. 2003. Attachment to the therapist. *Psychoanalytic Psychology*, 20, 271–286.

Pederson, D. R., Gleason, K. E., Moran, G. S. & Bento, S. 1998. Maternal attachment representations, maternal sensitivity, and the infant–mother attachment relationship. *Developmental Psychology*, 34, 925–933.

Riggs, S. A., Jacobvitz, D. & Hazen, N. 2002. Adult attachment and history of psychotherapy in a normative sample. *Psychotherapy: Theory, Research, Practice, Training*, 39, 344–353.

Sandler, J., Holder, A. & Dare, C. 1970. Basic psychoanalytic concepts: IV. Countertransference. *British Journal of Psychiatry*, 117, 83–88.

Shane, M. G. & Shane, M. 2001. The attachment motivational system as a guide to an effective therapeutic process. *Psychoanalytic Inquiry*, 21, 675–687.

Shaver, P. R. & Mikulincer, M. 2002. Attachment-related psychodynamics. *Attachment & Human Development*, 4, 133–161.

Shaver, P. R. & Mikulincer, M. 2009. An overview of adult attachment theory. In Obegi, J. H. & Berant, E. (eds) *Attachment theory and research in clinical work with adults*. New York: Guilford Press.

Simpson, J. A. & Belsky, J. 2008. Attachment theory within a modern evolutionary framework. In Cassidy, J. & Shaver, P. (eds) *Handbook of attachment: Theory, research, and clinical applications*, 2nd ed. New York: Guilford Press.

Slade, A. 2008. The implications of attachment theory and research for adult psychotherapy: Research and clinical perspectives. In Cassidy, J. & Shaver, P. (eds) *Handbook of attachment: Theory, research, and clinical applications*, 2nd ed. New York: Guilford Press.

Solomon, J. & George, C. 2008. The measurement of attachment security and related constructs in infancy and early childhood. In Cassidy, J. & Shaver, P. (eds) *Handbook of attachment: Theory, research, and clinical applications*, 2nd ed. New York: Guilford Press.

Sroufe, L. A. & Waters, E. 1977. Attachment as an organizational construct. *Child Development*, 48, 1184–1199.

Thompson, R. A., Flood, M. F. & Lundquist, L. 1995. Emotional regulation: Its relations to attachment and developmental psychopathology. In Cicchetti, D. & Toth, S. L. (eds) *Emotion, cognition, and representation. Rochester symposium on developmental psychopathology, Vol. 6*. Rochester, NY: University of Rochester Press.

Tolmacz, R. 2009. Transference and attachment. In Obegi, J. H. & Berant, E. (eds) *Attachment theory and research in clinical work with adults*. New York: Guilford Press.

Tyrrell, C. L., Dozier, M., Teague, G. B. & Fallot, R. D. 1999. Effective treatment relationships for persons with serious psychiatric disorders: The importance of attachment states of mind. *Journal of Consulting and Clinical Psychology*, 67, 725–733.

Vogel, D. L. & Wei, M. 2005. Adult attachment and help-seeking intent: The mediating roles of psychological distress and perceived social support. *Journal of Counseling Psychology*, 52, 347–357.

Wallin, D. J. 2007. *Attachment in Psychotherapy*, New York: Guilford Press.

Zeifman, D. & Hazan, C. 2008. Pair bonds as attachments: Reevaluating the evidence. In Cassidy, J. & Shaver, P. (eds) *Handbook of attachment: Theory, research, and clinical applications*, 2nd ed. New York: Guilford Press.

Zimmermann, P. 1999. Structure and functions of internal working models of attachment and their role for emotion regulation. *Attachment & Human Development*, 1, 291–306.

Part II

Relational and narrative characteristics of attachment patterns

Chapter 3

Secure attachment

In contrast to insecure attachment patterns, which each pose different challenges in a treatment context, secure attachment in clients does not cause any particular problems. Generally, the secure client can be expected to have a constructive, cooperative, open, and perhaps even grateful approach, which for most treatment providers may constitute the 'ideal picture' of a treatment relationship. The reason why the secure pattern will still be described in line with the three insecure patterns is partly to illustrate contrast; the insecure patterns are best understood in light of how they differ from the secure pattern. Furthermore, it is to make clear a possible objective for long-term psychotherapeutic treatment. For a treatment provider working psychotherapeutically with insecurely attached clients, a goal can be to move towards the type of relationship and interaction that spontaneously arises with securely attached clients (Holmes, 2009, Wallin, 2007). Therefore, it is important to describe the special characteristics of treatment relationships with secure clients. Finally, describing the secure attachment pattern can help clarify what cannot and should not be expected from even the most secure of clients to ensure that secure attachment is not placed in an idealized or unrealistic light.

This and the following three chapters will describe the four primary attachment patterns and how these affect treatment under two main points. First, characteristics of the way in which clients with that particular attachment pattern interact on the interpersonal level will be described. Clients' characteristic way of approaching relationships, asking for help or not asking for help, dealing with conflicts and disagreements, etc. are of general relevance to all treatment relationships. Second, the narrative characteristics of the way in which clients talk about themselves and their situation will be described. The way clients talk about themselves and others, about events, thoughts, and feelings, is directly relevant to psychotherapy, different types of counselling, coaching, and to other treatment forms in which a client's experiential world is in focus. However, the relevance of this may prove more far-reaching, as most forms of treatment involve verbal communication between client and treatment provider, with the client's self-narrative inevitably playing a role.

Obviously, the interpersonal and narrative characteristics cannot be completely separated. Some of the interpersonal characteristics characterize ways of communicating which are intertwined with the narrative self-portrayal, while some of the narrative characteristics also have a considerable interpersonal effect on the listener. Thus there is no strict division between the two separate 'channels'; rather, these are two different domains treatment providers can consider. To some extent these two domains each draw on a particular research tradition within the field of attachment theory – the questionnaire method and interview method, respectively.

Whereas a secure attachment pattern is usually related to personal narratives about positive attachment experiences, there are people who are able to break with strongly negative childhood experiences and function securely in adulthood (Hesse, 2008, Roisman et al., 2002). This kind of 'earned' secure attachment has special implications and will therefore be treated separately at the end of this chapter.

The interpersonal dimension: openness and trust

A woman has sought out a psychotherapist for help after her son was killed in a road accident. She intimates that, although she and her husband are able to support each other in this difficult situation, there are things she feels unable to talk with her husband about. She says she is aware that it is irrational, but she has been tormented by thoughts that she could have done something to prevent the accident. Her husband says there is no use in thinking like that, but she is unable to get rid of these thoughts and believes she needs to talk about it more to be able to move on. In the first sessions, the woman alternates between crying a great deal and talking about her son, the accident, and life following the accident. She describes her emotions as alternating between anger and a feeling of unreality. When the psychotherapist inquires into some of the things she has related, she usually answers reflectively, but she also comments on the psychotherapist's questions if she feels they are slightly off target. She says that having a forum in which to talk about her reaction to the loss is very helpful and helps her in her everyday life. Her thoughts about being able to prevent the loss gradually become less insistent. She expresses that the feeling of powerlessness is distressing, and perhaps this is why she has struggled to let go of the idea that she could have done something.

In interpersonal interactions, people with secure attachment patterns are generally characterized by an immediate trusting and optimistic approach as well as openness and interest in getting involved with others and sharing thoughts and emotions (Mikulincer and Shaver, 2007). As mentioned in the previous chapter, secure attachment constitutes an obvious resource in treatment contexts, as securely attached clients generally meet the treatment provider with positive expectations and a readiness to receive help. Furthermore, secure attachment is linked to other qualities that are advantageous in a treatment context. Secure attachment is generally related to a higher degree of self-confidence than insecure attachment patterns, which can be an important resource during personal crises, just as secure attachment is also associated with a greater disposition to draw on a network of relationships. The following sections will present a number of characteristics of the way the securely attached person relates to and behaves in personal relationships.

Openness regarding feelings and vulnerability

Most adults who appear securely attached will have experienced that expressions of sadness, vulnerability, fear, and need for comfort were consistently met with care and support. One of the most important characteristics of secure attachment relationships in childhood is the attachment figure's responsiveness when it really matters, that is, when the child is distressed or needs care and security (Ainsworth et al., 1978, George and Solomon, 2008). As described in the previous chapter, repeated experiences of being met adequately when needed results in the formation of an inner 'secure base' – a feeling that help is available, which in itself can be calming in critical situations. This does not mean that secure people do not become upset, afraid, or distressed. However, it is less likely that they will believe that these feelings are 'wrong' – they do not think that showing their vulnerability or their actual feelings of distress or fear is problematic. Reliable care provided when needed has communicated to them that being vulnerable, needing help, and showing this is acceptable behaviour (Holmes, 1997, Wilkinson, 2003). Furthermore, the secure attachment figure's reliable response in these situations has conveyed that it is not necessary to manipulate or amplify the expression of vulnerability to get the needed care.

In a treatment situation, it is generally an advantage if clients feel secure expressing vulnerability and difficult feelings, as this supplies treatment providers with a more realistic 'bearing' of their emotional state. In some treatment contexts one might think it better if clients are 'brave' and refrain from displaying psychological vulnerability – for example, in somatic treatment at hospitals and in other areas. In most cases, however, clients' openness about their feelings will be a resource, because these feelings contain important information about circumstances that can affect a client's collaboration with treatment providers and, in some cases, the final outcome of treatment (Dozier, 1990, Levy et al., 2011, Zegers et al., 2006). A client, who is suffering violently in connection with treatment, but who due to avoidant attachment tendencies does not convey this to the treatment provider, may suddenly abandon and leave treatment without explanation. With securely attached clients, there is a greater chance that the treatment provider will be aware of the problems before reaching this point, and this paves the way for constructive dialogue about how the ongoing treatment can be adjusted or supported.

Although treatment providers may find it difficult and become emotionally strained when clients clearly express how much their current situation affects them, the securely attached client's communication of difficult emotions will usually be relatively clear and without a tendency to dramatize, as characteristic of ambivalent clients (Crittenden and Landini, 2011, Magai, 1999, Mikulincer et al., 2003).

Clear communication of emotional pain naturally warrants an emotional 'response' from the treatment provider – also from treatment providers whose role does not require them to 'do anything' with this emotional reaction – however, there will not be the same degree of pressure to react directly to the client's emotional state as with ambivalent clients. Whether a securely attached client chooses to spontaneously convey his or her vulnerability to a treatment provider will depend on the specific situation and the treatment relationship. Under all circumstances, however, it is likely that the securely attached client will be open to the treatment provider, if he or she finds it relevant to inquire into the client's feelings.

Self-worth and conflict management

Although attachment between children and caregivers is first and foremost about security, this security – when supported by the relationship – has other important consequences for the child. When parents of insecurely attached children ignore, reject, or react out of step with the child's attachment needs, they simultaneously convey that there are important aspects of the child's emotional life and needs that they do not want to or cannot be concerned with or which are not 'acceptable'. In contrast, through their reliable care for their children, secure parents convey that the child is a person who 'deserves' to be loved and taken care of, which promotes the development of a healthy self-esteem (Bartholomew and Horowitz, 1991, Berlin et al., 2008, Bowlby, 1969). Secure attachment relationships also support a child's feeling of competence in the world, partly in attachment situations where the child learns that expressing one's problems leads to being helped, but also on a more general level due to the connection between the attachment system and the exploration system described in Chapter 1. Because of securely attached children's trust in their parents' availability, they are free to explore their surroundings, learn new things, and engender a feeling of mastery (Grossmann et al., 1999). Insecurely attached children's exploration of the world is more impeded, because they must spend energy considering their parents' lack of availability or unreliable support.

In correspondence with theoretical expectations, a large number of studies indicate that secure adult attachment patterns are related to higher self-esteem and greater confidence in one's own ability to deal constructively with adversity in life (Mikulincer and Shaver, 2007: 155–163). This contrasts with insecure attachment, which is generally associated with lower self-esteem, whether the person's self-image is unequivocally negative or the person attempts to maintain an 'inflated' positive self-image to cover underlying feelings of inadequacy. Adults with insecure attachment patterns are also more inclined to either deny adversity or be gripped by panic and feel incapable of coping with difficult situations.

In a treatment context, clients' self-esteem and confidence in their own ability to get through hardships can have great significance. A securely attached client with fundamentally positive expectations of himself and others will be more ready to take up the challenge of treatment, and be more 'free' to focus on the treatment itself, rather than worry about how it will progress or whether the treatment provider will fail. In emotionally strained situations it is a great advantage to not simultaneously have to struggle with fundamental doubts about whether one is acceptable as a human being and deserving of love and care, just as it is an advantage to be confident in one's ability to tackle difficulties in a productive way.

The difference between secure and insecure attachment also manifests itself in different strategies for dealing with conflict, where self-esteem as well as confidence in others' reliability and positive intentions imply that securely attached people are generally more open and constructive in their encounter with interpersonal conflicts (Creasey, 2002). Because securely attached people have usually experienced that their needs were taken seriously by their attachment figures, they will feel safer drawing attention to their needs than insecurely attached people. If they experience others hurting them or ignoring their wishes, they will be more inclined to assume that this was a mistake or a one-off incident, which will be 'fixed' if they draw attention to their feelings. This contrasts with insecurely attached people, who will be more inclined to conclude that others have bad intentions, that they do not deserve better, or perhaps both. Securely attached people are thus more inclined to explain disagreements with others based on features of the specific situation – "He was just tired after a long day at work" – rather than more permanent features of the people or relationships – "He doesn't love me anyway" or "We just aren't compatible."

This more positive approach to interpersonal conflicts can easily become significant in a treatment relationship, where it may affect clients' inclination to draw attention to their needs if the treatment provider does not acknowledge them. Of course, treatment providers do not always meet all the client's needs or wishes, nor should they, but in such cases it is more expedient to discuss this openly, rather than the client feeling let down without the treatment provider being aware of it. With securely attached clients there is thus a smaller risk of the treatment alliance being ruptured without the treatment provider noticing.

At the same time, there is less risk of the client panicking if conflicts of interest or opinion arise between client and treatment provider; for example, disagreements concerning the treatment strategy that the treatment provider advocates. Here the securely attached client will both be inclined to trust the treatment provider's good intentions and to feel confident that they can find a solution together. So, although the securely attached client may not accept everything the treatment provider suggests, or necessarily be especially 'compliant', the climate of collaboration is likely to be positive.

Willingness to seek support

Securely attached people have usually experienced how others can provide help and support in difficult and threatening situations, and therefore it makes sense and feels natural for them to approach others if they feel vulnerable (Wilkinson, 2003).

Studies of the relation between attachment patterns and the tendency to seek help and support indicates that secure attachment is not just connected with a greater inclination to seek support from actual attachment figures, such as parents, close friends, or partners, but also from other persons such as teachers, mentors, or counsellors (Larose and Bernier, 2001, Lopez et al., 1998, Riggs et al., 2002, Vogel and Wei, 2005). Here securely attached people especially diverge from people with avoidant attachment patterns. However, research also indicates that the outcome from seeking help is greater for people with secure attachment, who are more calmed by this contact. Unlike ambivalently attached people, who are also inclined to seek help and support but find it hard to be calmed by the support they receive because they constantly fear an unpleasant outcome, the secure person will instead associate contact with others with a 'promise' that things will improve. Therefore, securely attached people are most likely to take the initiative to seek out treatment, to contribute constructively to this treatment, and to feel helped by treatment providers.

In treatment contexts, this inclination to lean on others and find real comfort and relief in contact is an obvious resource. First of all, this means that the client will often be able to use the contact with the treatment provider constructively. Second, it means that the client will likely draw on a wider network of supporting people – spouse, friends, family, etc. – which can lighten the pressure on the treatment provider and be very valuable in many courses of treatments. For example, for a client who is in therapy because she experienced a bank robbery it makes a great difference whether she has a boyfriend and good friends with whom she can discuss her experiences, or lives alone without close social contacts.

Of course, secure attachment patterns are not synonymous with a large social network. However, research indicates that securely attached people are inclined to have more and closer social relationships to draw on in difficult situations, also in adulthood (Mikulincer and Shaver, 2007: 271–319). In the AAI, secure people especially differ from avoidant people in their clear and explicit appreciation of attachment and attachment relationships, which are also acknowledged as being crucial to the person's life and well-being (Main et al., 2008). Securely attached people are thus motivated to establish and maintain close emotional relationships. By virtue of their emotional openness, their general self-esteem, and their constructive strategies for handling conflicts, they have especially good conditions for establishing and maintaining deep and mutually committed relationships.

The narrative dimension: coherence and credibility

A man works for an organization where, following a number of layoffs, work has become exceedingly busy for the remaining employees. This has hit him hard, and he has been off work due to stress for a prolonged period of time. In this connection he has an interview with his caseworker, who asks him to give an account of how he is doing and how he aims to move on. The man answers: "Taking time off to rest has definitely helped me, but I still feel stressed inside. The other day, for example, I noticed that I flinched whenever the phone rang, which can't exactly be a sign of good health, right? I definitely think things are improving, and my wife has really helped me put things into perspective. I'm sure you'd like to know whether I can see myself returning to my job? I've really thought about it a lot, because I feel I'm beginning to see that breaking down like that had both something to do with me but also with the workplace itself. I probably said yes to far too many things to make myself indispensable, but then there wasn't really room to say no if all our tasks were to be completed. I'm afraid that I'll end up in the same situation if I return, but what are my alternatives? Is it possible to be provided with some form of support if I give it another go?"

The manner in which parents of securely attached children recount their story in the AAI is first and foremost characterized by coherence and credibility (Main et al., 2008, Hesse, 2008). Security is not necessarily related to articulate or elaborate descriptions of thoughts and feelings or to a highly reflective approach. Nor is there any immediate connection between secure attachment and verbal intelligence (Bakermans-Kranenburg and van Ijzendoorn, 1993, Sagi et al., 1994). What is central is that different parts of the narrative are not contradictory, that the narrative is intelligible and the listener is able to empathize, and that the information provided is appropriate and relevant to the context.

Even during the AAI, where the attachment system is activated because of the extensive inquiry into attachment experiences, the securely attached person is able to communicate a coherent and credible narrative adapted to the listener's understanding and to what is required in the specific situation. In treatment relationships with secure clients, one may therefore generally expect a clear and open communication – even about difficult and vulnerable topics – as well as the narrative being adapted to what is appropriate and constructive in the given context.

Connection between general descriptions and specific examples

As described in Chapter 1, internal working models consist of different types of knowledge at different levels of generality. The internal working models of secure people are characterized by integration of and agreement between information at different levels and in different representational systems (Bretherton and Munholland, 2008, Crittenden and Landini, 2011). This implies that knowledge on a *general, semantic* level – assumptions about and views of relationships – will be aligned with knowledge on a *specific, episodic* level – recollections of concrete episodes of interaction. On one hand, this means that if securely attached people give a general description of a relationship, they will likely be able to mention concrete examples of interaction with this person that illustrate and support this picture. On the other hand, it means that if securely attached people relate specific episodes, they will usually be good at summarizing the essence of these episodes according to reasonable, general characteristics (Holmes, 1999).

The ability to tell a story whose different levels are aligned and interconnected is crucial to the ability to communicate effectively and constructively with others, including with a treatment provider. For the treatment provider aiming to understand a client's difficulties, it will prove important to be able to empathize with the client's narrative on some level. It is necessary to hear about specific episodes and examples to form a more concrete picture of how difficulties manifest themselves, as well as to hear more abstract summaries of the general essence of the problem, so one can understand the import the clients ascribes to their difficulties (Holmes, 2001, Slade, 2008). If one of these levels is missing in the narrative, or if the two levels do not correspond, treatment providers will struggle to gain a picture of what to focus on in treatment. When research generally indicates that secure clients make better use of treatment and have stronger treatment alliances, this may to some degree be related to the fact that reaching a clear and mutual problem understanding can be easier with a securely attached client.

It is important to bear in mind that integration between types and levels of knowledge is context-specific: a secure person's narrative will not stand out as especially coherent and integrative unless the subject turns to attachment (Crowell et al., 1996). There is no evidence to suggest that the lack of coherence between the semantic and episodic levels in insecurely attached people's narratives is caused by general difficulties with generalizing or exemplifying, which would also manifest itself in a work context or when talking about hobbies, for example. Secure attachment is specifically tied to coherent and integrative narratives about close emotional relationships, which has obvious relevance in some treatment contexts. In psychotherapy or other treatments where a client's self-image and relationships are in focus, the client's ability to present a coherent and integrative narrative about self and others plays a significant role. This is less crucial in somatic treatment, but can still be important to the treatment provider's contact with the client, and thus also for treatment alliances and in the end perhaps for the final outcome.

'Mentalization' and reflection in the moment

Although not always the case, securely attached people's narrative about themselves and their relationships will often be characterized by a higher degree of 'metacognitive monitoring' and 'mentalization' than insecurely attached people's narratives. 'Metacognitive monitoring' is the ability to 'monitor' one's own narrative while it takes shape – for example, being aware of and explicitly considering mutually contradicting information or drawing attention to the parts of the narrative that make up one's own perspective, but which may be imprecise or change with time (Main, 1991). This will often involve taking the listener's perspective into account. The person narrating may say, "I realize I sound slightly self-contradictory here, but generally I am very independent, just not when it comes to my finances …" The concept 'metacognitive monitoring' partly overlaps with the concept 'mentalization', although 'mentalization' has a broader meaning, being a general ability to understand and describe one's own and others' thoughts, emotions, and intentions (Allen, 2003, Fonagy et al., 2002). In a narrative, mentalization is indicated by descriptions of one's own mental states, assumptions about others' mental states, and thoughts about the connection between mental states and actions.

According to theory, secure attachment is linked with a higher degree of mentalization than insecure attachment because of special properties of the secure parent–child relationship, which presumably promote the child's ability to mentalize. Research has shown that parents of securely attached children are more inclined to talk to their child about thoughts and feelings, and more precisely 'mirror' the child's feelings (Bretherton, 1990, Fonagy et al., 2007, Meins and Fernyhough, 1999). For instance, if their child is afraid of a new toy, they will say, "Oh, that scared you a bit, did it?" rather than ignoring the child's expression of emotion, by smiling and shaking the toy or maybe saying, "Oh, how upset you are with Mummy!" Through such exchanges with parents, children gradually learn to connect their emotional states with concepts and situations. Parents of securely attached children are also easier to 'read', as the emotions reflected in their facial expressions and body language usually correspond more closely to emotions expressed verbally than it does for parents of insecurely attached children (Roisman et al., 2004). Thus, in several different ways, secure attachment relationships form an environment that is especially conducive to developing the ability to identify and consider one's own and others' mental and emotional states.

In a treatment relationship, the ability to mentalize is important for the clarity of communication, that is, for the clients' ability to clearly communicate their situation. A narrative poor on mentalization may be a narrative about a number of events and actions without descriptions of subjective reactions to the events or motives behind the actions. It could also be a narrative where thoughts and feelings are perhaps mentioned, but where events and actions are not connected to thoughts and feelings, or where these thoughts and feelings appear 'feigned' or 'cliché-ridden' rather than seeming to be personal reactions and observations – for example, "Of course I was upset when my mother died. People usually get upset when they lose a family member." Narratives poor on mentalization mean that treatment providers trying to gain a picture of the client's inner life are left to conjecture and make assumptions that may prove completely erroneous.

In contrast to this, a securely attached client's narrative will usually provide a genuine and nuanced picture of the person's subjective life, which gives the treatment provider a good basis for understanding and empathizing with the client's situation. This is crucial in treatment contexts where the client's thoughts and emotional life are in focus. However, it can also be important in other kinds of treatment. For example, understanding why a client systematically neglects taking his or her prescribed medicine is important when aiming for a more strict observance of a treatment plan. The more inclined clients are to narratively connect their own actions with underlying motives, thoughts, and feelings, the more relevant information treatment providers will have access to when planning and adjusting a course of treatment.

When making assumptions about others' subjective life, the securely attached person's narrative will usually acknowledge that it is not possible to know exactly what another person thinks and feels (Hesse, 2008, Main, 1991). Treatment providers will most likely be able to form an impression of important people in the client's life and above all of which assumptions the client makes about these people's thoughts, feelings, and motives. This disposition to consider other people's perspective combined with modesty with regard to one's ability to have certain knowledge of it is clearly a resource in treatment relationships. The secure client will also tend to be aware of the treatment provider having a different perspective than the client's own, which the client cannot simply 'figure out' in advance. It is therefore less likely that a secure client will disregard that the treatment provider is also a person and meet the treatment provider with an unshakable, prejudiced assumption such as "You are only out to discover all my flaws so you can feel superior to me", or similar.

'Balance' and appropriate 'dosing' of information

In addition to the readiness to consider different perspectives and put oneself in other people's shoes, securely attached people's descriptions of themselves and others they are close to will usually be characterized by balance between constructive and less constructive features and actions (Blatt et al., 1997, Main et al., 2008). Because the secure person's self-worth is relatively robust, it is not necessary to cling to ideas of personal infallibility or perfection. At the same time, the securely attached person will not give in to a negative spiral of self-reproach and feelings of inadequacy. In secure people's representation of themselves, there will therefore be room for considering personal flaws and for taking responsibility for problems experienced, while at the same time maintaining a basic self-worth. As described earlier, a feeling of self-worth is an obvious resource in many contexts, also in a treatment situation. On the narrative level, this balance and ability to bring out nuances is an advantage because the client thus communicates a more 'whole' picture to the treatment provider, rather than painting an idealized image or drawing a purely negative picture that gives no impression of strengths or competences.

This 'balance' is also present in descriptions of close personal relationships, where descriptions of others are nuanced rather than being 'black and white' – either completely wonderful or utterly awful (Calabrese et al., 2006). In line with this, a securely attached person is unlikely to describe either a spouse or parent as solely responsible for his or her problems, although their roles may be examined in the narrative. In marriage counselling, for example, it is likely that secure clients will describe relational problems as something that both parties have contributed to and share responsibility for. In the description of self as well as others, the secure person's narrative balance is indicated by the good and less positive aspects being integrated into the total description. Thus, the narrative will not alternate chaotically between black and white with changing perspectives from one moment to the next, but constitute a comprehensive picture where different sides are related to each other (Crittenden and Landini, 2011, Wallin, 2007).

Narratives classified as 'secure' in the AAI are characterized by including an appropriate amount of detail that enables the listener to follow and empathize with the narrative account (Hesse, 2008). The narrative is neither sketch-like and superficial nor flooded by unnecessary details or digressions. This ability to narrate with an appropriate 'dosing' of information may be linked to the secure person's ability to assume the listener's perspective and willingness to share his or her subjective perspective with others. Even in difficult situations, the securely attached client will often be able judge how much information the treatment provider needs in order to react adequately, as well as what information the treatment provider does not need. Furthermore, secure persons' immediate, interpersonal openness will mean that, rather than keeping things to themselves, they are generally willing to share their thoughts and feelings with the treatment provider when this is appropriate.

There will naturally be individual differences with regard to how talkative clients are in treatment contexts, also among securely attached people. However, more talkative secure clients will still generally include material relevant to the given context. Similarly, less talkative secure clients will not systematically omit information relevant in the situation. This is a contrast to ambivalent clients' inclination to go off on narrative 'tangents' when their attachment system is activated and to avoidant clients' inclination to avoid sharing feelings or specific relationship episodes, even when asked directly. Just as with the integration of different systems of knowledge – episodic and semantic information – securely attached clients are only expected to excel in nuanced, appropriately dosed, and relevant information when describing close, personal relationships or in situations where the attachment system is activated (Crowell et al., 1996).

Notes on 'earned' secure attachment

An important point regarding adult attachment patterns, as they are defined in both the questionnaire and interview traditions, is that they describe a person's current approach to dealing with and engaging in attachment relationships, rather than the person's background and childhood attachment (Crowell et al., 2008, Main et al., 1985). As mentioned in Chapter 1, although there is a tendency towards developmental continuity, meaning that secure and insecure attachment in childhood is related to secure and insecure adult attachment respectively, there is no narrow determinism, and movements in both directions occur (Crowell and Hauser, 2008, Hamilton, 2000, Waters et al., 2000a, 2000b). There are thus people who appear securely attached in adulthood, but who in the past have experienced insecure attachment relationships. This 'earned' secure attachment is interesting in a treatment context for two reasons. First of all, it is relevant to ask whether 'earned' secure attachment has any particular implications for treatment compared to 'continuous' secure attachment. Do 'earned' secure people handle crises just as well, or does their insecure background constitute a vulnerability factor? Second, understanding the phenomenon 'earned' secure attachment may provide a hint as to what is needed to help insecurely attached clients when working psychotherapeutically with their attachment history and pattern.

Only a limited number of studies have compared people with 'continuous' and 'earned' security. However, the studies that do exist indicate that the two patterns do not differ with regard to the ability to function as a security-providing parent – not even under pressure (Phelps et al., 1998, Roisman et al., 2002, 2007). This has especially been the focus in developmental psychological research investigating whether coherent narratives about difficult childhoods are reliable indicators of a person actually 'breaking' the unfortunate pattern through which insecurity is communicated and passed on to future generations. The question of whether 'earned' secure people are more disposed to suffer from different psychological difficulties than 'continuously' secure persons – such as a tendency to depression in difficult situations – has led to more contradictory results. However, this question is difficult to answer definitively without the use of longitudinal studies, which require considerable resources as they involve following individuals from childhood to adulthood. The dilemma is that people's retrospective account of their childhood attachment history must be assumed to be potentially affected by their current psychological well-being. In other words, a depressed person will be inclined to present his or her attachment history more negatively, and may therefore wrongfully end up appearing as 'earned' secure rather than 'continuous' secure.

Due to the great methodological challenges related to examining the factors that contribute to people with negative attachment histories developing a secure attachment pattern in adulthood, there is limited empirical evidence in the area. It is likely that biologically conditioned 'resilience', that is, an inborn resistance in some children, plays a role in this context (Hesse, 2008). It is also likely to be the case that these people as children or later in life were fortunate enough to have access to other and more positive relationships than the relationship to their parents – for example, an aunt who served as an attachment figure or later experiences of secure attachment in romantic relationships. Finally, psychotherapy can play a role for some in changing the 'track' initially laid down by an insecure childhood. This will be treated in more depth in Chapter 9.

References

Ainsworth, M. S., Blehar, M. C., Waters, E. & Wall, S. 1978. *Patterns of attachment: A psychological study of the strange situation*. Hillsdale, NJ: Lawrence Erlbaum.

Allen, J. G. 2003. Mentalizing. *Bulletin of the Menninger Clinic*, 67, 91–112.

Bakermans-Kranenburg, M. J. & van Ijzendoorn, M. H. 1993. A psychometric study of the Adult Attachment Interview: Reliability and discriminant validity. *Developmental Psychology*, 29, 870–879.

Bartholomew, K. & Horowitz, L. M. 1991. Attachment styles among young adults: A test of a four-category model. *Journal of Personality and Social Psychology*, 61, 226–244.

Berlin, L. J., Cassidy, J. & Appleyard, K. 2008. The influence of early attachments on other relationships. In Cassidy, J. & Shaver, P. (eds) *Handbook of attachment: Theory, research, and clinical applications*, 2nd ed. New York: Guilford Press.

Blatt, S. J., Auerbach, J. S. & Levy, K. N. 1997. Mental representations in personality development, psychopathology, and the therapeutic process. *Review of General Psychology*, 1, 351–374.

Bowlby, J. 1969. *Attachment and Loss: Vol. 1. Attachment*. London: Pimlico.

Bretherton, I. 1990. Communication patterns, internal working models, and the intergenerational transmission of attachment relationships. *Infant Mental Health Journal*, 11, 237–252.

Bretherton, I. & Munholland, K. A. 2008. Internal working models in attachment relationships: Elaborating a central construct in attachment theory. In Cassidy, J. & Shaver, P. (eds) *Handbook of attachment: Theory, research, and clinical applications*, 2nd ed. New York: Guilford Press.

Calabrese, M. L., Farber, B. A. & Westen, D. 2006. The relationship of adult attachment constructs to object relational patterns of representing self and others. *Journal of the American Academy of Psychoanalysis and Dynamic Psychiatry*, 33, 513–530.

Creasey, G. 2002. Associations between working models of attachment and conflict management behavior in romantic couples. *Journal of Counseling Psychology*, 49, 365–375.

Crittenden, P. M. & Landini, A. 2011. *Assessing adult attachment. A dynamic maturational approach to discourse analysis*, New York: W.W. Norton & Company.

Crowell, J. A., Fraley, R. C. & Shaver, P. 2008. Measurement of individual differences in adolescent and adult attachment. In Cassidy, J. & Shaver, P. (eds) *Handbook of attachment: Theory, research, and clinical applications*, 2nd ed. New York: Guilford Press.

Crowell, J. A. & Hauser, S. T. 2008. AAIs in a high-risk sample: Stability and relation to functioning from adolescence to 39 years. In Steele, H. & Steele, M. (eds) *Clinical Applications of the Adult Attachment Interview*. New York: Guilford Press.

Crowell, J. A., Waters, E., Treboux, D., O'Connor, E., Colon-Downs, C. & Feider, O. 1996. Discriminant validity of the Adult Attachment Interview. *Child Development*, 67, 2584–2599.

Dozier, M. 1990. Attachment organization and treatment use for adults with serious psychopathological disorders. *Development and Psychopathology*, 2, 47–60.

Fonagy, P., Gergely, G., Jurist, E. L. & Target, M. 2002. *Affect regulation, mentalization, and the development of the self*, New York: Other Press.

Fonagy, P., Gergely, G. & Target, M. 2007. The parent–infant dyad and the construction of the subjective self. *Journal of Child Psychology and Psychiatry*, 48, 288–328.

George, C. & Solomon, J. 2008. The caregiving system. A behavioral systems approach to parenting. In Cassidy, J. & Shaver, P. R. (eds) *Handbook of attachment: Theory, research, and clinical applications*, 2nd ed. New York: Guilford Press.

Grossmann, K. E., Grossmann, K. & Zimmermann, P. 1999. A wider view of attachment and exploration: Stability and change during the years of immaturity. In Cassidy, J. & Shaver, P. R. (eds) *Handbook of attachment: Theory, research, and clinical applications*. New York: Guilford Press.

Hamilton, C. E. 2000. Continuity and discontinuity of attachment from infancy through adolescence. *Child Development*, 71, 690–694.

Hesse, E. 2008. The Adult Attachment Interview: Protocol, method of analysis, and empirical studies. In Cassidy, J. & Shaver, P. (eds) *Handbook of attachment: Theory, research, and clinical applications*, 2nd ed. New York: Guilford Press.

Holmes, J. 1997. Attachment, autonomy, intimacy: Some clinical implications of attachment theory. *British Journal of Medical Psychology*, 70, 231–248.

Holmes, J. 1999. Defensive and creative uses of narrative in psychotherapy: An attchment perspective. In Roberts, G. & Holmes, J. (eds) *Healing stories: Narrative in psychiatry and psychotherapy.* London: Oxford University Press.

Holmes, J. 2001. *The search for the secure base. Attachment theory and psychotherapy,* London: Brunner-Routledge.

Holmes, J. 2009. From attachment research to clinical practice: Getting it together. In Obegi, J. H. & Berant, E. (eds) *Attachment theory and research in clinical work with adults.* New York: Guilford Press.

Larose, S. & Bernier, A. 2001. Social support processes: Mediators of attachment state of mind and adjustment in late adolescence. *Attachment & Human Development*, 3, 96–120.

Levy, K. N., Ellison, W. D., Scott, L. N. & Bernecker, S. L. 2011. Attachment style. *Journal of Clinical Psychology*, 67, 193–201.

Lopez, F. G., Melendez, M. C., Sauer, E. M., Berger, E. & Wyssmann, J. 1998. Internal working models, self-reported problems, and help-seeking attitudes among college students. *Journal of Counseling Psychology*, 45, 79–83.

Magai, C. 1999. Affect, imagery, and attachment: Working models of interpersonal affect and the socialization of emotion. In Cassidy, J. & Shaver, P. R. (eds) *Handbook of attachment: Theory, research, and clinical applications.* New York: Guilford Press.

Main, M. 1991. Metacognitive knowledge, metacognitive monitoring, and singular (coherent) vs multiple (incoherent) model of attachment: Findings and directions for future research. In Parkes, C. M. & Stevenson-Hinde, J. (eds) *Attachment across the life cycle.* New York: Tavistock/Routledge.

Main, M., Hesse, E. & Goldwyn, R. 2008. Studying differences in language usage in recounting attachment history: An introduction to the AAI. In Steele, H. & Steele, M. (eds) *Clinical applications of the Adult Attachment Interview.* New York: Guilford Press.

Main, M., Kaplan, N. & Cassidy, J. 1985. Security in infancy, childhood, and adulthood: A move to the level of representation. *Monographs of the Society for Research in Child Development*, 50, 66–104.

Meins, E. & Fernyhough, C. 1999. Linguistic acquisitional style and mentalising development: The role of maternal mind-mindedness. *Cognitive Development*, 14, 363–380.

Mikulincer, M. & Shaver, P. R. 2007. *Attachment in adulthood: Structure, dynamics, and change,* New York: Guilford Press.

Mikulincer, M., Shaver, P. R. & Pereg, D. 2003. Attachment theory and affect regulation: The dynamics, development, and cognitive consequences of attachment-related strategies. *Motivation and Emotion*, 27, 77–102.

Phelps, J. L., Belsky, J. & Crnic, K. 1998. Earned security, daily stress, and parenting: A comparison of five alternative models. *Development and Psychopathology*, 10, 21–38.

Riggs, S. A., Jacobvitz, D. & Hazen, N. 2002. Adult attachment and history of psychotherapy in a normative sample. *Psychotherapy: Theory, Research, Practice, Training*, 39, 344–353.

Roisman, G. I., Fraley, R. C. & Belsky, J. 2007. A taxometric study of the Adult Attachment Interview. *Developmental Psychology*, 43, 675–686.

Roisman, G. I., Padron, E., Sroufe, L. A. & Egeland, B. 2002. Earned-secure attachment status in retrospect and prospect. *Child Development*, 73, 1204–1219.

Roisman, G. I., Tsai, J. L. & Chiang, K.-H. S. 2004. The emotional integration of childhood experience: Physiological, facial expressive, and self-reported emotional response during the Adult Attachment Interview. *Developmental Psychology*, 40, 776–789.

Sagi, A., van Ijzendoorn, M. H., Scharf, M. & Koren-Karie, N. 1994. Stability and discriminant validity of the Adult Attachment Interview: A psychometric study in young Israeli adults. *Developmental Psychology*, 30, 771–777.

Slade, A. 2008. The implications of attachment theory and research for adult psychotherapy: Research and clinical perspectives. In Cassidy, J. & Shaver, P. (eds) *Handbook of attachment: Theory, research, and clinical applications*, 2nd ed. New York: Guilford Press.

Vogel, D. L. & Wei, M. 2005. Adult attachment and help-seeking intent: The mediating roles of psychological distress and perceived social support. *Journal of Counseling Psychology*, 52, 347–357.

Wallin, D. J. 2007. *Attachment in Psychotherapy*, New York: Guilford Press.

Waters, E., Hamilton, C. E. & Weinfield, N. S. 2000a. The stability of attachment security from infancy to adolescence and early adulthood: General introduction. *Child Development*, 71, 678–683.

Waters, E., Merrick, S., Treboux, D., Crowell, J. & Albersheim, L. 2000b. Attachment security in infancy and early adulthood: A twenty-year longitudinal study. *Child Development*, 71, 684–689.

Wilkinson, S. R. 2003. *Coping and complaining. Attachment and the language of disease.* New York: Brunner-Routledge.

Zegers, M. A. M., Schuengel, C., van Ijzendoorn, M. H. & Janssens, J. M. A. M. 2006. Attachment representations of institutionalized adolescents and their professional caregivers: Predicting the development of therapeutic relationships. *American Journal of Orthopsychiatry*, 76, 325–334.

Chapter 4

Avoidant attachment

The avoidant attachment pattern is characterized by an effort to scale down the attachment system and the emotional and behavioural dispositions that are connected to it. This pattern has its origin in experiences in which showing obvious attachment behaviour, such as crying or clinging to one's caregiver, proved inappropriate or risky (Crittenden, 1999, Mikulincer et al., 2009). A person may have had parents who were preoccupied with their respective careers and who wanted domestic life to function without difficulties, like a 'well-oiled machine'. As a child, this person learned not to be an encumbrance and to take care of himself if he was upset by something. In this way he ensured that he received the best possible support from his emotionally unavailable parents and, as an adult, he will carry this strategy with him into situations where the attachment system is activated.

The predisposition for attempting to 'downregulate' the attachment system influences the general way in which a person approaches relationships. This chapter will first examine how avoidant attachment is expressed in interpersonal interactions and, subsequently, how it manifests itself on a narrative level.

The interpersonal dimension: withdrawal and invulnerability

A man goes to see his general practitioner with complaints of shortness of breath and heart palpitations. These symptoms occur most frequently in the evening, after he has gone to bed and occasionally at work. Initially, when asked how long these symptoms have persisted, the man reluctantly answers, "A while." However, it eventually becomes clear that this has been going on for a year, and that the man's visit to the doctor was prompted by the insistence of his spouse. The man does not seem to consider the symptoms a real problem. He states that he has always been in excellent health, stays in shape, and he does not expect that there is anything wrong with him. The doctor asks whether anything has been troubling him lately in either his personal life or at work; is there perhaps something he worries about when lying in bed at night, or has anything in particular been at stake during the times he has experienced the symptoms at work? The questions clearly make the man uncomfortable, and he avoids eye contact with the doctor.

He replies that everything is fine; he has everything under control and asks whether the doctor cannot just simply give him a physical examination. During the rest of the consultation, the man only communicates using single-syllable words, and he hurries out the door as soon as the doctor has finished the examination.

Most of the relational behaviour patterns connected to avoidant attachment can be considered 'by-products' of the effort to keep the attachment system at bay. The person may, for example, emphasize independence, avoid emotional intimacy, and avoid directing attention to his own or others' vulnerability (Main, 2000, Muller, 2010). This is not necessarily a conscious strategy. Rather, it is a way of managing one's emotions and attention that generally operates automatically and that the person may only be aware of in some instances. Whereas the securely attached person achieves security primarily through intimacy with compassionate others, the avoidantly attached person obtains a secondary feeling of security through experiencing independence and strength (Main, 1995). This strategy for attaining security can easily become relevant in a treatment context, and it is important to understand how central components of the relationship to treatment providers can be more problematic for people with a history of avoidant attachment.

Emphasis on independence and personal strength

When attachment figures reject and demean children or withdraw from contact when they show vulnerability and seek comfort, the children are forced to adapt their behaviour to this local 'reality'. If the experience of being rejected is systematic, so that the children are certain of the hopelessness of seeking intimacy and comfort, the most expedient strategy the children can adopt is to strive to tone down their overt attachment behaviour in order to increase the probability of the attachment figure's continued availability (Main, 1995, Weinfield et al., 2008). For a small child, this 'choice of strategy' takes place on a behavioural level and not as the result of reflective deliberation. The child directs attention away from feelings of vulnerability, away from threats, and away from the figures of attachment in their capacity as attachment figures, not based on a decision to be 'strong and brave', but because of simple, emotional necessity.

However, this approach, which initially occurs purely on an operational level of action, will eventually be expanded by a conceptual self-image and a set of values that contribute to supporting the strategy. Some components of this self-understanding may be adopted directly from the parents, who may perhaps have admonished the child not to be a 'cry baby'. Other components might be conclusions drawn by the person himself. For example, "If that's the case, never mind then; I don't need them, I can take care of myself ..." This type of conviction will end up forming a part of the person's conscious approach to seeking support and comfort from others. Avoidant people ascribe value to strength and toughness and take pride in not being dependent on others (Main et al., 2008, Mikulincer and Shaver, 2008, Waldinger et al., 2003). This attitude affects both the avoidant person's approach to new attachment relations, including romantic relationships, and their approach to many types of treatment situations. For example, studies suggest that avoidant people are significantly less inclined to turn to psychotherapy than others are and, similarly, they tend to endure somatic symptoms for a longer period before seeking help from their doctor (Feeney and Ryan, 1997, Riggs et al., 2002).

The aversion to entering into a dependent relationship or to showing weakness means that when treatment providers actually meet a person with avoidant attachment the person in question may be somewhat 'out of her depth' already. The avoidant person's general way of handling stress is to further intensify their self-reliance and to isolate themselves from others, as opposed to asking for help, which they may not even see as an option (Larose and Bernier, 2001, Lopez et al., 1998, Vogel and Wei, 2005). An avoidantly attached person may, for example, have experienced difficulties at work for a long time without a murmur, before at last succumbing to a stress reaction. Seeking treatment may be accompanied by a strong feeling of defeat, in addition to the stress-related symptoms. The tenacious effort to 'take care of oneself' and 'be strong' has failed, and the breakdown cannot be reconciled with the person's favoured self-image.

A number of studies suggest that people with avoidant attachment patterns are inclined to rely on a defensively 'augmented' image of themselves as being particularly outstanding, strong, etc. (Lopez, 2001, Mikulincer and Shaver, 2007: 160–163). This self-image contributes to maintaining the feeling of not needing other people, a need that is downplayed and devalued. However, because this self-confidence has a partially defensive function and therefore deviates from the more ingrained self-esteem of securely attached people, it is vulnerable to collapsing under the pressure of stressful situations. In these cases, the avoidant person's apparent strength and self-assurance may suddenly give way to doubt, inferiority, and shamefulness, which have previously been hidden from awareness (Mikulincer et al., 2009, Wallin, 2007). For treatment providers, it is important to have an understanding for the intense shamefulness some people can experience when finding themselves in a vulnerable and dependent position, which they cannot merely 'brush aside'. One result of the struggle to avoid feeling vulnerable may be a devaluation and criticism of the treatment provider. A client's hostility toward a treatment provider may be a desperate attempt to defend the sense of invincibility, which is an important part of avoidant people's way of managing their attachment system.

The desire to avoid seeking help can easily lead the person with avoidant attachment to resist treatment in different ways or to abandon it prematurely. Being in a dependent relationship, which is often part of a course of treatment, is a constant challenge for these people, and therefore cooperating constructively and engaging with the treatment can be difficult for them (Dozier et al., 2001, Muller, 2010). A treatment provider may have a sense, and rightly so, that they already 'have one foot out the door' and that they are only reluctantly taking part in treatment.

Limited attention to feelings

One way in which children with avoidant attachment patterns avoid overt attachment behaviour, such as crying or clinging to caregivers, is to make an effort to suppress the emotional sensations that trigger this behaviour. People with a history of avoidant attachment behaviour will carry the inclination to suppress or ignore their own emotions in attachment-related situations into their adult life. In fact, neurophysiological research suggests that avoidant people suppress emotional responses on a physiological level (Dozier and Kobak, 1992, Fox and Hane, 2008, Roisman, 2007, Roisman et al., 2004). Thus, they are not only less disposed to express feelings openly to others, but they are also less disposed to *feel* emotions. Therefore, when people with avoidant attachment claim not to be distressed in strained situations, it is, to some extent, true: they do not experience anxiety or sadness. At the same time, however, other parts of their physiology suggest that they are under emotional strain – for example, their heart rate and 'galvanic skin response', a change in the skin's electrical conductance, which usually accompanies emotional arousal. This physiological response to strain, which is not associated with verbal or behavioural expression of emotion, may partly explain the connection between avoidant attachment and a number of psychosomatically conditioned disorders (Maunder and Hunter, 2001, Waller et al., 2004). In other words, avoidantly attached people simply do not react to their bodies' signals, and this can lead to physiological symptoms or even illnesses in some cases.

The experiences avoidant people have drawn from attachment relations have not given them cause to trust emotions as a helpful guide for their actions. Usually a child's feeling of sadness caused by, for example, being teased by other children will serve as an incentive to seek comfort and support from his parents. However, if the child has reason to expect that he will be ignored or perhaps even reproached for 'whining', this feeling becomes useless and cannot be acted upon. Thus, for the avoidantly attached person, feelings become an unreliable 'information channel'. This explains the avoidant person's preference for 'cooler', more rational approaches to decision-making and deliberation (Crittenden, 1997, 1999). In a treatment setting, clients with an avoidant attachment pattern will not spontaneously speak of their feelings, even in difficult situations, nor will they care to be asked about them. From the avoidant person's point of view, feelings are simply 'in the way' – they are not an aid to moving forward.

Compared to secure and ambivalent attachment, avoidant attachment is strongly related to a lack of emotional expressiveness (Magai, 1999, Mikulincer and Shaver, 2007: 264–268). Feelings of sadness, anger, and shame, in particular, are rarely expressed through words or behaviour such as through tears. On the contrary, in difficult situations, avoidant people are inclined to display 'false cheerfulness' and conceal experienced difficulty behind a smile (Crittenden, 1995). Consequently, in a treatment context, the treatment provider will often have a limited and unclear picture of where an avoidantly attached client 'is' emotionally.

This is not necessarily because avoidant people consciously wish to hide the way they are feeling – they are simply neither very practised in sensing how they feel, nor do they expect that their articulation of feelings will have a positive or relevant effect. As with other characteristics connected to avoidant attachment, there is reason to expect that the avoidant person's tendency to suppress or discount emotions will be especially prominent in situations where there is a risk of the attachment system being activated, for example, in connection with illness, bereavement, and other crises.

The limited attention paid to emotions does not just pertain to the avoidant people themselves – avoidant people are also less likely to be aware of and empathize with other people's feelings (Collins and Read, 1990, Lopez, 2001). This partially explains avoidant parents' limited response to the attachment behaviour of their own children. Studies also show that avoidant people are less caring towards partners experiencing emotional difficulty (Simpson et al., 1992, 2002, 2007), presumably because identifying with the partner's painful emotions involves the activation of feelings that the avoidant person would rather avoid. Therefore, it is to be expected that, in a treatment setting, avoidant clients will have a limited awareness of or empathy with the treatment provider's emotional state. Of course, this is not usually a requirement in treatment. However, treatment providers may be affected by working with people who exhibit limited empathy or consideration for the way they are feeling, and there is a risk of acting in parallel to the clients and 'punishing' them by displaying similarly limited empathy or consideration (Diamond et al., 2003, Wallin, 2007).

Unease with interpersonal openness and intimacy

People with avoidant attachment patterns dislike getting too close to others (Cassidy, 2001, Hazan and Shaver, 1987, Holmes, 1997). Nearness and intimacy are a threat to the independence they perceive as being essential to their psychological survival. Compared to both securely and ambivalently attached people, avoidant people tend to appraise close relationships as a less important part of life (Main et al., 2008). Instead, they make it known that being emotionally close to other people is not greatly significant to them. They may even associate intimacy with a sense of being trapped and a feeling of discomfort rather than security and happiness. Accordingly, avoidant people, as a rule, have fewer intimate relationships, and their romantic relationships are generally shorter and more superficial compared to those of securely attached people (Mikulincer and Shaver, 2007: 308–315, Treboux et al., 2004). Consequently, avoidant people often do not have the strong foundation of a supportive network common for securely attached people. This scant social network leaves avoidant people with a lack of support to be called upon in times of crisis or illness.

Avoidant people prefer to keep others at a distance, both psychologically and physically. Thus, for instance, they have the largest physical 'comfort zone' – the physical distance they prefer to maintain between themselves and others (Kaitz et al.,

2004). One of the ways in which to maintain the *psychological* distance to others is by perceiving oneself as 'different' and not having much in common with others. Avoidant people are more disposed to view themselves as 'special' and to believe that other people are relatively dissimilar to themselves (Mikulincer et al., 1998). For this reason, avoidant people are substantially sceptical of the possibility of others understanding them. This will inevitably affect their attitude to treatment providers. They will be inclined to expect that, even if they manage the difficult task of 'opening up', they will certainly be misunderstood and possibly even scorned or ridiculed.

Despite the ostensible spurning of intimate relationships and the inclination to keep their distance from others, avoidantly attached people may still feel lonely. Studies suggest that all forms of insecure attachment, including avoidant attachment, are connected with a higher degree of experienced loneliness than secure attachment (Larose and Bernier, 2001, Mikulincer and Shaver, 2007: 280–282). Although avoidant people 'choose' emotional distance as the seemingly lesser of two evils, they are not necessarily content or happy about their isolated state. Therefore, avoidant people's assurance that they are unaffected by being alone and taking care of themselves should not necessarily be trusted. While they may deal with isolation better than others, there is an underlying desire for closeness, yet this is considered too risky to act upon. Still, this longing for intimacy does not have the desperate quality characteristic of the disorganized attachment pattern in which interpersonal avoidance is combined with a strong feeling of being lost in one's loneliness. People with avoidant attachment patterns generally experience that they are able to 'take care of themselves' alone.

In addition to the avoidant person's tendency to avoid intimacy, the lack of close, personal relations may be a result of ineffective social problem-solving skills that tend to push others away. Discomfort with the negatively charged feelings, and the intense, direct interaction often involved in interpersonal conflicts, may cause the avoidant person to steer clear of direct confrontation. At times, this can prove problematic, as when important issues in relationships are not discussed and remain unresolved. The inclination to ignore their own as well as others' feelings also means that people with avoidant strategies are poorly equipped to solve problems in close relationships. A number of studies suggest that people with avoidant attachment patterns are not as good at constructively solving interpersonal conflicts as securely attached people (Creasey, 2002, Mikulincer and Shaver, 2007: 268–279, Roisman, 2007, Simpson et al., 1996). The reason for this is that they are, to a great extent, disposed to 'stick their head in the sand' and evade these conflicts. Over time, a friend or partner may find this response frustrating.

The narrative dimension: abstraction and minimization

A woman has been afforded a couple of sessions with a psychologist via the crisis centre at the hospital where she works. A patient, whom she had nursed for a long time, has died in connection with a risky operation. Subsequently, the woman appears to be affected by this event. For example, she has made quite a few mistakes, which is very atypical for her. However, during the first therapy session, she says that she cannot quite see the point of talking about what has happened: "This kind of thing happens – in this profession, you just have to be prepared for it. Of course it isn't pleasant when something like this happens, but you just can't go around worrying about it." The woman smiles and looks down at the table. The psychologist asks how she reacted when she was informed of the patient's death? "I don't know," says the woman. "I don't really remember." A long pause follows. When asked whether the woman sees a connection between the patient's death and the problems she subsequently experienced at work, the woman answers, "I don't know. It's conceivable of course, but I don't really know. I think it's starting to get better again, though. It wasn't that bad, after all." The psychologist is left with a sense that the woman is still affected by the death, but that she is very reluctant to talk about the subject. The woman is not motivated to partake in additional therapy sessions, and says that she believes she has worked through everything.

The inclination to downregulate the attachment system and thereby the associated feelings of vulnerability and dependence on others also affects the way in which avoidant clients present themselves and their story. When such feelings are explored in the AAI, avoidant people attempt to evade the subject or close it quickly in various ways (Main, 1995). Analogous to the avoidant child in the Strange Situation, the discomfort related to the attachment-activating situation is handled with an effort to direct attention elsewhere and suppress overt emotional reactions. The resulting narratives are impersonal and marked by limited emotional expression.

Brevity and superficiality

Securely attached people freely and fluently tell of their experiences in attachment relationships, whereas avoidant people's narrative style is often more brief – reading like a telegram (Holmes, 1999, Main et al., 2008). This narrative style is related to the desire to quickly move on to other subjects, to avoid 'dwelling' on attachment-related experiences, which activate unwanted associations. Occasionally, avoidant people will abruptly change the subject from attachment relationships to less 'dangerous' subjects. This is relatively rare in the AAI, as it contains a strong signal that the interviewee is expected to talk about attachment. However, it is highly likely that this kind of 'strategic' change of subject commonly appears in more loosely structured conversations. Again, the avoidance is not necessarily a wilful reaction to consciously experienced discomfort. It just as well may be a case of a relatively automatic, unconscious reaction, in which the avoidant person is not necessarily aware that she is steering the conversation away from more emotional and relational topics.

When avoidant people choose or feel compelled to talk about attachment topics, they usually do so in superficial terms. Questions are answered briefly and generally. For example, "What was my relationship with my parents like? Well, it was fine, normal, the way parent–child relationships usually are, I think." Even if avoidant people are asked to elaborate on these superficial descriptions, they will often keep description at this level. This is often done by appealing to a poorly remembered childhood when asked to give illustrative examples in the AAI – either by intimating a limited recollection of their childhood in general or by intimating that an example cannot be recalled in that moment (Hermans et al., 2005, Hesse, 2008).

The description of others and the relationship with them is often expressed by means of 'clichés' or reference to what is normal or ordinary (Main et al., 2008). This can be seen as a way to distract attention from potentially emotional attachment relationships. If everything really was "normal" and the family was a "typical nuclear family", where the mother bandaged wounds "like all mothers do", there would be no reason to give it more thought or study it more closely. The brevity and superficiality of the communication implicitly urges the interviewer to "let it lie" and "move on".

Others listening to the avoidant person's narrative may get the sense of not really being allowed to get close to the person, and that the avoidant person does not ascribe the conversation or narrative any value, nor have they properly elaborated on it. In this way, the avoidant person's narrative style also serves to keep others at a distance (Main, 1995, Slade, 2008). In the context of treatment, this narrative style also covertly urges the treatment provider to cease any further questioning and leave emotionally sensitive topics alone. However, acting on this implicit plea can have negative consequences for treatment, as the treatment provider will lack important information about the client's true perspective on things.

Generalization and abstraction rather than specific memories

A major way in which the avoidant person's narrative differs from that of the securely attached person is by the relative absence of specific recollections that give insight into the nature of their relationship with their caregivers (Hesse, 2008, Holmes, 2001). The securely attached person can often recount many concrete incidents during the AAI, whereas the avoidant person often answers evasively and reports that she cannot remember any concrete episodes. However, as noted earlier, the difference in reporting cannot be explained by a difference in general recall ability between persons with avoidant and secure attachment (Bakermans-Kranenburg and van Ijzendoorn, 1993, Sagi et al., 1994). Therefore, there are two ways of explaining this phenomenon. One explanation is that avoidant people, consciously or unconsciously, block access to concrete memories. The second explanation is that, because of their inclination to turn their attention away from attachment-related interactions, avoidant people have not 'encoded' episodes of this kind in memory when they originally occurred. Experimental studies suggest that both mechanisms are at play (Fraley and Brumbaugh, 2007, Mikulincer and Orbach, 1995).

A narrative that primarily takes place on a general, abstract level makes it difficult to get a vivid picture of what the person is talking about. This means that listeners may find it challenging to get a clear idea of how an interaction actually played out between the avoidant person and other people. The narrative is not fleshed out and remains more like a sketch. Listeners will feel inclined to make assumptions and form their own picture based on what they know or have experienced themselves. Therefore, a narrative containing a scant number of memories of concrete episodes puts listeners at increased risk of painting an imprecise picture.

In addition to a relative absence of concrete memories, the avoidant person's narrative in the AAI is usually marked by a lack of coherence or by conflict between general, abstract descriptions and the few specific episodes that do figure in the narrative (Main et al., 2008). Typically, general descriptions are positive – "My mother was very loving" – but they are poorly connected to the concrete episodes remembered; at least they seem so from an outsider's point of view. For example, the person may relate how he was badly bullied in school while, at the same time, recounting that he never told his mother, because he was afraid she would criticize him for being an easy target. It seems as if the general description and the concrete episodes exist in two separate 'streams' of the narrative, which cannot enter into dialogue with each other, and in which the abstract, overarching stream generally takes priority.

Due to the general tendency of avoidant people to idealize their parents and other attachment figures in the AAI, some attachment literature concludes that avoidant persons generally have an unrealistically positive picture of their attachment figures. This is inconsistent with research findings based on questionnaires, which, as already mentioned, largely suggest that avoidantly attached people are disposed to devalue others, including their own partners. Based on these findings, the question becomes whether this overly positive representation of caregivers is in fact primarily a way to avoid dealing with the relation in greater depth. In daily conversation, quickly answering a question by saying, "Everything's fine," normally constitutes a 'protection' from potentially more probing questions. This also applies to other typical answers of avoidant persons, such as "My childhood was very normal" and "My mother and father acted like everyone else."

When these narrative dispositions are brought into a treatment context, treatment providers may have a hard time finding out what underlies the abstract descriptions. Naturally, this is more important in some treatment contexts than in others. However, when treatment success relies on having a picture of the client's emotional or relational reality, the avoidant person's abstractions and generalizations can cause great difficulty. The AAI demonstrates that concrete events and interactions can be a far cry from descriptions on an abstract, semantic level. Therefore, treatment providers cannot simply assume that they know what lies behind the client's general descriptions.

Downplaying negative experiences and emotions

In the AAI, people with avoidant attachment patterns are usually reluctant to disclose difficult experiences with their caregivers. Nevertheless, when they do talk about difficult episodes, they often downplay these experiences or strive to conclude on a 'positive' note – for example, "Yes, my father hit me sometimes, but it wasn't that bad. In fact it probably made me stronger" (Main et al., 2008, Muller, 2010). On a theoretical level, this can be understood as part of an effort to avoid activating the attachment system. In situations in which it is impossible to ignore difficult experiences by suppressing the emotional reactions, the need for comfort can be denied instead.

The inclination to downplay negative experiences depends on the specific subjects being discussed. In the AAI, the interviewee is asked directly about experiences of being scared, upset, or feeling rejected in childhood – experiences that are generally connected with the activation of the attachment system and, therefore, also with the evasion mechanisms of avoidantly attached people (Mikulincer et al., 2009). This does not necessarily mean that people with avoidant attachment patterns always express things positively and optimistically without griping or describing negatively charged emotional states. There are many forms of complaints and many negatively charged emotional states that are not directly pertinent to attachment. Outrage over social injustice or anger towards thoughtless drivers, for example, do not directly indicate attachment behaviour and therefore are not 'threatening' emotional states for avoidantly attached people.

Typically, the more difficult a situation people find themselves in, the more they will intensify their complaints and expressions of negative feelings. However, for avoidantly attached people, the more threatened and vulnerable they feel, the *more* they will be disposed to denying or downplaying negative feelings (Mikulincer et al., 2003). Therefore, it is when something goes too deep that the avoidant person is most likely to recount a trivialized or businesslike narrative void of all negative feelings and evaluations.

For avoidant people the reluctance to express difficult emotions has a long developmental history. Over time, this emotional reserve leads to a lack of ability in emotional expression in people with avoidant attachment, especially compared to securely attached people. A number of studies connect avoidant attachment with *alexithymia*, which is a lack of ability to verbalize one's emotional states (Mallinckrodt and Wei, 2005, Picardi et al., 2005). Therefore, when avoidant persons 'skate over' difficulties in their narrative, it may be due to both a lack of will and ability. In psychotherapeutic work with avoidantly attached people, one will often observe how expressions of emotion are experienced as being 'alien' and 'unnatural' for them and require quite some getting used to.

As described earlier, people with avoidant attachment patterns will be less inclined to feel they need help, and they will also be less inclined to in fact seek help. *When* they do seek help, they will be reticent in expressing vulnerability, anxiety, anger, or sadness (Muller, 2010, Wallin, 2007). In treatment work with avoidant clients, this inclination to omit or make light of negative feelings can cause the treatment provider to underestimate the burden of the client. In many cases, the treatment provider will tend to accept the avoidant client's trivialization at face value. However, if perceived as a trivialization, which covers up true experienced strain, one may end up in the paradoxical situation of trying to convince the client that he is in fact suffering or has a problem, while the client maintains that it is "really not particularly important". Thus, communication can go awry in several different ways.

References

Bakermans-Kranenburg, M. J. & van Ijzendoorn, M. H. 1993. A psychometric study of the Adult Attachment Interview: Reliability and discriminant validity. *Developmental Psychology*, 29, 870–879.

Cassidy, J. 2001. Truth, lies, and intimacy: An attachment perspective. *Attachment & Human Development*, 3, 121–155.

Collins, N. L. & Read, S. J. 1990. Adult attachment, working models, and relationship quality in dating couples. *Journal of Personality and Social Psychology*, 58, 644–663.

Creasey, G. 2002. Associations between working models of attachment and conflict management behavior in romantic couples. *Journal of Counseling Psychology*, 49, 365–375.

Crittenden, P. M. 1995. Attachment and psychopathology. In Goldberg, S. & Muir, R. (eds) *Attachment theory: Social, developmental, and clinical perspectives*. Hillsdale, NJ: Analytic Press.

Crittenden, P. M. 1997. Truth, error, omission, distortion, and deception: The application of attachment theory to the assessment and treatment of psychological disorder. In Dollinger, S. M. C. & Dilalla, L. F. (eds) *Assessment and intervention issues across the life span*. Mahwah, NJ: Lawrence Erlbaum.

Crittenden, P. M. 1999. Danger and development: The organization of self-protective strategies. *Monographs of the Society for Research in Child Development*, 64, 145–171.

Diamond, D., Clarkin, J. F., Stovall-McClough, K. C., Levy, K. N., Foelch, P. A., Levine, H. & Yeomans, F. E. 2003. Patient–therapist attachment: Impact on the therapeutic process and outcome. In Cortina, M. & Marrone, M. (eds) *Attachment theory and the psychoanalytic process*. London: Whurr Publishers, Ltd.

Dozier, M. & Kobak, R. R. 1992. Psychophysiology in attachment interviews: Converging evidence for deactivating strategies. *Child Development*, 63, 1473–1480.

Dozier, M., Lomax, L., Tyrrell, C. L. & Lee, S. W. 2001. The challenge of treatment for clients with dismissing states of mind. *Attachment & Human Development*, 3, 62–76.

Feeney, J. A. & Ryan, S. M. 1997. Attachment style and affect regulation: Relationships with health behavior and family experiences of illness in a student sample. *Health Psychology*, 13, 334–345.

Fox, N. A. & Hane, A. A. 2008. Studying the biology of human attachment. In Cassidy, J. & Shaver, P. (eds) *Handbook of attachment: Theory, research, and clinical applications*, 2nd ed. New York: Guilford Press.

Fraley, R. C. & Brumbaugh, C. C. 2007. Adult attachment and preemptive defenses: Converging evidence on the role of defensive exclusion at the level of encoding. *Journal of Personality*, 75, 1033–1050.

Hazan, C. & Shaver, P. 1987. Romantic love conceptualized as an attachment process. *Journal of Personality and Social Psychology*, 52, 511–524.

Hermans, D., Defranc, A., Raes, F., Williams, J. M. G. & Eelen, P. 2005. Reduced autobiographical memory specificity as an avoidant coping style. *British Journal of Clinical Psychology*, 44, 583–589.

Hesse, E. 2008. The Adult Attachment Interview: Protocol, method of analysis, and empirical studies. In Cassidy, J. & Shaver, P. (eds) *Handbook of attachment: Theory, research, and clinical applications*, 2nd ed. New York: Guilford Press.

Holmes, J. 1997. Attachment, autonomy, intimacy: Some clinical implications of attachment theory. *British Journal of Medical Psychology*, 70, 231–248.

Holmes, J. 1999. Defensive and creative uses of narrative in psychotherapy: An attachment perspective. In Roberts, G. & Holmes, J. (eds) *Healing stories: Narrative in psychiatry and psycohtherapy*. London: Oxford University Press.

Holmes, J. 2001. *The search for the secure base. Attachment theory and psychotherapy*, London: Brunner-Routledge.

Kaitz, M., Bar-Haim, Y., Lehrer, M. & Grossman, E. 2004. Adult attachment style and interpersonal distance. *Attachment & Human Development*, 6, 285–304.

Larose, S. & Bernier, A. 2001. Social support processes: Mediators of attachment state of mind and adjustment in late adolescence. *Attachment & Human Development*, 3, 96–120.

Lopez, F. G. 2001. Adult attachment orientations, self–other boundary regulation, and splitting tendencies in a college sample. *Journal of Counseling Psychology*, 48, 440–446.

Lopez, F. G., Melendez, M. C., Sauer, E. M., Berger, E. & Wyssmann, J. 1998. Internal working models, self-reported problems, and help-seeking attitudes among college students. *Journal of Counseling Psychology*, 45, 79–83.

Magai, C. 1999. Affect, imagery, and attachment: Working models of interpersonal affect and the socialization of emotion. In Cassidy, J. & Shaver, P. R. (eds) *Handbook of attachment: Theory, research, and clinical applications*. New York: Guilford Press.

Main, M. 1995. Recent studies in attachment: Overview, with selected implications for clinical work. In Goldberg, S. & Muir, R. (eds) *Attachment theory: Social, developmental, and clinical perspectives*. Hillsdale, NJ: Analytic Press.

Main, M. 2000. The organized categories of infant, child, and adult attachment: Flexible vs inflexible attention under attachment-related stress. *Journal of the American Psychoanalytic Association*, 48, 1055–1096.

Main, M., Hesse, E. & Goldwyn, R. 2008. Studying differences in language usage in recounting attachment history: An introduction to the AAI. In Steele, H. & Steele, M. (eds) *Clinical Applications of the Adult Attachment Interview*. New York: Guilford Press.

Mallinckrodt, B. & Wei, M. 2005. Attachment, social competencies, social support, and psychological distress. *Journal of Counseling Psychology*, 52, 358–367.

Maunder, R. G. & Hunter, J. J. 2001. Attachment and psychosomatic medicine: Developmental contributions to stress and disease. *Psychosomatic Medicine*, 63, 556–567.

Mikulincer, M. & Orbach, I. 1995. Attachment styles and repressive defensiveness: The accessibility and architecture of affective memories. *Journal of Personality and Social Psychology*, 68, 917–925.

Mikulincer, M., Orbach, I. & Iavnieli, D. 1998. Adult attachment style and affect regulation: Strategic variations in subjective self–other similarity. *Journal of Personality and Social Psychology*, 75, 436–448.

Mikulincer, M. & Shaver, P. 2008. Adult attachment and affect regulation. In Cassidy, J. & Shaver, P. (eds) *Handbook of attachment: Theory, research, and clinical applications*, 2nd ed. New York: Guilford Press.

Mikulincer, M. & Shaver, P. R. 2007. *Attachment in adulthood: Structure, dynamics, and change*, New York: Guilford Press.

Mikulincer, M., Shaver, P. R., Cassidy, J. & Berant, E. 2009. Attachment-related defensive processes. In Obegi, J. H. & Berant, E. (eds) *Attachment theory and research in clinical work with adults*. New York: Guilford Press.

Mikulincer, M., Shaver, P. R. & Pereg, D. 2003. Attachment theory and affect regulation: The dynamics, development, and cognitive consequences of attachment-related strategies. *Motivation and Emotion*, 27, 77–102.

Muller, R. T. 2010. *Trauma and the avoidant client. Attachment-based strategies for healing*, New York: W. W. Norton & Company.

Picardi, A., Toni, A. & Caroppo, E. 2005. Stability of alexithymia and its relationships with the "Big Five" factors, temperament, character, and attachment style. *Psychotherapy and Psychosomatics*, 74, 371–378.

Riggs, S. A., Jacobvitz, D. & Hazen, N. 2002. Adult attachment and history of psychotherapy in a normative sample. *Psychotherapy: Theory, Research, Practice, Training*, 39, 344–353.

Roisman, G. I. 2007. The psychophysiology of adult attachment relationships: Autonomic reactivity in marital and premarital interactions. *Developmental Psychology*, 43, 39–53.

Roisman, G. I., Tsai, J. L. & Chiang, K.-H. S. 2004. The emotional integration of childhood experience: Physiological, facial expressive, and self-reported emotional response during the Adult Attachment Interview. *Developmental Psychology*, 40, 776–789.

Sagi, A., van Ijzendoorn, M. H., Scharf, M. & Koren-Karie, N. 1994. Stability and discriminant validity of the Adult Attachment Interview: A psychometric study in young Israeli adults. *Developmental Psychology*, 30, 771–777.

Simpson, J. A., Rholes, W. S. & Nelligan, J. S. 1992. Support seeking and support giving within couples in an anxiety-provoking situation: The role of attachment styles. *Journal of Personality and Social Psychology*, 62, 434–446.

Simpson, J. A., Rholes, W. S., Orina, M. M. & Grich, J. 2002. Working models of attachment, support giving, and support seeking in a stressful situation. *Personality and Social Psychology Bulletin*, 28, 598–608.

Simpson, J. A., Rholes, W. S. & Phillips, D. 1996. Conflict in close relationships: An attachment perspective. *Journal of Personality and Social Psychology*, 71, 899–914.

Simpson, J. A., Winterheld, H. A., Rholes, W. S. & Orina, M. M. 2007. Working models of attachment and reactions to different forms of caregiving from romantic partners. *Journal of Personality and Social Psychology*, 93, 466–477.

Slade, A. 2008. The implications of attachment theory and research for adult psychotherapy: Research and clinical perspectives. In Cassidy, J. & Shaver, P. (eds) *Handbook of attachment: Theory, research, and clinical applications*, 2nd ed. New York: Guilford Press.

Treboux, D., Crowell, J. A. & Waters, E. 2004. When "new" meets "old": Configurations of adult attachment representations and their implications for marital functioning. *Developmental Psychology*, 40, 295–314.

Vogel, D. L. & Wei, M. 2005. Adult attachment and help-seeking intent: The mediating roles of psychological distress and perceived social support. *Journal of Counseling Psychology*, 52, 347–357.

Waldinger, R. J., Seidman, E. L., Gerber, A. J., Liem, J. H., Allen, J. P. & Hauser, S. T. 2003. Attachment and core relationship themes: Wishes for autonomy and closeness in the narratives of securely and insecurely attached adults. *Psychotherapy Research*, 13, 77–98.

Waller, E., Scheidt, C. E. & Hartmann, A. 2004. Attachment representation and illness behavior in somatoform disorders. *Journal of Nervous & Mental Disease*, 192, 200–209.

Wallin, D. J. 2007. *Attachment in Psychotherapy*. New York: Guilford Press.

Weinfield, N. S., Sroufe, L. A., Egeland, B. & Carlson, E. A. 2008. Individual differences in infant–caregiver attachment: Conceptual and empirical aspects of security. In Cassidy, J. & Shaver, P. (eds) *Handbook of attachment: Theory, research, and clinical applications*, 2nd ed. New York: Guilford Press.

Chapter 5

Ambivalent attachment

In many ways, the ambivalent attachment pattern is the avoidant pattern 'in reverse' – that is, the diametrically opposite way of managing the attachment system. Whereas avoidant people emphasize independence, ambivalent people seek intimacy and desire to merge with others; and whereas avoidant people suppress negative feelings, ambivalent people are disposed to intensify these (Mikulincer et al., 2003). Yet the two patterns also have a number of characteristics in common. This is because they share a background of insecure attachment experiences. Thus the experience that caregivers are not always reliable is a common experience, which necessarily leads to doubts about treatment providers and treatment contexts.

Whereas avoidant attachment is assumed to be rooted in childhood experiences where attachment behaviour proved predictably fruitless, that is, was invariably met with dismissal or neglect, ambivalent attachment is assumed to be rooted in more unpredictable childhood experiences, where attachment behaviour sometimes triggered the desired care and protection but at other times did not (Cassidy and Berlin, 1994). A woman may have had parents who were preoccupied with their infighting and therefore often inattentive or unavailable, but who would at times suddenly become attentive and caring, with her being unable to work out which of the two responses to expect.

A well-known phenomenon in the psychology of learning is that when a specific behaviour is intermittently and unpredictably rewarded, it will result in an intensification of the behaviour (Crittenden, 1999). One has to keep trying, because one never knows when the 'reward' will suddenly be given. Therefore, whereas the avoidant child 'turns down' attachment behaviour, the ambivalent child 'turns it up'. The child becomes concerned with securing the caregiver's attention and will be hypervigilant of the caregiver's availability and state of mind. However, even when succeeding in securing the caregiver's attention and comfort, it will not have the calming effect experienced by the securely attached child – having experienced the caregiver's unreliability, the ambivalent child is never able to feel completely calm and safe (Weinfield et al., 2008). In ambivalently attached adults, this pattern is continued at both an interpersonal and narrative level. In the following, the first section will examine a number of general features of the ambivalent person's interpersonal interaction. The next section will examine general features of the ambivalent person's narrative style.

The interpersonal dimension: entanglement and drama

In the wake of her divorce, a woman has been affected by symptoms of depression – she finds everyday life overwhelming and constantly ponders what went wrong between her and her ex-husband. As her oldest daughter has had problems at school, she and her daughter are called in for a meeting with the school psychologist in order to clarify what is troubling her daughter. The woman complains at length about how difficult the husband's abandonment has been for her and her daughters. She recounts that she feels unfairly treated and that she finds it hard to be blamed for her daughter's problems – the person to blame is her ex-husband. The school psychologist assures the woman that the meeting's objective is not to place blame with anyone, but to gain insight into the girl's situation. However, the woman does not seem to register this – she is not calmed, but starts crying saying that she cannot take any more. During the conversation, the woman answers on her daughter's behalf on several occasions, explaining how the daughter feels let down by her father. She expresses a feeling that the school psychologist probably thinks she is a bad mother but that she is doing her best, even though it is incredibly difficult, as she is all on her own. The school psychologist struggles to get the woman to focus on her daughter's situation.

The ambivalent child has learned that if he or she complains bitterly, loudly, and long enough, the caregiver may just 'reward' this with comfort and care. Where the avoidant child attempts to become emotionally independent of the caregiver, the ambivalent child becomes extra dependent because the child must constantly be aware of the caregiver and put much effort into maintaining the caregiver's attention. In adulthood this pattern is continued in the shape of extensive focus on interpersonal relationships; a desire for constant closeness and a feeling of being unable to function without close proximity to another (Hazan and Shaver, 1987). Ambivalent people attempt to hold on to others by appealing to their care and empathy and through strong emotional expressions.

Insecurity and relational demands

Whereas securely attached people have generally had reliable caregivers and avoidant people have managed their caregivers' unreliability through a strategy of independence, people with ambivalent attachment are doubly exposed: they do not find others reliable but they do not feel able to 'take care of themselves' either. This results in a strong feeling of insecurity and in issues relating to self-esteem and self-confidence. Ambivalent people have a generally negative self-image, feel emotionally dependent on others, and are simultaneously very afraid of being rejected or abandoned by the people who matter to them. Whereas securely attached

people have had a stable feeling of self-worth 'installed' in them throughout childhood, ambivalent people's childhood experiences have not provided the same
foundation for forming a stable self-esteem. More than other people, they base their
self-worth on continual feedback from others and are therefore particularly sensitive to rejection or criticism, which can easily undermine their shaky self-esteem
(Bartholomew and Horowitz, 1991, Collins and Read, 1990, Mikulincer and
Shaver, 2007: 155–168, Treboux et al., 2004).

This unstable self-esteem means that people with ambivalent attachment often
seek confirmation from others, including partners, but also treatment providers.
Ambivalent people will tend to be 'on the lookout' for the way other people see
them and they are also likely to explicitly request feedback and confirmation of
other people's interest and dedication (Davila, 2001). In romantic relationships, for
example, this could manifest itself through constant questions about the strength of
their partners' feelings for them – "Do you really love me?" Treatment providers
may experience strong demands from ambivalent people to assure them that they
are doing well, as well as assuring them of sufficient attention to their needs. A
characteristic of people with ambivalent attachment is that – even when they
receive the attention and confirmation sought – they are only calmed temporarily,
because the underlying insecurity endures. This can often lead to unsatisfactory
interactions with other people, who after a while become tired of the ambivalent
person's 'insatiable' need for affirmation. This is also a risk in treatment relationships, where time and resources will often be inadequate in relation to the degree
of care and attention the ambivalent person demands.

Because ambivalent people were unable to control whether necessary care and
protection was given to them, they developed a general feeling of helplessness
and lack of control (Dykas and Cassidy, 2011, Gamble and Roberts, 2005,
Mickelson et al., 1997). The feeling of helplessness is further intensified by a
tendency to focus on negative information, such as one's own flaws and defects
or the most unfortunate or insoluble aspects of a given situation. Both contribute
to intensifying the feeling of being dependent on and at the mercy of other people,
which again increases vigilance to possible threats or rejections. When meeting a
person with ambivalent attachment, treatment providers will thus often be faced
with someone who is extremely keen to make his or her need for help clear, and
who simultaneously fears and partially expects poor treatment. For this reason,
people with ambivalent attachment may approach treatment providers with an
accusing tone even from the very first contact, as if they have already let them down.
In such cases it is extremely important to be aware of the underlying feeling of
helplessness and hopelessness that motivates this behaviour.

The term 'ambivalent' originally referred to the type of behaviour observed in
the Strange Situation, where children on the one hand demand the caregivers'
comfort and reassurance and on the other hand 'put up a struggle' or become
physically aggressive, when the caregivers try to provide comfort (Ainsworth
et al., 1978). This paradoxical reaction recurs in adults with ambivalent attachment. In contrast to people with avoidant attachment, they will often clearly and

insistently seek care and attention. However, when it is given to them, they will receive it with a mixed, critical attitude, as if it is not quite good enough or does not correspond to what they actually asked for (Lopez, 2009, Wallin, 2007). And, whereas avoidant people may be inclined to keep treatment providers and others at arm's length, when it comes to ambivalent people, treatment providers may experience the feeling of simultaneously being drawn in and pushed away or rejected. This reaction can easily give rise to feelings of inadequacy in treatment providers, who may also be inclined to experience ambivalent people as 'tiresome' and 'ungrateful'.

Alternatively, treatment relationships with ambivalently attached people can initially be marked by great cooperativeness and gratefulness, where clients give off strong signals of trust and a sense of being helped. This may later be replaced by disappointment and reproach if the treatment provider makes a mistake, which can result in a 'fall' from the idealized position of 'infallible saviour', which the client initially assigned to the treatment provider.

Intensification of negative emotions

Whereas avoidant people downregulate the attachment system and the negative emotions related to an active attachment system, the ambivalent person is inclined to intensify and upregulate negative emotional states (Mikulincer and Shaver, 2008). This may seem slightly puzzling – why would intensifying feelings such as helplessness and frustration be in anyone's interest? However, this inclination makes sense when understood on the basis of attachment experiences where care and protection were available at times – but without being predictable or dependable. The intensification of negative emotional states has an expressive function and serves to maximize the possibility of receiving the wanted care. Even though this reaction can cause irritation in caregivers, negative attention is better than no attention in threatening situations. The ambivalent child's intensification of his own insecurity to secure the caregiver's attention will, with time, become part of the person's readiness and resources to cope with unsafe situations, thereby intensifying the experience and expression of insecurity which, paradoxically, becomes a source of secondary security for the ambivalent person. For ambivalent people, focusing attention on the feeling of being threatened and being very vocal in their complaints feels the 'most secure' (Cassidy and Berlin, 1994, Crittenden and Landini, 2011, Main, 1995).

A number of studies have shown that people with ambivalent attachment patterns are inclined to 'ruminate', that is, worry about and ponder experienced difficulties (Mikulincer and Shaver, 2007: 200–203). Ambivalent attachment is similarly connected to a tendency for catastrophizing – expecting the worst possible scenarios. For example, if a partner seems less attentive than usual, this is immediately considered a sign of infidelity and of an impending break-up. When something is difficult or unpleasant, the ambivalent person will not try to ignore it like the avoidant person, but instead spend time and energy worrying about it.

Compared to the securely attached person, the ambivalent person lacks faith in both his own problem-solving abilities and others' reliability. This is one of the reasons why ambivalent people are more inclined to 'hang on' to such worries without seeing a way out. This results in a vicious circle where experienced difficulties lead to rumination and catastrophizing, which in turn intensifies the experience of difficulties resulting in increased emotional suffering.

When ambivalent people fall ill, or experience loss or adversity in life, they will easily become greatly 'marked by crisis' (Wilkinson, 2003). They will be overwhelmed by feelings such as anxiety, anger, sorrow, and confusion, which are experienced as being out of their control. These feelings will often be conveyed to other people, whom the ambivalent people will attempt to involve in regulating their anxiety and solving their problems. Whereas avoidant people put on a brave front and attempt to function normally until they 'break down', ambivalent people who face difficulties will quickly struggle to cope with the challenges of life.

The aforementioned intensification of difficult feelings and lack of faith in their ability to 'cope' mean that ambivalent people are significantly more inclined to seek help and support from treatment providers and they will clearly express their experience of being in a crisis (Pianta et al., 1996, Schmidt et al., 2002, Vogel and Wei, 2005). Paradoxically, this loud insistence on undergoing great suffering and needing help makes it hard for the treatment provider to assess the actual need for help as well as where to initially focus treatment. The atmosphere of crisis can be overwhelming and obscure factual information of what is causing trouble.

Unclear boundaries between self and others

Whereas avoidant people are inclined to see themselves as significantly different from others, ambivalent people are more inclined to overestimate other people's likeness to themselves, for example, with regard to opinions or preferences (Lopez, 2001, Mikulincer et al., 1998). Theoretically this can be understood as an offshoot of ambivalent people's great need for interpersonal proximity. Such unclear boundaries or distinctions between self and others contribute to a feeling of fusion and connectedness, which the ambivalent person prefers because the thought of differences in perspective, or even potential ruptures, is intensely anxiety-provoking. For this reason, attachment figures to some degree end up appearing as 'extensions' of ambivalent people, who can be very unsure which features, opinions, or feelings belong to themselves and which belong to the attachment figures.

The unclear boundaries between self and others entail a degree of emotional over-involvement, where the ambivalent person is easily 'infected' with others' feelings. This especially affects their ability to care for others, as their disposition to be strongly influenced by emotions means they struggle to function as security-providing caregivers for their children or their own partners (Feeney and Hohaus, 2001, George and Solomon, 2008). If a partner is sick or troubled in other ways, ambivalent people can become so suffused by their worries that they become unable to reassure their partner or function as his or her 'resource person'.

Whereas people with avoidant attachment tend to ignore or be inattentive to others' feelings, ambivalent people are very aware of others' feelings, although they may be inclined to be mistaken about these. Among other things, this is related to the ambivalent person's unclear boundaries between self and others, as ambivalent people will often assume or 'sense' that others share their feelings in a given situation. Several studies indicate that people with ambivalent attachment more often than others misjudge others' feelings, either with respect to the type of feelings or their intensity (Mikulincer et al., 2001). In treatment relationships this can manifest itself by ambivalent clients believing that they 'know' how the treatment provider feels about them, or how the treatment provider feels in general in different situations – without the treatment provider necessarily agreeing with this assessment.

Treatment providers may also experience that ambivalent people assume that their frustration or anxiety is shared by the treatment provider, or that treatment providers somehow share their perspective of the situation. Ambivalent clients can be inclined to draw you in as an ally, who is expected to be on their side and to have complete insight into the way they experience the situation (Crittenden and Landini, 2011, Wallin, 2007). Treatment providers may thus be included in a 'we' without any particular basis in the treatment relationship or an established mutual understanding.

The narrative dimension: confusion and verbosity

A man with a physically exhausting job has reported sick for some time due to a back injury. He has started physiotherapy aimed at rehabilitation. The first treatment was marked by the man's account of how distressing his physical problems had been for him. He left treatment with a couple of exercises to do at home. At the following session, the physiotherapist asks how the man got on with the exercises. The man answers, "Well, you know, it isn't easy to get the exercises done with things being as they are at the moment. I mean, it can be quite difficult to find the time to do them, you see, because – of course, I've tried to do them, Carol has been so busy, so I've had to take care of loads of things. She says I should take care of dinner since I'm at home doing nothing. It's enough to drive me crazy! Do you know that feeling? And I just think, that in my situation and with everything I've been through, I deserve more understanding, she could at least ..., but no, her head is full of her own things and projects, and then there is this and that, and couldn't you take a look at the basement stairs and blah, blah, blah. There is always something."

Just as ambivalent attachment seems diametrically opposed to the avoidant pattern on the interpersonal level, the narrative characteristics of ambivalent attachment are also in complete contrast to the avoidant pattern. In the AAI, the ambivalent person's narratives are often long and complex, with many 'tangents' and private accounts. In contrast to downplaying negative experiences as seen in avoidant interviews, the ambivalent interviews often contain a complaining or reproachful tone, where troubles and difficult feelings are accentuated rather than downplayed.

Verbosity and associational 'tangents'

Whereas avoidant people seem unwilling to talk about attachment in the AAI, ambivalent people tend to become 'sucked in' by this particular subject and often have much to say about it (Main et al., 2008). This is why interviews with ambivalent people usually last longer than interviews with secure or avoidant people – ambivalent people simply talk more.

Part of the reason for this seems to be the ambivalent person's preoccupation with the topic of attachment as well as a tendency to lose perspective and get carried away when the attachment system is activated. A spread of associations towards different emotional thoughts and recollections occurs, which draws the ambivalent person's attention and often leads the person 'astray' from answering the interviewer's questions, as ambivalent people pursue these 'tangents' in their narrative (Hesse, 2008, Holmes, 1999). If an ambivalent person is asked to talk about her childhood relation to her mother, she may for instance be reminded of an incident where her mother fought with her sister and then give a detailed account of this, and then move on to talk about the sister and the sister's relationship to their grandfather, etc., until the original question is lost from sight.

The narrative tangents followed will often be emotional. They may, for example, involve long recounts of all the times a parent proved inadequate in some way or other (Crittenden and Landini, 2011). In other cases, people with ambivalent attachment may lose themselves in more peripheral considerations and start talking about the toaster in their childhood home, as if passively following their immediate associations. According to the theory, this lack of ability to limit oneself to what is relevant in the given situation is rooted in the AAI's capacity to activate the attachment system, which for an ambivalent person entails a tendency to be carried away and lose perspective. Thus, an ambivalent person cannot be expected to be just as talkative or inclined to go off on tangents if the conversation were about something other than attachment or if the situation was not attachment-relevant.

In a treatment context, there is reason to expect similar verbosity from ambivalent clients when talk turns to relational problems and conflicts, or when the attachment system is activated in other ways; for example, if the client feels exposed and vulnerable. Whereas avoidant clients will be inclined to 'clam up' and secure clients will express their problems in a contextually fitting manner, ambivalent clients will easily lose themselves in long and often complaining descriptions. For treatment providers it can prove hard to interrupt or regulate the conversation, because the ambivalent client is so engulfed and has little sense of which information is relevant to the treatment provider or to the treatment. Whereas one may face a lack of information with avoidant clients, one will often end up with an information overload when treating clients with ambivalent attachment (Lopez, 2009, Slade, 2008).

Enlisting and narrative 'chaos'

Perhaps partly because of the tendency towards unclear boundaries between self and others, and partly because of a lack of discernment when the attachment system is activated, ambivalent people will often present their attachment narratives in private and enlisting ways (Main et al., 2008). Sometimes the listener will not be presented with enough information to understand the narrative, and at other times ambivalent people will attempt to engage the listener in their personal perspective by using comments such as "You must recognize this from your own life?" or similar. In the AAI, a characteristic of the ambivalent person's narrative is that the listener is implicitly expected to share the narrator's perspective or understanding without the necessary prerequisites being present in the account given.

One of the ways this tendency manifests itself is through 'slips' in time, person, or theme, where the person suddenly begins talking about other times or people, without making this clear to the listener. New people or incidents are abruptly brought into play without any previous introduction. The person may perhaps say, "This is exactly like that time with John; the way he treated me was completely out of order," without explaining that John is the person's brother or explaining exactly what was "out of order". In this way, the ambivalent person's narratives quickly become messy or chaotic, because subjects, people, incidents, and times are jumbled together without any effort to create or convey a coherent overview.

The narrative may also contain long 'quotes' from other people or from what the interviewee has said to others in the past, without clear indication of it being a quote or of who is being quoted. This may contribute to making the narrative 'dynamic' and function as a form of dramatization, but for the listener it can come across as confusing, because it does not clearly emerge which person a given perspective belongs to or from which perspective the narrative is being told (Holmes, 2001).

Another feature that contributes to the sense of narrative 'chaos' is frequent occurrence of words and phrases whose meaning is unclear in the context, as well as a tendency of leaving sentences unfinished. This can also give an impression of enlisting the treatment provider, as if he or she ought to understand what is meant if the client says, "She always said dadadada and stuff like that to me," or if an unfinished sentence is left 'hanging in the air'. People with ambivalent attachment patterns may also switch personal pronouns around – for instance, saying "I" instead of "he" – thus further contributing to the confusion about who is being referred to (Hesse, 2008).

The result of these inclinations to narrate in an enlisting and 'chaotic' way is that the listener is put to work trying to 'keep up' and keep track of the narrative's many threads. Depending on temperament, this can cause confusion, frustration, or irritation. Whereas avoidant people's narratives are typically poor on episodic material – that is, descriptions of specific people and incidents – ambivalent people's narratives will be teeming with this kind of material. However, it can be difficult to create an overview and find coherence in the narrative because this material is not organized and introduced in a way that enables the listener to keep up. In treatment contexts this may obviously become problematic, not merely because the listener may become frustrated due to the complex and enlisting narratives, but also because the listener may overhear important information about the client's condition and circumstances.

Furthermore, the ambivalent person's narrative chaos can lead to problems in prioritizing material. As a listener, one is not in doubt that the person is experiencing emotional distress, but it can be much harder to determine what the central problem or problems are. In a conversation with an ambivalent person, it can be difficult to know where to begin because there are many different threads to pursue, and it is unclear how they are related or whether some material is more important than other material.

Disorganizing affectivity

In contrast to the avoidant person, the ambivalent person's narratives in the AAI are often emotional. Ambivalently attached people are engrossed by their own story and often attempt to emotionally engage the listener as well (Holmes, 1999, Main, 1995). In the AAI, the ambivalent person's narratives are often dominated by negative emotions such as anger or anxiety and may be marked by a plaintive or reproachful tone. It is as if the narrator is 'caught up' in these negative emotions in a way that derails the narrative, just as ambivalent children are unable to 'let go' of their frustration and insecurity in the Strange Situation (Ainsworth et al., 1978).

The tendency to get caught up in negative emotions when these arise means that people with ambivalent attachment patterns often pursue associations – for example, from one anger-inducing episode to another – without considering whether the additional material is relevant to the listener. At times, the awakened emotions make the narrative 'fall apart', for example, when sentences are unfinished, talk becomes enlisting or private, and people and incidents are brought into play without previous introduction. Furthermore, some emotional subjects can take up so much of the ambivalent person's focus that they are broached again and again even out of context, as if any subject becomes an association to the way "my mother never respected me" or similar.

Even though the ambivalent person's narratives can be very emotional, this does not necessarily mean that the emotions are named or explicitly described. Thus a number of studies connect avoidant as well as ambivalent attachment with alexithymia – that is, the inability to verbalize emotional states (Mallinckrodt and Wei, 2005, Picardi et al., 2005). An ambivalent narrative marked by anger will not necessarily contain a clear description of this anger in which its source is identified, rather demonstrate anger through a large number of accusations and complaints. In this way ambivalent narratives differ from secure narratives that also include emotional material, but in which emotions are named and contextualized so they can even serve to organize the narrative rather than flowing freely with disorganizing effects on the narrative. In a treatment context, this tendency to free-flowing and potentially disorganizing affectivity when the attachment system is activated may easily affect the relationship between treatment provider and client. Whereas the avoidant person's unemotional narrative keeps the treatment provider at a distance, the ambivalent person's emotional, narrative chaos contributes to engaging and captivating the treatment provider, while simultaneously making it harder to find a bearing (Lopez, 2009, Wallin, 2007). The ambivalent client's narratives can easily awaken a multitude of feelings in the treatment provider. However, whereas it is easier to identify the source of these feelings in conversations with secure clients (for example, feeling empathy with a client in a difficult situation), it can be hard to determine exactly why the ambivalent client's narrative causes the listener to feel despondent, frustrated, annoyed, or frightened. This is, at least partially, due to the fact that the client's expressions of emotion are not integrated in a clear narrative structure, but rather destabilize narrative order.

References

Ainsworth, M. S., Blehar, M. C., Waters, E. & Wall, S. 1978. *Patterns of attachment: A psychological study of the strange situation.* Hillsdale, NJ: Lawrence Erlbaum.

Bartholomew, K. & Horowitz, L. M. 1991. Attachment styles among young adults: A test of a four-category model. *Journal of Personality and Social Psychology,* 61, 226–244.

Cassidy, J. & Berlin, L. J. 1994. The insecure/ambivalent pattern of attachment: Theory and research. *Child Development,* 65, 971–981.

Collins, N. L. & Read, S. J. 1990. Adult attachment, working models, and relationship quality in dating couples. *Journal of Personality and Social Psychology,* 58, 644–663.

Crittenden, P. M. 1999. Danger and development: The organization of self-protective strategies. *Monographs of the Society for Research in Child Development,* 64, 145–171.

Crittenden, P. M. & Landini, A. 2011. *Assessing adult attachment. A dynamic maturational approach to discourse analysis.* New York: W.W. Norton & Co.

Davila, J. 2001. Refining the association between excessive reassurance seeking and depressive symptoms: The role of related interpersonal constructs. *Journal of Social and Clinical Psychology,* 20, 538–559.

Dykas, M. J. & Cassidy, J. 2011. Attachment and the processing of social information across the life span: Theory and evidence. *Psychological Bulletin,* 137, 19–46.

Feeney, J. A. & Hohaus, L. 2001. Attachment and spousal caregiving. *Personal Relationships,* 8, 21–39.

Gamble, S. A. & Roberts, J. E. 2005. Adolescents' perceptions of primary caregivers and cognitive style: The roles of attachment security and gender. *Cognitive Therapy and Research,* 29, 123–141.

George, C. & Solomon, J. 2008. The caregiving system. A behavioral systems approach to parenting. In Cassidy, J. & Shaver, P. R. (eds) *Handbook of attachment: Theory, research, and clinical applications,* 2nd ed. New York: Guilford Press.

Hazan, C. & Shaver, P. 1987. Romantic love conceptualized as an attachment process. *Journal of Personality and Social Psychology,* 52, 511–524.

Hesse, E. 2008. The Adult Attachment Interview: Protocol, method of analysis, and empirical studies. In Cassidy, J. & Shaver, P. (eds) *Handbook of attachment: Theory, research, and clinical applications*, 2nd ed. New York: Guilford Press.

Holmes, J. 1999. Defensive and creative uses of narrative in psychotherapy: An attchment perspective. In Roberts, G. & Holmes, J. (eds) *Healing stories: Narrative in psychiatry and psychotherapy*. London: Oxford University Press.

Holmes, J. 2001. *The search for the secure base. Attachment theory and psychotherapy*. London: Brunner-Routledge.

Lopez, F. G. 2001. Adult attachment orientations, self–other boundary regulation, and splitting tendencies in a college sample. *Journal of Counseling Psychology*, 48, 440–446.

Lopez, F. G. 2009. Clinical correlates of adult attachment organization. In Obegi, J. H. & Berant, E. (eds) *Attachment theory and research in clinical work with adults*. New York: Guilford Press.

Main, M. 1995. Recent studies in attachment: Overview, with selected implications for clinical work. In Goldberg, S. & Muir, R. (eds) *Attachment theory: Social, developmental, and clinical perspectives*. Hillsdale, NJ: Analytic Press.

Main, M., Hesse, E. & Goldwyn, R. 2008. Studying differences in language usage in recounting attachment history: An introduction to the AAI. In Steele, H. & Steeele, M. (eds) *Clinical Applications of the Adult Attachment Interview*. New York: Guilford Press.

Mallinckrodt, B. & Wei, M. 2005. Attachment, social competencies, social support, and psychological distress. *Journal of Counseling Psychology*, 52, 358–367.

Mickelson, K. D., Kessler, R. C. & Shaver, P. R. 1997. Adult attachment in a nationally representative sample. *Journal of Personality and Social Psychology*, 73, 1092–1106.

Mikulincer, M., Gillath, O., Halevy, V., Avihou, N., Avidan, S. & Eshkoli, N. 2001. Attachment theory and reactions to others' needs: Evidence that activation of the sense of attachment security promotes empathic responses. *Journal of Personality and Social Psychology*, 81, 1205–1224.

Mikulincer, M., Orbach, I. & Iavnieli, D. 1998. Adult attachment style and affect regulation: Strategic variations in subjective self–other similarity. *Journal of Personality and Social Psychology*, 75, 436–448.

Mikulincer, M. & Shaver, P. R. 2007. *Attachment in adulthood: Structure, dynamics, and change*. New York: Guilford Press.

Mikulincer, M. & Shaver, P. 2008. Adult attachment and affect regulation. In Cassidy, J. & Shaver, P. (eds) *Handbook of attachment: Theory, research, and clinical applications*, 2nd ed. New York: Guilford Press.

Mikulincer, M., Shaver, P. R. & Pereg, D. 2003. Attachment theory and affect regulation: The dynamics, development, and cognitive consequences of attachment-related strategies. *Motivation and Emotion*, 27, 77–102.

Pianta, R. C., Egeland, B. & Adam, E. K. 1996. Adult attachment classification and self-reported psychiatric symptomatology as assessed by the Minnesota Multiphasic Personality Inventory – 2. *Journal of Consulting and Clinical Psychology*, 64, 273–281.

Picardi, A., Toni, A. & Caroppo, E. 2005. Stability of alexithymia and its relationships with the "Big Five" factors, temperament, character, and attachment style. *Psychotherapy and Psychosomatics*, 74, 371–378.

Schmidt, S., Strauss, B. & Braehler, E. 2002. Subjective physical complaints and hypochondriacal features from an attachment theoretical perspective. *Psychology and Psychotherapy: Theory, Research and Practice*, 75, 313–332.

Slade, A. 2008. The implications of attachment theory and research for adult psychotherapy: Research and clinical perspectives. In Cassidy, J. & Shaver, P. (eds) *Handbook of attachment: Theory, research, and clinical applications*, 2nd ed. New York: Guilford Press.

Trebousx, D., Crowell, J. A. & Waters, E. 2004. When "new" meets "old": Configurations of adult attachment representations and their implications for marital functioning. *Developmental Psychology*, 40, 295–314.

Vogel, D. L. & Wei, M. 2005. Adult attachment and help-seeking intent: The mediating roles of psychological distress and perceived social support. *Journal of Counseling Psychology*, 52, 347–357.

Wallin, D. J. 2007. *Attachment in Psychotherapy*. New York: Guilford Press.

Weinfield, N. S., Sroufe, L. A., Egeland, B. & Carlson, E. A. 2008. Individual differences in infant–caregiver attachment: Conceptual and empirical aspects of security. In Cassidy, J. & Shaver, P. (eds) *Handbook of attachment: Theory, research, and clinical applications*, 2nd ed. New York: Guilford Press.

Wilkinson, S. R. 2003. *Coping and complaining. Attachment and the language of disease*. New York: Brunner-Routledge.

Chapter 6

Disorganized attachment

As described in Chapter 1, a theoretical and empirical distinction is made between organized attachment patterns (secure, avoidant, and ambivalent) and disorganized attachment patterns. Whereas avoidant and ambivalent attachment are both specific, organized ways of deviating from a fundamentally secure pattern by either deactivating or hyperactivating the attachment system, there is something more complex afoot in disorganized attachment (Lyons-Ruth and Jacobvitz, 2008). The interview and questionnaire traditions differ slightly in their conceptualization of the insecure patterns that go beyond the purely avoidant or ambivalent patterns. The AAI employs the category 'unresolved with respect to loss or trauma' as well as the category 'cannot classify', which is primarily used for interviews exhibiting strong avoidant/deactivating as well as strong ambivalent/hyperactivating tendencies (Hesse, 1996, 2008). The questionnaire tradition operates with the category 'fearful', which covers the simultaneous presence of a significant degree of attachment-related avoidance and a significant degree of attachment-related anxiety (Bartholomew and Horowitz, 1991, Brennan et al., 1998).

To some extent, the AAI category 'cannot classify' and the questionnaire tradition's category 'fearful' resemble each other, at least with regard to the theoretical understanding of these. Furthermore, the AAI category 'unresolved with respect to loss or trauma' predicts disorganized attachment in children, which in the Strange Situation manifests itself through a breakdown in the child's action strategies, often through the presence of conflicting action impulses towards approaching and distancing from the caregiver (Hesse and Main, 2000). This can also be interpreted as the concurrent presence of avoidance and ambivalence. Thus, theoretically and developmentally there is a degree of kinship between the different ways of conceptualizing the patterns deviating from the organized patterns, in which a single 'strategy' for handling the attachment system is in charge.

Even though the categories and concepts mentioned do not cover completely identical phenomena, they will all be treated under the heading 'disorganized' in this chapter. The term 'disorganized' will be used to describe more complex patterns with conflicting tendencies, which either appear simultaneously or in quick shifts, or with isolated or more fundamental breakdowns in the person's readiness and resources to cope with attachment-related problems. Thus the features and dispositions treated in this chapter form a less coherent 'pattern' than seen in the previous chapters. They are rather a collection of different, distinct deviations from the three organized 'main' patterns. These deviations and complications can be greatly significant in a treatment context. As in the previous chapters, the different features of interpersonal interaction will be treated first, followed by the different characteristics of narrative style.

The interpersonal dimension: 'breakdown' and fragility

A woman, who has enjoyed great success as an independent businesswoman, has recently given birth to her first child, and the changeover to life as a mother to an infant has not been easy. She is, therefore, followed closely by a nurse, who frequently visits and talks to her about everyday life with the baby after the woman's boyfriend has returned to work. The woman is generally very quiet and the nurse struggles to establish a close relationship with her. The woman conveys that every-thing is fine, but the nurse suspects that she is keeping much to herself. Sometimes when the child cries the woman gets a faraway look in her eyes and sits passively, and when the nurse encourages her to hold the baby the woman does it mechani-cally. During one of the nurse's visits, the woman suddenly works herself up and violently berates the nurse for not being genuinely concerned about her and for not helping enough. She yells at the nurse, calling her a stupid cow who has come to interfere and is self-righteous. When the nurse subsequently tries to talk to the woman about the incident, the woman answers that she really doesn't know what came over her, but that she is fine now. She resumes her quiet and reserved attitude.

The interpersonal characteristics of people with disorganized attachment are fundamentally about ways of regulating fear or about breakdowns in this regula-tion of fear. A common experiential background of people with disorganized attachment patterns are experiences with attachment figures who were either in themselves anxiety-provoking or who were unable to provide sufficient reassur-ance in anxiety-provoking situations. They may have experienced death, abuse, mental illness in the family, or merely had parents who were too overwhelmed and helpless to serve as secure bases and safe havens for their children.

With regard to disorganized attachment in children, it is important to mention that some studies indicate that a biologically determined vulnerability also plays a part and contributes in determining whether traumatic experiences in attachment relationships lead to attachment-related disorganization or not (Lyons-Ruth and Jacobvitz, 2008). Thus, there is likely a biological component that plays a part in some types of disorganized attachment, which in a large number of studies has been found to be more widespread in groups with mental problems or with actual psychopathology, although disorganized attachment is not in itself synonymous with mental illness (DeKlyen and Greenberg, 2008, Dozier et al., 2008).

Avoidance and longing

In the questionnaire tradition for measuring adult attachment patterns, the disorganized or 'fearful' pattern is operationalized as a strong tendency of both avoidance and ambivalence. We are dealing with people who simultaneously long for intimate emotional connections with other people and are afraid of allowing others to get too close. Of all the different patterns, this attachment pattern is connected with the highest degree of subjectively experienced suffering (Mason et al., 2005, Riggs et al., 2007). The avoidantly attached person gains secondary security through the experience of independence, the ambivalently attached person gains secondary security through striving to merge with others, but the disorganized person struggles to find security through any of these strategies. They thus find themselves between a rock and a hard place, and it is not surprising that they often suffer, for example, from depressions.

Of all four patterns, the disorganized attachment pattern is related to the greatest difficulties in developing open and trusting relationships with other people. People with this pattern may have experienced that relationships with those who were meant to provide security and care were not only inadequate in this respect, but even increased and deepened the feeling of insecurity. This results in great vigilance and reticence with regard to engaging with, or in any way depending on, other people (Cassidy and Mohr, 2001, Muller, 2010, Saypol and Farber, 2010). In contrast to the experience of self-sufficiency seen in avoidantly attached people, the disorganized pattern is related to a strong sense of inadequacy and helplessness. There is a great longing for proximity with others, yet this is at the same time anxiety-provoking, because such proximity is expected to bring about unpleasant consequences.

The conflicting impulses of seeking proximity while simultaneously being avoidant mean that people with disorganized attachment have a particularly hard time interacting smoothly and constructively with other people. Their behaviour can appear incomprehensible or contradictory, and their strategies for handling conflicts are often inadequate. Because of this, people with disorganized attachment usually only have a few close relationships, which, furthermore, are often marked by unsatisfactory interaction, for example arguments, frequent crises, or even violence (Hennighausen et al., 2011, Lyons Ruth and Jacobvitz, 1999, Lyons-Ruth et al., 2004).

In treatment relationships, the disorganized pattern can also result in marked difficulties in establishing constructive cooperation towards treatment. Treatment providers may struggle to relate to the combination of strong vigilance and great helplessness – it is as if two messages are being conveyed simultaneously: "stay away, but please come and help me" (Wallin, 2007). The disorganized person is also inclined to waver between deactivation and hyperactivation as the dominant strategy, and therefore the disorganized person's way of being in the treatment relationship can shift unpredictably. Just like the disorganized client, the treatment provider working with disorganized clients can easily come to feel that treatment is neither feasible nor realizable (Liotti, 2011). No matter what one does, one risks doing the wrong thing for the client who sends conflicting signals and whose wants and needs oppose each other.

Dissociation and 'collapse' in action strategies

At an interpersonal, behavioural level, disorganized patterns are characterized by an absence of usable action strategies in threatening or difficult situations. A kind of 'collapse' occurs, in which there are either no action strategies to draw on, or where opposing action strategies are activated simultaneously; for example, an inclination to cling to others and an inclination to avoid contact with others (Hesse and Main, 2000, Main and Solomon, 1986). Under all circumstances this results in the disorganized person struggling to find a suitable way of reacting to difficult or anxiety-provoking situations. Correspondingly, several empirical studies indicate that people with disorganized attachment patterns have the most problematic coping strategies for dealing with adversity, and in some contexts completely lack strategies for dealing with problems.

Theory and research have associated the disorganized attachment pattern in children with recurring experiences of 'fear without solution' – that is, experiences where the child is afraid, but has no suitable action against fear; for instance, if the parent who is available for comfort and protection is simultaneously the person who causes the fear (Cassidy and Mohr, 2001, Hesse and Main, 2006). This impossible situation, in which the child experiences violent insecurity but has no ready strategy, leads to a collapse in the child's regulation of emotions, which results in atypical behavioural patterns. As described in Chapter 1, in the Strange Situation this collapse may manifest itself with the child coming to a standstill and sitting motionless or collapsing helplessly on the floor. With time, the child learns that attachment-activating situations are both 'dangerous' and 'hopeless' and impossible to regulate (Lyons-Ruth and Jacobvitz, 2008).

A behavioural pattern especially connected to disorganized attachment is to dissociate, that is, to 'split up' one's consciousness or attention and, for instance, enter a trance-like state (Liotti, 1999, Stovall-McClough and Cloitre, 2006). This reaction becomes especially prominent in frightening and attachment-activating situations, where the person may 'space out' and become hard to reach because he or she is in a private world. Anyone may potentially react with dissociative symptoms in overwhelming and traumatizing situations. However, for people with disorganized attachment patterns, the inclination to do so will be stronger and the reaction will be more widespread (Liotti, 2011).

For the clients themselves, dissociation will be related to an experience of 'unrealness' or of not being present in their own bodies, which can feel secure and frightening at the same time: secure because it feels as if no one and nothing can hurt them, but frightening because they get a sense of falling apart or 'going mad'. Furthermore, dissociation hinders constructive problem solving because the person is unable to act when he or she feels unconnected to the world.

The treatment provider working with a disorganized client in a serious crisis will likely be faced with someone who is partially or completely unable to approach the crisis with a conscious focus on a possible solution. Instead the person may be more or less 'frozen' in a state of shock, without necessarily being able to ignore feelings of fear or insecurity. At the same time, this person will feel unable to act constructively in the situation and will either experience conflicting action impulses or a complete absence of strategies for action (Hesse and Main, 2000). This can significantly complicate cooperation in a treatment context and will often necessitate more intensive or long-term treatment or special support measures.

Controlling behaviour and role reversal

In research into the further development of children's early attachment, it has been established that several children, who at the age of 1 appear disorganized in the Strange Situation, develop a marked controlling behaviour towards their caregivers later in childhood (Lyons-Ruth and Jacobvitz, 2008). This 'control' manifests itself in a partial inversion of roles, where the child assumes certain behaviours that usually belong to the parents' domain. This controlling behaviour can assume different forms, including a 'punitive' form, where the child is critical of and orders the caregiver around, and a 'caregiving' form, where the child takes care of and looks after the caregiver. Both behaviours can be interpreted as an attempt to take control of situations, where the caregiver, for some reason, has proven unable to provide the child with the basic security needed for the child to develop. Whereas the young child is defenceless against frightening or helpless caregivers and therefore appears disorganized in the Strange Situation, older children have more resources at their disposal and are therefore able to organize other ways of behaving.

This distinctive developmental shift in the way disorganized attachment manifests itself contributes to further complicating the picture of disorganized attachment. Whereas some children with a disorganized background continue to appear chaotic in their attachment behaviour, other children – especially the ones who assume a controlling-caregiving role towards their parents – will, to the untrained eye, appear especially well-functioning. Children with this pattern can to some degree succeed in 'keeping together' a badly functioning family by compensating for the parents' inadequacies (Hennighausen et al., 2011). However, emotionally, other things are at stake, and disorganized people may experience serious problems with regard to regulating feelings of fear and insecurity, which they attempt to deal with by controlling other people. Therefore these seemingly 'well-functioning' people with disorganized attachment patterns are also vulnerable and at risk of serious psychological problems if the pressure becomes too great.

To the extent treatment providers assume the role of caregiver, treatment providers may experience similar reactions in clients with disorganized attachment patterns who, in an attempt to control their own fear, will turn attention towards 'controlling' or managing the treatment provider (Liotti, 2011, Wallin, 2007).

This attention may be of a controlling, critical quality and the client may both 'instruct' the treatment provider with regard to what he or she should do, while at the same time criticizing this effort. Or there may be a sense of misplaced care, where the client inquires into the treatment provider's well-being and tries to take care of him or her. Both reactions can seem puzzling when facing them as a treatment provider. However, they will start to make sense when one understands that the clients are trying to avoid unbearable fear by instead concentrating on being attentive to and 'handling' the treatment providers as protection against being let down by them.

The narrative dimension: trauma narratives and unintegrated 'voices'

A man has undergone a successful bypass operation and is soon ready to be discharged. He speaks to a nurse about the operation and the rehabilitation process to come. The man's own father died from a heart attack at age 55, which has been mentioned in the case history. Apart from this, however, the man has not spoken about his father's death to the staff. The nurse asks about the after-effects of the operation and whether the man is in good spirits. He answers: "Yes, I mean it has been a bit of a shock, both to me and the family. I still think there is some pain, but I guess I've been let off cheaply, when you consider ..." The man is quiet for a long time – the nurse waits for him to continue. "It didn't go as well for my dad, for example – and he was even younger than I am now – it's frightening, very frightening to think about. I don't really think I can ... It was the 14th of April. The daffodils had just come out in the garden. Mum told us to leave our bikes and come into the living room. She had on a blue dress with those small white dots. He, he ..." The man sighs and looks straight ahead. The nurse asks whether there is anything he needs to talk about. "Uhm, no, so, what were you saying about the rehabilitation process?"

As previously mentioned, there are two categories that fall outside the 'organized' patterns in the AAI – first the category 'unresolved with regard to loss or trauma' and second the category 'cannot classify' (Hesse, 2008). Common to these two types is a 'collapse' in the narrative's organization, either 'locally' or more generally. This may involve trauma-related material, which breaks into the narrative without being integrated meaningfully. Abrupt 'holes' in the narrative's progression may occur, in which words become inadequate to convey what is going on. Or sudden shifts between different 'voices' in the narrative may occur, with the narrator being unaware of, or failing to comment on, the shifting positions.

Whereas ambivalent attachment can also be related to narrative disorganization in the shape of chaotic or incomprehensible narratives, there is something more fundamental at work in disorganized attachment, as it is seemingly the ability to create overall meaning for oneself that is challenged, rather than simply the ability to communicate interpersonally (Holmes, 2001, Wallin, 2007). The general feeling that contributes to the narrative's disorganization seems to be anxiety or even pure terror rather than anger, longing, or irritation.

Breakthrough of trauma-related material

In the AAI, disorganized attachment first of all manifests itself in particular ways of talking about experiences, which in some sense or other were traumatic. This could, for example, be the loss of a close family member or acquaintance, or different types of abuse, such as violence or sexual assault committed by someone close to you. For some people with disorganized attachment, such traumatic experiences 'permeate' the narrative in such a way that these incidents are also referred to in contexts where they have no immediate relevance or relation to the questions asked (Hesse and Main, 2000, Main et al., 2008).

A number of different events with widely differing content can, for example, all be associated to a parent's suicide, or a person who has been subjected to sexual abuse may continue to focus on the themes of sexuality, danger, and power. For some disorganized people, traumatic experiences can be so intrusive that they are constantly brought to the foreground, as if the person is unable to 'shake them off' or 'leave them be' even though the conversation topic may be something else entirely. In a treatment context where these traumatic incidents are not at all in focus, it can become disruptive or even derail the conversation if such experiences are constantly brought up.

However, the influence of trauma-related material can also be more subtle, and may instead manifest itself through unclear and 'cryptic' references to a frightening experience which is not fully or unambiguously described. A man whose alcoholic father has physically assaulted him several times may talk about "the time the troubles began" without clarifying what the term 'troubles' signifies (Hesse and van Ijzendoorn, 1999, Main et al., 2008). Or it may appear as if the person only has conscious access to parts of the traumatic experience, without these being integrated in a coherent narrative account. A woman may say about her mother that she "often screamed and screamed", without this frightening image being connected to an account of what happened or why she screamed.

The more cryptic, partial references to traumatic material naturally become most striking in contexts where the actual purpose is to gain a more detailed overview of experiences of this nature. When they appear in conversations about other topics, there is a certain likelihood that treatment providers will fail to notice them, because they do not clearly refer to the underlying traumatic content. However, they may still attract attention as small glimmers of something that is ominous and unclear in the person's narrative. Because of the lack of narrative integration of the material, treatment providers may struggle to gain a clear picture of what the client has actually been through and how it has affected him or her.

At times, the mention of trauma-related material may take the form of more detailed flashbacks where the person talks about events in great detail as if they are etched into his or her consciousness (Hesse and Main, 2000, 2006, Main et al., 2008).

These may be a number of small observations relating to practical circumstances, which the person cites in great detail – seemingly without considering their relevance to the context – as if the person is transported back in time and merely reports his or her impressions.

Shifts between different 'voices' and wordless 'gaps'

In the AAI, one of the characteristics of disorganized or unclassifiable narratives is the occurrence of abrupt shifts between different 'voices' in the narrative, which the person does not seem to notice (Hesse, 2008, Hesse and van Ijzendoorn, 1999). This may occur in descriptions of deaths or other traumatic experiences, where the person will suddenly start talking in a different trance-like, engrossed way using imagery – for example, "If we did something wrong, his hands, hit, he ... those hands, hit and hit, run away ..." The person may suddenly start talking like a clergyman at a funeral, use uncharacteristic poetic language, or the person may get lost in long, atypically detailed accounts. Common to these shifts is the fact that they appear without warning and without the person being aware of or commenting on them. It is as if a collapse occurs in the person's active, conscious creation of meaning.

The collapse in meaning-making can also be expressed by seeming dissociation in the narrative and the occurrence of long, wordless gaps. This is especially significant when it occurs in connection with mention of a loss or other traumatic experiences, where the person seems to 'come to a halt' and then continue the narrative as if nothing had happened. Theoretically these marked breaks in the narrative's continuity are rooted in the presence of anxiety-provoking experiences or impulses that the person is unable to integrate with the rest of his or her meaning-making and in a breakdown of a metacognitive monitoring, that is, the ability to 'monitor' one's own narrative as it occurs, and to register changes in one's own state of mind (Hesse and Main, 2006, Liotti, 1999).

The person's narrative can be more or less globally disorganized – it may, for example, include abrupt shifts between entirely different perspectives on one's own attachment relationships, which may at one moment be described in strong emotional, hyperactivating language and the next in cold, deactivating language (Hesse, 1996, 2008). This differs from the acceptance of different perspectives found in securely attached people in that no meta-reflection or negotiation occurs between the different perspectives in disorganized narratives – they simply replace each other as if different personalities were expressing themselves without commenting on the discrepancy. Theory and research related to disorganized attachment indicate that this pattern is especially marked by an absence of meta-reflection or mentalization, since the traumatic experiences that are often at the root of the disorganized pattern also contribute to undermining the ability to mentalize (Fonagy, 2000, Fonagy et al., 2002).

In the original research on elements in the AAI that were able to predict disorganized attachment in children, focus was, as mentioned, on different types of unprocessed representations of attachment-related traumas or losses. In recent years, these findings have been extended by a research group including the psychologist Karlen Lyons-Ruth, who connected disorganized attachment to further markers, which they call 'hostile/helpless' positions in relation to attachment (Lyons-Ruth et al., 2004, Melnick et al., 2008). These 'hostile/helpless' positions are theoretically seen as a development of the controlling strategies seen in older children who were disorganized when they were younger.

On the narrative level, 'hostile/helpless' positions are, for example, expressed through devaluating and distancing descriptions of caregivers, while the person at other times expresses a connectedness and partial identification with the same caregivers. A woman may say that her mother was both "completely disturbed, way-out, made my life a living hell", and that she and the mother "resemble each other a lot and are very close". There may also be a strong, pervasive sense of fear or an inclination to describe oneself as "evil" or responsible for all the problems in a relationship. Or else there may be cool contempt for the person's own or others' suffering; the person may, for example, laugh immediately after talking about witnessing violence between his or her parents as a child.

For treatment providers working with clients with disorganized attachment patterns, such local or global tendencies to narrative disorganization can make it difficult to orientate oneself and form an overall picture of the client and the client's subjective world of experience. The client's sudden shifts can be surprising and disruptive and even frightening at times (Liotti, 2011, Wallin, 2007). When one is uncertain of where the client stands, it can be difficult to know how to approach the dialogue.

'Magical reasoning' and lapses in reality testing

Sometimes the discussion of traumatic events will be marked by a sense of unrealness, as if the person is not completely sure whether the incident has actually taken place or not, or is unsure of when it happened. A loss can, for example, have been so overwhelming and so hard to reconcile with a person's previous experiences in life that it never becomes fully integrated into the person's new sense of reality but continues to be imbued with a sense of doubt or unrealness (Fearon and Mansell, 2001, Hesse and van Ijzendoorn, 1999). This may then manifest itself through cryptic comments hinting that the deceased may still be alive or through confusion about the particular circumstances surrounding the death. A death may be referred to as taking place at two or more different times, or a deceased person may be mentioned several times in the present tense, even though this person passed away many years ago.

'Magical reasoning' or private logic about these incidents may also occur (Hesse, 2008, Main et al., 2008). A woman may, for example, believe that her father's car accident happened because she did not clean her room. Disorganized people may harbour notions that unpleasant occurrences for some reason or other are deserved – for example, that they prompted beatings from their own parents.

It can seem as if there is a 'lapse' in the reasoning surrounding traumatic events, which are not integrated with the rest of the person's reasoning and knowledge, but remain as a 'pocket' of something unclear and ominous in the collected narrative.

'Magical reasoning' is one of the markers for disorganized attachment that can be hard to evaluate in the AAI, because one has to consider the person's general system of beliefs, including religious beliefs. For example, different cultures and systems of beliefs relate differently to death. For some people, having a continued dialogue with their deceased mother will be perfectly normal and not a sign of disorganized attachment (Shaver and Fraley, 2008). However, a particular characteristic of the 'magical reasoning' that *is* a sign of unresolved loss or trauma is the sense of unrealness and lack of integration between the way in which the person relates to the trauma and the rest of the person's life view. This also results in these private logics remaining unexplained, whereas clients who are aware of operating from a particular religious or existential assumption, which the treatment provider does not necessarily share, will often explain their position to the treatment provider or alternatively choose to keep these thoughts and experiences to themselves.

When dealing with lapses in reality testing as a narrative marker of disorganized attachment, there is obviously a problem of delimitation in relation to actual psychosis with more general lapses in reality testing (Turton et al., 2001). This is complicated by the fact that, among clients with psychoses, there is an overrepresentation of disorganized attachment, and the fact that attachment-related disorganization is possibly part of the developmental background for psychoses (Dozier et al., 2008, Grossman et al., 2003, Read and Gumley, 2008). However, the lapses in reality testing connected with unresolved loss or trauma are usually more isolated and only appear in discussion of traumatic incidents. Thus we are not dealing with a more extensive collapse in the client's sense of reality, as we see in psychoses where 'magical thinking' or private logic dominates a person's meaning-making in other areas too.

References

Bartholomew, K. & Horowitz, L. M. 1991. Attachment styles among young adults: A test of a four-category model. *Journal of Personality and Social Psychology*, 61, 226–244.

Brennan, K. A., Clark, C. L. & Shaver, P. R. 1998. Self-report measurement of adult attachment: An integrative overview. In Simpson, J. A. & Rholes, W. S. (eds) *Attachment theory and close relationships*. New York: Guilford Press.

Cassidy, J. & Mohr, J. J. 2001. Unsolvable fear, trauma, and psychopathology: Theory, research, and clinical considerations related to disorganized attachment across the life span. *Clinical Psychology: Science and Practice*, 8, 275–298.

Deklyen, M. & Greenberg, M. T. 2008. Attachment and psychopathology in childhood. In Cassidy, J. & Shaver, P. (eds) *Handbook of attachment: Theory, research, and clinical applications*, 2nd ed. New York: Guilford Press.

Dozier, M., Stovall-McClough, C. & Albus, K. E. 2008. Attachment and psychopathology in adulthood. In Cassidy, J. & Shaver, P. (eds) *Handbook of attachment: Theory, research, and clinical applications*, 2nd ed. New York: Guilford Press.

Fearon, R. M. P. & Mansell, W. 2001. Cognitive perspectives on unresolved loss: Insights from the study of PTSD. *Bulletin of the Menninger Clinic*, 65, 380–396.

Fonagy, P. 2000. Attachment and borderline personality disorder. *Journal of the American Psychoanalytic Association*, 48, 1129–1146.

Fonagy, P., Gergely, G., Jurist, E. L. & Target, M. 2002. *Affect regulation, mentalization, and the development of the self.* New York: Other Press.

Grossman, A. W., Churchill, J. D., McKinney, B. C., Kodish, I. M., Otte, S. L. & Greenough, W. T. 2003. Experience effects on brain development: Possible contributions to psychopathology. *Journal of Child Psychology & Psychiatry & Allied Disciplines*, 44, 33–63.

Hennighausen, K. H., Bureau, J.-F., David, D. H., Holmes, B. M. & Lyons-Ruth, K. 2011. Disorganized attachment behavior observed in adolescence: Variation in relation to Adult Attachment Interview classifications at age 25. In Solomon, J. & George, C. (eds) *Disoganized attachment and caregiving.* New York: Guilford Press.

Hesse, E. 1996. Discourse, memory, and the Adult Attachment Interview: A note with emphasis on the emerging cannot classify category. *Infant Mental Health Journal*, 17, 4–11.

Hesse, E. 2008. The Adult Attachment Interview: Protocol, method of analysis, and empirical studies. In Cassidy, J. & Shaver, P. (eds) *Handbook of attachment: Theory, research, and clinical applications*, 2nd ed. New York: Guilford Press.

Hesse, E. & Main, M. 2000. Disorganized infant, child, and adult attachment: Collapse in behavioral and attentional strategies. *Journal of the American Psychoanalytic Association*, 48, 1097–1127.

Hesse, E. & Main, M. 2006. Frightened, threatening, and dissociative parental behavior in low-risk samples: Description, discussion, and interpretations. *Development and Psychopathology*, 18, 309–343.

Hesse, E. & van Ijzendoorn, M. H. 1999. Propensities towards absorption are related to lapses in the monitoring of reasoning or discourse during the Adult Attachment Interview. *Attachment & Human Development*, 1, 67–91.

Holmes, J. 2001. *The search for the secure base. Attachment theory and psychotherapy.* London: Brunner-Routledge.

Liotti, G. 1999. Disorganization of attachment as a model for understanding dissociative psychopathology. In Solomon, J. & George, C. (eds) *Attachment disorganization.* New York: Guilford Press.

Liotti, G. 2011. Attachment disorganization and the clinical dialogue: Theme and variations. In Solomon, J. & George, C. (eds) *Disorganized attachment and caregiving.* New York: Guilford Press.

Lyons-Ruth, K. & Jacobvitz, D. 1999. Attachment disorganization: Unresolved loss, relational violence, and lapses in behavioral and attentional strategies. In Cassidy, J. & Shaver, P. R. (eds) *Handbook of attachment: Theory, research, and clinical applications.* New York: Guilford Press.

Lyons-Ruth, K. & Jacobvitz, D. 2008. Attachment disorganization: Genetic factors, parenting contexts, and developmental transformation from infancy to adulthood. In Cassidy, J. & Shaver, P. (eds) *Handbook of attachment: Theory, research, and clinical applications*, 2nd ed. New York: Guilford Press.

Lyons-Ruth, K., Melnick, S., Bronfman, E., Sherry, S. & Llanas, L. 2004. Hostile-helpless relational models and disorganized attachment patterns between parents and their young children: Review of research and implications for clinical work. In Atkinson, L. &

Goldberg, S. (eds) *Attachment issues in psychopathology and intervention*. London: Lawrence Erlbaum.

Main, M., Hesse, E. & Goldwyn, R. 2008. Studying differences in language usage in recounting attachment history: An introduction to the AAI. In Steele, H. & Steele, M. (eds) *Clinical Applications of the Adult Attachment Interview*. New York: Guilford Press.

Main, M. & Solomon, J. 1986. Discovery of a new insecure-disorganized/disoriented attachment pattern. In Brazelton, T. B. & Yogman, M. W. (eds) *Affective development in infancy*. Norwood, NJ: Ablex.

Mason, O., Platts, H. & Tyson, M. 2005. Early maladaptive schemas and adult attachment in a UK clinical population. *Psychology and Psychotherapy: Theory, Research and Practice*, 78, 549–564.

Melnick, S., Finger, B., Hans, S., Patrick, M. & Lyons-Ruth, K. 2008. Hostile-helpless states of mind in the AAI: A proposed additional AAI category with implications for identifying disorganized infant attachment in high-risk samples. In Steele, H. & Steele, M. (eds) *Clinical Applications of the Adult Attachment Interview*. New York: Guilford Press.

Muller, R. T. 2010. *Trauma and the avoidant client. Attachment-based strategies for healing.* New York: W. W. Norton & Co.

Read, J. & Gumley, A. 2008. Can attachment theory help explain the relationship between childhood adversity and psychosis? *Attachment: New Directions in Psychotherapy and Relational Psychoanalysis*, 2, 1–35.

Riggs, S. A., Paulson, A., Tunnell, E., Sahl, G., Atkison, H. & Ross, C. A. 2007. Attachment, personality, and psychopathology among adult inpatients: Self-reported romantic attachment style versus Adult Attachment Interview states of mind. *Development and Psychopathology*, 19, 263–291.

Saypol, E. & Farber, B. A. 2010. Attachment style and patient disclosure in psychotherapy. *Psychotherapy Research*, 20, 462–471.

Shaver, P. R. & Fraley, R. C. 2008. Attachment, loss, and grief: Bowlby's views and current controversies. In Cassidy, J. & Shaver, P. (eds) *Handbook of attachment: Theory, research, and clinical applications*, 2nd ed. New York: Guilford Press.

Stovall-McClough, K. C. & Cloitre, M. 2006. Unresolved attachment, PTSD, and dissociation in women with childhood abuse histories. *Journal of Consulting and Clinical Psychology*, 74, 219–228.

Turton, P., McGauley, G., Marin Avellan, L. & Hughes, P. 2001. The Adult Attachment Interview: Rating and classification problems posed by non-normative samples. *Attachment & Human Development*, 3, 284–303.

Wallin, D. J. 2007. *Attachment in Psychotherapy*. New York: Guilford Press.

Part III

Attachment patterns and treatment practice

Chapter 7

Assessment of client attachment patterns

The previous chapters have outlined how clients' attachment patterns can be a central dimension that influences the collaboration with clients in many treatment relationships. The more serious and insistent the client's problems are, and the longer the treatment relationship lasts, the more likely it is that the client's attachment pattern will affect the way treatment collaboration unfolds. For treatment providers who want to take this into consideration and be more systematically aware of this influence, the question of how and when a client's attachment pattern can be assessed naturally arises.

In some treatment contexts, it will make sense to formally assess clients' attachment patterns. The first section of this chapter therefore discusses when such assessment is relevant, how to conduct a formal assessment of attachment patterns, and which possibilities and risks are involved in this assessment. In other treatment contexts, a formal assessment will be irrelevant or unrealistic in practice. Sometimes it will only be possible to form an impression based on interaction with the client. Therefore, the chapter's second section discusses how and to what degree it is possible to assess client attachment solely based on treatment-related interaction.

Clients obviously differ on many other dimensions than attachment patterns alone, and some of these dimensions – for example, gender – may interact with attachment patterns or influence the appearance of these. The third section of this chapter deals with the relationship between attachment patterns and other client characteristics.

Finally, as with all assessment or diagnosis, questions arise as to how this activity influences the treatment relationship. A relevant question is also whether labelling the client according to a categorical system is constructive, when research increasingly indicates that a dimensional and perhaps process-related understanding of attachment is more appropriate. These questions will be treated in the fourth and last section of this chapter.

Formal assessment

In some contexts, treatment providers or treatment institutions may have an interest in assessing clients' attachment patterns at isolated points in time, for example, before starting treatment and perhaps at the end of treatment. There are several contexts in which an initial assessment of attachment patterns may be relevant for preparing a treatment plan – for example, when working with troubled youths. If attachment and attachment patterns are part of a treatment's focus – for instance, in treatment for parents with mental problems that might interfere with parenting skills – it can also be relevant to follow potential developments in attachment patterns through repeated assessments (Heinicke and Levine, 2008, Moran et al., 2008, Teti et al., 2008, Toth et al., 2008).

A formal assessment of clients' attachment patterns will usually entail that clients are asked about their attachment inclinations or experiences, either through interview or questionnaire. Of course, this has to be justifiable in the particular treatment context. Assessment of attachment involves probing highly personal information, and the assessment process itself can trigger many thoughts and feelings in the client. Therefore, formal 'measurement' of a client's attachment pattern in treatment is only advisable if this knowledge is important and has actual significance for planning treatment. Furthermore, it is best if there is a possibility of following up on the results of the assessment by providing relevant feedback to the client and offering an opportunity for discussing and processing potential reactions to the assessment and assessment process.

A number of tools for systematic assessments of adult attachment patterns have been developed. Many of these are mentioned in Chapter 1. There are four main groups of instruments: semi-structured interviews, projective tests, observation-based rating schemes, and questionnaires. There is a conceptual overlap between most of these; however, as also mentioned in Chapter 1, it has become clear that these different methods do not 'measure' the exact same thing (Roisman et al., 2007b). The particular choice of tool for a formal assessment will depend on the purpose and practical circumstances.

Among the semi-structured interviews, the AAI is the best known (George et al., 1996, Main et al., 2002). However, there are other types, such as the Current Relationship Interview (CRI), which is based on the AAI tradition, but which focuses on romantic relationships instead of relationships to parents (Crowell and Owens, 1996). The AAI is a resource-demanding tool, because the entire interview must be transcribed in detail to enable coding, and the coding itself is time-consuming. The total time spent on administration, transcription and coding of a single interview may amount to 10–30 working hours, depending on the interview's complexity and length.

George and West have developed a projective test that assesses attachment patterns on the basis of the stories a person tells about a number of images with attachment-related content. In contrast to the questionnaire tradition, this projec-tive test, the Adult Attachment Projective (AAP), corresponds well with the AAI (George and West, 2001, 2012). Compared to the AAI, administration, transcrip-tion and scoring of the AAP is significantly shorter and is expected to take around three hours (George and West, 2001), which means that it may be more practically accessible in some contexts. It does not provide the same rich and detailed insight into a client's attachment history that the AAI does, but to some clients it may be less threatening to be asked to provide stories in response to pictures rather than to talk directly about experiences in attachment relationships.

Another option that may be relevant, and which does not necessitate special assessment sessions dedicated to evaluating attachment, is the use of observation-based coding schemes. One such system has been elaborated by Pilkonis and colleagues (Pilkonis, 1988, Pilkonis et al., 2014). Their Adult Attachment Rating Scales are used to rate the attachment dynamics described by a client in the context of an ordinary social and developmental history recorded as part of the intake in a psychiatric treatment context. These scales mainly focus on the interpersonal dimension of adult attachment and are applied by a group of raters, with final evaluations based on consensus. In the context of psychotherapy, Talia and colleagues have developed a promising new tool, the Patient Attachment Coding System, which allows for the classification of client attachment based on a single transcribed therapy session (Talia et al., 2014). Attachment is assessed based on the interpersonal function of client discourse in adjusting emotional proximity to the therapist, and attachment evaluations using this system have been found to correspond well to independently administered and evaluated AAIs. A detailed overview of the Patient Attachment Coding System can be found in the Appendix.

In an everyday treatment context, all of the above-mentioned instruments share the disadvantage that extensive training is required for them to be used reliably. For some of them, this training is followed by a demanding authorization process. Transcription and coding is also time-consuming, although to different degrees. In treatment environments where the developmental aspects of clients' attachment patterns are of special interest and relevance – for example, work with mothers and children in an infant psychiatric ward – it makes sense to invest time and resources in the training required for the AAI or AAP, because they measure attachment patterns in a way which developmental psychological studies have connected to a number of central features of parent–child relationships (van Ijzendoorn, 1995). In psychiatric or psychotherapeutic contexts where there are resources for research or documentation of attachment and attachment changes, training in an instrument such as the Patient Attachment Coding System may also prove highly relevant.

In the majority of treatment contexts, however, the assessment of client attachment patterns is most realistically conducted either via the use of questionnaires or through attachment-oriented interviews without the use of formal coding systems. For this reason, these two options will be discussed in more detail in the following. However, thorough knowledge of the attachment literature, as well as of one more of the established coding systems – or access to supervision from someone with this knowledge – will be a great advantage in relation to such assessment.

Interview-based assessment

Although only few contexts will be conducive to application of the research-based coding systems to attachment-oriented interviews, it is still possible to use interviews when assessing client attachment patterns. Compared to questionnaires, there are both advantages and disadvantages in using the interview method. Whereas questionnaires only give access to the conclusions that people are ready to draw about themselves, an interview may give access to information that clients are not aware of or perhaps do not wish to admit to (Jacobvitz et al., 2002). Interviews also allow for further probing of unclear points and may serve as a basis for establishing a relationship to a client before embarking on a longer course of treatment (Steele and Steele, 2008).

In many treatment contexts, different types of interviews are traditionally conducted as part of the initial assessment or in the chronicling of case history. Attention to attachment patterns could easily be included here. The specific questions to include will naturally depend on the treatment provider's particular interest in the given treatment context. In the following, three different approaches to this kind of interview will be described: 1) to inquire into the client's attachment history, 2) to inquire into the client's current approach to attachment relationships, and 3) to examine coherence and incoherence in the internal working models, drawing inspiration from the AAI. In practice these can easily supplement each other.

In some contexts, it will make sense to systematically inquire into the client's attachment history. Relevant questions might be: "Who took care of you as a child?" "What was your relationship to your parents like?" "Were there any important shifts in this relationship?", and "Have you experienced loss or abuse?" The aim is that the client's early experiences of attachment relationships are described and elaborated, which will give an impression of the client's attachment-related 'baggage'. Obviously this is a personal and, for many, a sensitive area, into which a treatment provider cannot simply inquire without reason. It is also important to remember that there is no one-to-one relationship between particular childhood experiences and particular attachment patterns. It is, for example, perfectly possible to exhibit a secure attachment pattern in adulthood despite not having received all the care needed as a child, and vice versa (Hesse, 2008, Roisman et al., 2002, Waters et al., 2000a). To the extent that a client recounts attachment experiences openly and sincerely, such an interview can provide an impression of the internal working models the client draws upon in attachment contexts.

A different line of approach would be to focus more on the client's current way of engaging in close relationships. This could be done by using parts of a questionnaire, such as the ECR (Brennan et al., 1998), as an interview guide, and inquire into fear of being abandoned, discomfort if others get too close, desires for emotional independence, etc. This differs from just using a questionnaire, since this form of interview may pave the way for establishing a relationship to the client and makes it possible to ask further questions in relation to the client's answers; for example, asking for specific examples to get a better understanding of how the client understands the topic and to correct potential misunderstandings. It will also be possible to inquire into different relationships and perhaps into changes over time.

Finally, one may focus on coherence in internal working models by using the AAI, either in its entirety or in excerpt, without subsequent transcription and coding with the formal coding system. It is important to understand that there is a reason why the training required for reliably coding this interview takes a long time. Thus, an accurate assessment of clients' attachment patterns cannot be carried out through a more 'loose' application of the AAI, not even by clinicians who are well versed in the attachment literature (Hughes et al., 2000). Furthermore, many of the aspects that are important in the formal coding of the AAI can be hard to spot without a detailed transcription of the interview. Nonetheless, the AAI can be a source of much useful information about the coherence or lack thereof in clients' internal working models. A possible line of approach could be to use only the part of the interview where clients are asked to give five adjectives that describe their relationship to childhood caregivers, followed by probing for specific examples illustrating these adjectives.

Even though the described strategies for clinical interviews may form part of a formalized assessment of clients' attachment patterns, none of these assessment strategies are as reliable as questionnaires and other standardized methods for measuring attachment patterns. Thus, they cannot be used in a formal measurement of treatment effect, for instance, since it is not possible to ensure that different assessors will reach the same results, or that the assessment is conducted consistently at different times. However, through a clinical interview it is possible to gain detailed information about attachment and attachment patterns, and the chance of learning about unique characteristics of the client's attachment experience as well as clearing up misunderstandings and elaborating unclear points is greater than when simply handing clients a questionnaire.

Assessment using questionnaires

The simplest method of evaluating clients' attachment patterns is to ask them to fill out one of the many existing questionnaires designed to assess adult attachment. As described in Chapter 1, multiple questionnaires exist. Since most of the international literature uses the Experiences in Close Relationships Scale (ECR) (Brennan et al., 1998), which was developed on the basis of a factor analysis of a large number of previous questionnaires, it may be most relevant to use this scale. The ECR also exists in a revised edition, ECR-R (Fraley et al., 2000), as well as in a shorter form (Wei et al., 2007). Other scales may have advantages in some contexts, but generally the agreement between the established questionnaires is good.

The ECR questionnaire consists of 36 statements, which the person is asked to assess on a seven-point scale from "strongly disagree" to "strongly agree", which makes it easy for most people to respond. The statements deal with close relationships in general – partners, close friends, or family members – rather than relationships to specific persons; the questionnaire can therefore also be answered by people who are not currently in a romantic relationship or who are not in contact with their family. Scoring of the questionnaire is simple and does not require complicated calculations. If more relation-specific patterns are of particular interest, it is also possible to change the wording of the instructions and questions to inquire into specific relationships, such as parents or partners (Fraley and Phillips, 2009). Thus, the ECR can assess 'general' attachment patterns as well as attachment patterns in more specific relationships.

The responses to the 36 statements in ECR form the basis for the calculation of two independent scales, *avoidance* and *anxiety*. The avoidance scale measures reservedness in relation to opening up to other people or allowing oneself to enter into a dependency relationship with them. The anxiety scale measures fear of being abandoned, uncertainty of partners' love, and general worry about close relationships. Low scores on both scales reflect a secure pattern, while heightened scores on one or both scales reflect an insecure pattern. Scores on the two ECR scales can be 'translated' into categorical assessments of attachment patterns. However, it is standard to report results as scores on each of the two dimensions, an approach which is also supported by the existing research (Crowell et al., 2008).

As mentioned in Chapter 1, it is important to be aware that questionnaires such as ECR primarily tap into a person's current attitudes and inclinations with respect to engaging in close emotional relationships. There are no grounds for assuming that these patterns reflect particular childhood conditions or experiences or that they correspond to a person's childhood attachment pattern. Thus, when assessing a client's attachment patterns with a questionnaire, one cannot 'translate' this to assumptions about the client's childhood or general attachment history. Furthermore, since questionnaires and the AAI do not overlap (Roisman et al., 2007b), one should not necessarily expect a correlation between attachment patterns assessed with questionnaires and the narrative characteristics that are primarily tied to interview-based assessment.

The information gained through questionnaires is predominantly information the respondent is aware of and is willing to admit to. If one works in a context where clients have an interest in portraying themselves in a certain light – for example, as either very well-functioning or very distressed – this can affect the information gathered from a response to a questionnaire. Likewise, people's self-knowledge differs, and some people's image of how they function in close relationships deviates slightly – or perhaps strongly – from the way they are described by people who know them. Nonetheless, questionnaires are generally a simple and accessible method for assessing client attachment, and can profitably be used in treatment contexts as long as the treatment provider is aware of the method's limitations.

Process diagnosis – assessment based on the interaction

In treatment contexts where there is no reason for or possibility of conducting a formal assessment of client attachment, it is still possible to be attentive to attachment and to conduct a more informal assessment as part of interacting with the client (Ammaniti et al., 2008, Lopez, 2009, Slade, 2008). Whereas formal assessments will be conducted at delimited times – typically at the beginning of a course of treatment and perhaps again at the end – an informal assessment may constitute a 'process diagnosis', in which the treatment provider is continually attentive to and considers the client's attachment inclinations and how these affect the treatment relationship. Many of the characteristics of attachment patterns outlined in the previous chapters are phenomena that treatment providers can gain a qualified impression of through a certain measure of interaction with clients. It will, for example, be clear whether a client presses for care and attention or instead shuts off and insists on handling things alone.

A further argument for the tenability of conducting continuous process diagnosis with regard to client attachment patterns is that adult attachment is to some degree context- and relationship-specific (Bretherton and Munholland, 2008, Collins et al., 2004, Stein et al., 1998). This will be elaborated in this chapter's last section about attachment patterns as categories or processes. Although research has shown that people's general attachment inclinations are systematically connected to general ways of being in relationships, the way that clients behave in specific treatment relationships can deviate from what would be predicted on the basis of their general attachment pattern. Psychotherapy research has developed methods for assessing clients' attachment to their specific therapist, which often – but far from always – corresponds to their general attachment pattern when measured with standard tools (Diamond et al., 2003, Mallinckrodt et al., 1995). In many treatment contexts, it will be more relevant to consider clients' actual attachment as it plays out in specific treatment situations rather than clients' general attachment patterns. Therefore, a process diagnosis may, in many contexts, be the most appropriate form of assessment.

In an informal process diagnosis of client attachment patterns, it makes sense to focus on the dimensions that the formal assessment tools tap into, namely the *interpersonal patterns* and *narrative patterns* that were outlined in the previous chapters. Since these two dimensions draw on different research traditions, which only overlap to a limited extent – the questionnaire method and the AAI, respectively – it is of course important to ask whether they can be united and point in the same direction in more informal assessments. A relevant study conducted by Westen and colleagues (Westen et al., 2006) sheds some light on this question. These researchers asked a large number of practising psychologists and psychiatrists to assess their clients on a number of features including interpersonal characteristics as well as some of the narrative characteristics related to attachment patterns. They subsequently conducted a factor analysis to examine whether and how these different descriptive dimensions were connected and found that the descriptions were meaningfully accounted for by four factors, which corresponded well to the four main attachment patterns. There is thus a strong indication that the interpersonal and narrative characteristics of attachment patterns are systematically and meaningfully connected in treatment providers' assessment of clients.

Attending to the interpersonal process

In Chapters 3 to 6 it was described how the four attachment patterns typically manifest themselves in interpersonal interaction. These features can form the basis for an informal assessment of client attachment patterns based on the way that clients engage – or do not engage – in the treatment interaction. One of the most important dimensions to consider in this assessment is the client's attitude and behaviour with regard to interpersonal proximity or distance. The more intensely a client seeks out proximity, the more it points towards an ambivalent/hyperactivating pattern; and the more a client prefers distance, the more it points towards an avoidant/deactivating pattern. An open, trustful attitude with positive expectations towards the treatment provider will indicate secure attachment, whereas distrust and fear of being let down will indicate insecure attachment. Table 7.1 sums up the most important interpersonal characteristics of the four primary attachment patterns.

An obvious source of error in process diagnosis based on the interpersonal process is that the treatment provider is also part of this process and thus the assessment will, for better or for worse, be affected by the treatment provider's own role and inclinations, and may therefore deviate from the way an outsider would describe the process (Gabbard, 2001, Slade, 1999). If a treatment provider, for example, finds a client demanding and emotionally overwhelmed or over-whelming, it may be a sign that the client's attachment pattern is marked by ambivalent features. However, it may also to some degree reflect that the treatment provider has an avoidant inclination and is uncomfortable with emotional proximity and interpersonal demands. Discussing such impressions either during supervision or with colleagues may be important, especially if these impressions are ascribed importance in interaction with clients. 'Process diagnosis' based on interpersonal interaction is not an infallible method and it is important to be aware that assessment of client attachment patterns on this basis must necessarily be a 'working hypothesis' open to continuous revision.

Treatment providers should also be wary of assuming that a client's way of interacting with them or with the treatment team reflects the client's way of inter-acting in all relationships. The more one knows about a client's other relation-ships, the more complete a picture can be formed of the client's attachment inclinations and the way in which these appear in a broader range of interpersonal interactions. Finally, it must be emphasized that a client's interpersonal behaviour will not just be motivated by attachment patterns. For example, a client who is sexually attracted to his or her treatment provider may be emotionally expressive and 'insistent' for very different reasons than an ambivalently attached client, for whom this relationship style is only motivated by activation of the attachment system. Attention to attachment dynamics and attachment patterns should thus not lead to one becoming blind to other relationship dimensions and motivational systems.

Table 7.1 Interpersonal markers of the four attachment patterns.

	Secure	Avoidant	Ambivalent	Disorganized
Proximity/distance	Value and are comfortable with proximity	Prefer distance and are uncomfortable with proximity. Consider self 'different'	Strive for proximity, but are not comfortable when it is achieved. Tendency to interpersonal 'fusion'	Fear proximity but feel lost without it
Trust/expectations to others	Are trusting and have positive expectations	Fear rejection or ridicule, but try to ignore feelings of insecurity	Fear being abandoned or losing attention – expect the worst	Strong distrust of others, fear of boundaries being breached or violated
Attitude to seeking and receiving help	Are open to seeking help	Prefer to handle things themselves	Strong desire for help or support	Afraid of getting involved, but feel helpless
Expression and regulation of emotions	Balanced expressions of both positive and negative emotions	Limited expression of emotions, false positivity, suppression of negative emotions	Frequent and dramatic expressions, focus on and intensify negative emotions	Absent or chaotic expressions of emotions, difficulties in regulating emotions
Self-image/self-esteem	Nuanced self-image and solid self-esteem	Tendency to a defensively 'magnified' self-image to compensate for low self-esteem	Low self-esteem with a strong need for interpersonal validation	Low self-esteem, incoherent self-image
Openness and self-disclosure	Are pleased to share thoughts and feelings, but 'dose' these according to the situation	Are reticent about sharing thoughts and feelings	Share thoughts and feelings, but not always adapted to the context	Are reticent about sharing thoughts and feelings, but involuntary 'breakthroughs' may occur
Dependence/independence	Feel comfortable in committed relationships, but are also capable of autonomy	Greatly value independence from others	Feel dependent on others – seek out relationships	Strong conflict between the desire for independence and feelings of dependence
Conflict management	Constructive strategies for handling conflicts	Uncomfortable with potential conflicts, attempt to ignore these	Great attention to conflicts, may be inclined to escalate these	Conflicts may lead to breakdowns and inappropriate behaviour
Empathy	Empathy with and care for others	Limited empathy and interpersonal 'coldness'	Preoccupied by others, but inclined to misattribute and project	Own fear/helplessness hinders empathy and solicitude with others

Attending to narrative features

If clients are being treated in a context that includes longer conversations, it will become increasingly possible to use narrative characteristics of the way in which they talk about themselves and their problems in an informal assessment of attachment patterns. Again, such assessment may take its starting point in the narrative characteristics of the four attachment patterns described in Chapters 3 to 6. An important dimension with regard to narrative characteristics is the general coherence and credibility of a narrative. More coherent and credible narratives indicate secure attachment, while different types of narrative incoherence indicate insecure attachment. Another important dimension is how emotions are integrated or not integrated in narratives about interpersonal interactions. Table 7.2 summarizes the most important narrative characteristics of the four primary attachment patterns.

Some of the narrative characteristics related to attachment can be difficult to notice for treatment providers, who will usually be paying attention to content, rather than to the way in which it is expressed. Furthermore, a number of the narrative markers included in the AAI and other coding systems are quite subtle and do not become clear until the conversation is transcribed. Treatment providers may, for example, fail to hear that a client refers to a deceased person in the present tense – it is just a single, small word that does not quite fit, and one may easily assume to have misheard the client. Continuous attention to a client's narrative style thus requires training a special 'ear' for such details – something that is typically part of the training of psychologists and psychotherapists, though not necessarily in a highly systematic fashion.

An important point in relation to continuous attention to narrative markers of client attachment patterns is that the different narrative characteristics described in this book are primarily observed when people's attachment systems are activated or when the conversation topic is attachment-related (Crowell et al., 1996). Thus, the narrative characteristics do not necessarily have the same implications if displayed in other contexts where attachment is not in play (Daniel, 2009). Even though treatment situations will often be inherently attachment-relevant and involve attachment system activation, there may be situations and phases of treatment where attachment is not as pertinent; thus, treatment providers need to be context-conscious in their assessment.

Just as with the interpersonal features that can serve as 'markers' for the different attachment patterns, the narrative 'markers' described here may sometimes be rooted in something other than attachment. Therefore it is important to be discerning when assessing these. People differ in their narrative abilities, and these differences can be rooted in many different things; for example, intelligence, personality, etc. Some forms of narrative incoherence may be due to psychotic illness or different forms of brain damage, which can also influence a client's narrative style. Thus, it is not advisable to infer a given attachment pattern from a certain narrative style without taking other potential contributing factors into account as well.

Table 7.2 Narrative markers of the four attachment patterns.

	Secure	Avoidant	Ambivalent	Disorganized
Coherence and credibility	Coherence between the narrative levels – the narrative appears credible	Contradictions between general descriptions and specific episodes	Incoherence due to absence of convincing generalization and 'common thread'	Trauma-related material is unintegrated in the narrative and destabilizes it
Balance in descriptions	Balance between negative and positive features in descriptions of self and others	Inclination to present self and attachment figures in positive light – marked by clichés	Often negative, reproachful descriptions of others – exaggerated 'authoritative' descriptions	Incoherent, contradictory or suddenly changing descriptions of self and others
Dramatization/downplaying	Openness about difficult aspects without appeal to pity	Downplaying of difficult incidents or feelings	Dramatizes difficulties and appeals to pity and involvement	Sudden shifts between dramatization and downplaying
Description of emotions	Descriptions of incidents include 'well-regulated' descriptions of emotions	Few and undifferentiated descriptions of emotions	The narrative is permeated by emotions 'demonstrated' rather than described	Absence of integrated descriptions of emotions, anxiety may 'leak' unintentionally
Abstraction/specificity	Balance between abstraction/generalization and specific details	Relatively abstract, poor on specific episodic material	Rich on specific episodic material, but often in fragments and without a common thread	Both abstraction and episodic fragments are present, but are poorly integrated
Consideration of interlocutor/listener	Can put self in the listener's place and give necessary introductions	Inclination to 'shut down topics' and cut off the interlocutor	Are carried away by the narrative and often talk about something other than what is asked for	Can be in 'own world' without a sense of the interlocutor, may at times frighten the listener
Verbosity	Appropriate amount of relevant information	Relatively short and telegram-like descriptions	Long accounts, including much irrelevant information	Can shift between reticence and verbosity
Narrative 'orderliness'	The narrative is well-organized – time, place, and persons are marked and introduced	The narrative is organized, but can be hard to follow because of internal contradictions	Jumps in time and place and/or persons, private phrases and unclear 'filler words'	Abrupt shifts in the narrative in connection with trauma-related material
Mentalization	Self and others are described as thinking and feeling – eye for different perspectives	Few and sketch-like accounts of people's thoughts and feelings, emphasis on the concrete	Many accounts of thoughts and feelings, often with authoritative 'mind-reader' quality	Magical reasoning and absence of mentalization in connection with trauma-related material

Attachment patterns and other client characteristics

Although attachment patterns can be an important dimension in treatment relationships, they are far from the only thing a client brings to a treatment context. Attachment patterns co-exist with, and are affected by, a large number of a client's other features. In this section, some of the additional client features that interact with clients' attachment patterns or influence the assessment of these are described.

Age and gender

As outlined in Chapter 1, attachment patterns are dynamic and develop over time. Thus the concept 'attachment pattern' does not cover the same in children as it does in adults. Development also takes place in adulthood – both development occurring as a result of a person's unique attachment experiences, but also more general developments tied to common developmental phases of a human life (Crowell et al., 2008, Magai, 2008).

The empirical evidence indicates that adolescents' attachment patterns are characterized by a greater prevalence of avoidant attachment than found in adults – at least when measuring attachment patterns with the AAI (Bakermans-Kranenburg and van Ijzendoorn, 2009). Theoretically this makes sense when considering the developmental phase in which adolescents typically find themselves. Breaking away from parents and transitioning to taking care of oneself is in focus at this age. A certain degree of deactivation of the attachment system and appreciation of emotional independence may in fact be conducive to this life task. Treatment providers who work with adolescents can therefore expect to encounter a greater frequency of avoidant attachment, which for some will be a passing 'phase' rather than a general pattern that will follow them for life.

In contrast to this, the disorganized attachment pattern as operationalized by the AAI category 'unresolved with respect to loss' becomes more frequent with age. The most obvious explanation is that older persons have experienced more losses, which they may not be resolved about (Bakermans-Kranenburg and van Ijzendoorn, 2009). It is not completely clear whether attachment-related disorganization is not 'triggered' until a loss is experienced, or whether the AAI is merely poorer at detecting disorganization when there are no losses to inquire about (Lyons-Ruth and Jacobvitz, 2008). However, younger adults, who have not yet experienced loss of close relations, can still display many of the other signs of disorganized attachment described in Chapter 6.

Many have focused on the possible connection between gender and attachment patterns. It is thus often put forward that avoidant attachment is more common in men, whereas ambivalent attachment is more common in women. At least in Western societies, this seems to correspond to cultural stereotypes of 'masculine' and 'feminine' ways of handling emotional difficulties. The inclination to downplay emotional vulnerability and pain is considered typically masculine, while the inclination to get carried away by emotions and perhaps to dramatize is considered a typical feminine feature. Thus, some authors have claimed that the difference between avoidant and ambivalent attachment is not so much between two different attachment patterns, but rather a gender difference. In attachment patterns as measured with the AAI, there does not seem to be a gender difference in the distribution of the patterns (Bakermans-Kranenburg and van Ijzendoorn, 2009). However a meta-analysis of studies conducted with questionnaires has demonstrated a difference: men are more avoidant and women more ambivalent – a difference which is greatest in early adulthood and diminishes with age (Del Giudice, 2011). In other words, when inquiring into the relation between attachment and gender, the method of measurement makes a difference. There are also studies which indicate that attachment patterns interact with gender in the sense that ambivalent attachment, for example, is expressed differently by men and women (Collins and Read, 1990, Simpson, 1990).

Gender stereotypes may affect treatment providers' assessment of clients' attachment patterns, as they may find it harder to detect avoidant features in women than in men and, conversely, find it harder to detect ambivalent features in men than in women, because they will generally look for features that correspond to cultural expectations. When detecting less culturally expected characteristics, there may be a tendency to consider avoidant features in women and ambivalent features in men as more 'problematic', because they do not correspond to the features that the culture typically values in men and women respectively. Of course, a given attachment pattern's 'adaptiveness' and appropriateness is not independent of such cultural evaluations. Therefore it is not unlikely that ambivalent attachment may actually prove more problematic for a man in today's society, while avoidant attachment may prove more problematic for a woman.

Socioeconomic and cultural background

The attachment literature is inclined to emphasize all the advantages of secure attachment. However, it is important to note that attachment patterns first and foremost constitute a functional adaption to a given childhood environment, and that attachment patterns' 'appropriateness' thus cannot be considered independently of their context (Belsky, 1999, Crittenden, 1988, Simpson and Belsky, 2008). This context does not just include parents' personality and parenting style, but also the wider context in which the family lives, including socioeconomic circumstances.

Many studies point to a greater prevalence of insecure attachment patterns in children living in difficult socioeconomic circumstances (Kobak and Madsen, 2008, Mickelson et al., 1997, van Ijzendoorn and Kroonenberg, 1988, Weinfield et al., 2008). This may be related to limited resources, as parents simply lack the practical and emotional energy necessary for providing an adequate secure base and safe haven for their children. However, it is also possible to regard parenting styles that are conducive to insecure attachment patterns in children as appropriate in some circumstances. For example, in contexts marked by poverty or danger, harsh or deactivating parenting may teach children strategies that are conducive to their survival in the given context (Simpson and Belsky, 2008). If you live in a rough environment with a high crime rate where trusting others or showing vulnerability can be dangerous, it may prove advantageous to have learned an avoidant style from your parents.

When working with people with other living conditions than the relatively secure and affluent reality of the middle classes, it is important to take note of this and not simply transfer the logic that secure attachment is necessarily the most adaptive and appropriate pattern. People with reason to be uncertain of the environment in which they live – for example, refugees waiting for a decision regarding a residence permit – have good reason to maintain patterns marked by insecurity, although of course this does not constitute a conscious 'choice' of strategy.

While existing studies have generally found the same percentage of secure attachment in populations throughout the world – about 55 per cent when measured with AAI – there are indications that some forms of insecure attachment are more prevalent in some cultures than others (Bakermans-Kranenburg and van Ijzendoorn, 2009, Del Giudice, 2011, van Ijzendoorn and Sagi-Schwartz, 2008). Although there is no basis for drawing firm conclusions in the area, several studies of North European populations found a relatively high percentage of avoidant attachment and smaller percentages of ambivalent attachment compared to the North American norm. In contrast, higher prevalence of ambivalent attachment was found in Japan and Israel. Thus, there is reason to believe that there may be cultural differences with regard to the prevalence of different attachment patterns, likely as a result of different norms and practices in bringing up children as well as different family patterns. However, this may also to some degree reflect different cultural norms regarding what it is acceptable to report in a conversation such as the AAI or when responding to questionnaires, rather than actual differences in the processing of information, regulation of emotion, etc.

Arguably, some of the features associated with the different attachment patterns are features that are valued differently in different cultures and subcultures. Independence is, for example, highly valued in many Western societies, while other parts of the world rate it much less favourably. Cultural norms differ greatly concerning which feelings are acceptable in public and how to express them. This means that particular attachment patterns will have different sets of 'side-effects' depending on one's culture. This can be important to understand if you work with clients from other cultures than your own. Something that from one culture's normative perspective may seem like an unhealthy degree of 'merging' or lack of boundaries between individuals may be a completely normal family pattern in another culture. In some cultures it may be common to be emotionally 'reserved', while the same stance towards emotional relationships will be considered a dismissing, highly avoidant style in other cultures.

Thus, the overall message is that one would be well advised to take context into account and assume a wider perspective in the assessment of attachment patterns, as with all assessment. A careful consideration of context will reduce the risk of assessment errors and serve to avoid an unsubstantiated normativity, in which it is uncritically assumed that you know what is most appropriate for a given person. The importance of this is emphasized by the theoretical point that attachment patterns first of all constitute appropriate adaptions or attempts to optimize a situation that may in itself be challenging or unsafe.

Categories or processes?

Like all other kinds of diagnosis or categorization of people, assessment of clients' attachment patterns holds risks and uncertainties worth considering. As with other types of psychological assessment, the level of accuracy is never 100 per cent. In other words, assessments can always turn out to be incorrect in specific cases, even though the method generally and usually works well. When dealing with psychological assessments that in some way or other affect the way in which treatment providers approach clients, there is the special complication that the assessment may in fact affect the client, both directly and indirectly.

Similar to the way in which the interpersonal expectations related to different attachment patterns can become self-fulfilling prophecies, treatment providers' evaluation of clients as belonging to a certain category may unfortunately contribute to 'locking' the clients in behavioural patterns corresponding to this categorization. Categorization processes may perpetuate or maintain a treatment provider's view of a client, because once a client has been identified as, for example, disorganized, the treatment provider will be more inclined to notice behaviour and features that correspond to this categorization and less inclined to notice features contrary to this conclusion.

Often a treatment provider's inflexible categorization can be an understandable response to working with clients who in some sense or other are challenging or 'difficult'. Categorizing such clients as, for instance, being 'disorganized' helps make sense of the difficulties experienced in relation to the clients and may help the treatment provider maintain understanding and patience. However, categorization can also end up serving as an excuse and a way of explaining away failed treatments. Treatment providers may conclude, "There was nothing I could do anyway, because his disorganized attachment pattern hindered establishing a proper treatment relationship." In such cases, a categorization can have a destructive effect and be used to 'label' and reject clients, rather than help them. There is a fine line between the two and there is good reason for treatment providers to act with care and continued reflection.

In addition to these general risks and points to be wary of regarding unnecessary or rigid categorization, attachment patterns also involve theoretical and research-related arguments for vigilance. In this book, attachment patterns have primarily been described and discussed as separate categories – both because this way of presenting them is most prevalent in the literature, but also for communicative reasons, as 'thinking' in categories or types can be easier when trying to understand something. However, as mentioned in Chapter 1, research in the area indicates that attachment patterns are less clearly delimited, less stable, and more complex than often assumed, which will be discussed in more depth below.

Categorical versus dimensional understanding

In the earliest literature about attachment patterns, describing and discussing these as separate categories was clearly the most widespread approach. However, Ainsworth's system for assessing the Strange Situation already included a certain dimensionality in the shape of subcategories; for example, secure with a slight tendency to ambivalence or a degree of avoidance (Ainsworth et al., 1978). The same applies to the AAI, which operates with subgroups that may be regarded as expressing a form of continuum, just as it includes a number of features that the coder assesses on nine-point scales (Hesse, 2008). Two interviews, which are both categorized as dismissing/avoidant, for example, may differ in that one is assessed as having an 'idealization' score of 6, while the other has an 'idealization' score of 8 and is thus in some respects considered 'more' avoidant. All newer questionnaires similarly include gradual transitions.

In addition to the fact that dimensionality is already completely or partially inbuilt in the assessment instruments, a number of relatively sophisticated studies of this question have also been conducted using different forms of mathematical verification (Fraley and Waller, 1998, Haydon et al., 2011, Roisman et al., 2007a). None of these studies suggest the existence of actual, underlying categories, but rather support the idea of attachment features being dimensionally distributed. Thus, although researchers who use the AAI ultimately decide on a category and, for example, code an interview as either secure or ambivalent, there is no empirical documentation for drawing the line precisely at a particular degree of presence of ambivalent features. In other words, there is no point on the 'ambivalence continuum' that corresponds to water's freezing point, which makes a significant qualitative difference in the properties of water. Therefore, solely operating with general categories can be misleading, especially when dealing with people who may be located on the borderline between two different categories.

Thus, even though categories and descriptions of 'prototypical' secure, avoidant, ambivalent, and disorganized patterns can contribute to a better understanding of the dynamics at play in attachment patterns, there are many good reasons to remember that in practice there will hardly ever be sharp boundaries between distinct categories, but rather a greater or lesser presence of a number of different features, with the possibility of 'mixtures' and in-between positions.

Stable traits or momentary snapshots?

Several studies of attachment patterns' stability have been conducted – both as part of psychometric validation of different research tools for assessing attachment patterns, and as part of longitudinal studies in which groups of people were followed for a longer period of time. The studies conducted as part of psychometric validation generally found a high 'test–retest stability' for both the AAI and questionnaires. In other words, if a person is interviewed with AAI and is then re-interviewed two months or a year later, there is a relatively high chance (about 75–90 per cent) that the person will be evaluated as belonging to the same category (Bakermans-Kranenburg and van Ijzendoorn, 1993, Hesse, 2008, Sagi et al., 1994). For the group not assessed as belonging to the same category in the second assessment, the discrepancy may partly be explained by measurement error – that is, that the assessment instrument is not completely accurate – and partly by actual changes in attachment.

Studies aimed at psychometric validation are usually conducted in 'normal populations', which likely increases the impression of stability. Other studies in which people's attachment patterns are followed over time indicate that attachment patterns are most stable in middle-class populations without special social or mental problems, while they are significantly less stable in groups that live under more risk-filled circumstances (Pinquart et al., 2013). Thus, some studies following people who grew up with poverty, violence, abuse, and other difficult conditions, or who experienced serious mental problems, have found relatively low stability in attachment patterns – especially, but not only, with regard to shifts between different insecure categories (Benoit and Parker, 1994, Crowell and Hauser, 2008, Hamilton, 2000, Waters et al., 2000a, 2000b).

Furthermore, there are indications that different attachment patterns have different degrees of stability, that is, some patterns may entail more stable features while others are more momentary or state-like. With regard to attachment patterns measured with the AAI, disorganized attachment is a relatively unstable category – that is, it varies more from measurement to measurement. Ambivalent attachment is also more unstable than secure and avoidant attachment, which are the most stable categories (Klohnen and Bera, 1998, Mickelson et al., 1997). A recent study suggests that, even though attachment patterns vary over time, for the individual it is more a question of 'variations on a theme', where an underlying prototype pulls towards a certain stability (Fraley et al., 2011).

In treatment contexts, it is important not to equate a given attachment pattern with presently experienced security or insecurity. Security is in a constant state of change, and it is important to be aware of the client's actual state. Just because a client has a tendency towards a secure attachment pattern, he or she will not necessarily feel secure in all relationships or situations. Conversely, clients with a mainly insecure attachment pattern will be able to engage in a secure treatment relationship if the right conditions are present.

Relational specificity

As described in Chapter 1, an infant's attachment patterns are relationship-specific, whereas adult attachment patterns are traditionally regarded as generalized phenomena that cut across relationships and, with time, develop into something that resembles personality traits. In some interpretations of attachment theory it is described as if the internal working models – and thereby attachment patterns – with experience become so 'cemented' that people will always experience relationships 'through' these models as part of a self-fulfilling prophecy. This view has been theoretically criticized; adults relate differently to different people and the better one knows another person, the more one's behaviour in the relationship with the person will depend on specific experiences with this person, rather than generalized expectations (Tronick, 2003). The view has also been challenged empirically. Thus, studies of adults' attachment to different people – parents, partners, and therapists – generally indicate that person-specific attachments do not necessarily correspond (Diamond et al., 2003, Mallinckrodt et al., 1995, Owens et al., 1995, Roisman et al., 2005, Treboux et al., 2004). Thus, it is not likely that adults are furnished with a single, unitary working model that is 'employed' in all relationships as a matter of course. Nor is it likely that adult attachment patterns are closed to input and adjustment in regard to the specific people that one relates to.

Despite the evidence that adult attachment patterns are to some degree relationship-specific, there is still a lot of research demonstrating a relationship between adults' behaviour in emotional and relational contexts and their general attachment patterns (Mikulincer and Shaver, 2007) – so how can these two observations be reconciled? The answer may emerge from a better understanding of the relationship between generalized and more specific working models and of which situations make people draw on their more general versus their more relationship-specific models. It is likely that both processes are in play: people *do* form unique relationships to specific others *and* draw on generalized internal working models in the process. Whether general or relationship-specific models dominate may depend on both person-specific and contextual conditions (Brumbaugh and Fraley, 2006, 2007, Collins et al., 2004, Grossmann, 1999, Pietromonaco and Barrett, 2000).

One of the differences between secure and insecure attachment patterns is the degree of flexibility in processing of information and in regulation of emotion. Secure attachment is characterized by a greater openness and flexibility, whereas one of the characteristics of insecure attachment patterns is a greater inclination to draw rigidly on generalized working models, even though they are not particularly constructive in the given context (Bretherton and Munholland, 2008, Main, 2000). For example, a person with a markedly avoidant attachment pattern will meet most people and situations with a reserved and downplaying style, whereas people with secure attachment are more able to modulate their relational style according to the situation and the people they are with.

Apart from such individual differences, there are likely to be situational factors that contribute to determining when people draw on relationship-specific and more generalized working models respectively. People may be more inclined to draw on the generalized models if they are under pressure, are stressed out, feel threatened, or when they are forced to act quickly. A man who has formed a generalized ambivalent pattern based on the majority of his experiences in attachment contexts may, for example, in time be able to establish a secure relationship with his girlfriend. His behaviour towards and expectations of his girlfriend will be guided by the specific experiences of her being reliable; he has developed a relationship-specific secure pattern. However, if he is one day presented with threatening information – for example, hints that his girlfriend has been unfaithful to him – there is a strong likelihood that he will be inclined to draw on his generalized ambivalent pattern and base his actions on this. Being in a threatened position may lead a person to resort to more well-learned, old strategies, momentarily losing contact with more recent patterns. Thus, in assessment of clients' attachment patterns it is generally a good idea to distinguish between general and more relationship-specific patterns, as both may turn out to have relevance in treatment.

References

Ainsworth, M. S., Blehar, M. C., Waters, E. & Wall, S. 1978. *Patterns of attachment: A psychological study of the strange situation*. Hillsdale, NJ: Lawrence Erlbaum.

Ammaniti, M., Dazzi, N. & Muscetta, S. 2008. The AAI in a clinical context: Some experiences and illustrations. In Steele, H. & Steele, M. (eds) *Clinical Applications of the Adult Attachment Interview*. New York: Guilford Press.

Bakermans-Kranenburg, M. J. & van Ijzendoorn, M. H. 1993. A psychometric study of the Adult Attachment Interview: Reliability and discriminant validity. *Developmental Psychology*, 29, 870–879.

Bakermans-Kranenburg, M. J. & van Ijzendoorn, M. H. 2009. The first 10,000 Adult Attachment Interviews: Distributions of adult attachment representations in clinical and non-clinical groups. *Attachment & Human Development*, 11, 223–263.

Belsky, J. 1999. Modern evolutionary theory and patterns of attachment. In Cassidy, J. & Shaver, P. R. (eds) *Handbook of attachment: Theory, research, and clinical applications*. New York: Guilford Press.

Benoit, D. & Parker, K. C. H. 1994. Stability and transmission of attachment across three generations. *Child Development*, 65, 1444–1456.

Brennan, K. A., Clark, C. L. & Shaver, P. R. 1998. Self-report measurement of adult attachment: An integrative overview. In Simpson, J. A. & Rholes, W. S. (eds) *Attachment theory and close relationships*. New York: Guilford Press.

Bretherton, I. & Munholland, K. A. 2008. Internal working models in attachment relationships: Elaborating a central construct in attachment theory. In Cassidy, J. & Shaver, P. (eds) *Handbook of attachment: Theory, research, and clinical applications*, 2nd ed. New York: Guilford Press.

Brumbaugh, C. C. & Fraley, R. C. 2006. Transference and attachment: How do attachment patterns get carried forward from one relationship to the next? *Personality and Social Psychology Bulletin*, 32, 552–560.

Brumbaugh, C. C. & Fraley, R. C. 2007. Transference of attachment patterns: How important relationships influence feelings toward novel people. *Personal Relationships*, 14, 513–530.

Collins, N. L., Guichard, A. C., Ford, M. B. & Feeney, B. C. 2004. Working models of attachment: New developments and emerging themes. In Rholes, W. S. & Simpson, J. A.

(eds) *Adult attachment: Theory, research, and clinical implications*. New York: Guilford Publications, Inc.

Collins, N. L. & Read, S. J. 1990. Adult attachment, working models, and relationship quality in dating couples. *Journal of Personality and Social Psychology*, 58, 644–663.

Crittenden, P. M. 1988. Relationships at risk. In Belsky, J. & Nezworski, T. (eds) *Clinical implications of attachment. Child psychology*. Hillsdale, NJ: Lawrence Erlbaum Associates, Inc.

Crowell, J. A., Fraley, R. C. & Shaver, P. 2008. Measurement of individual differences in adolescent and adult attachment. In Cassidy, J. & Shaver, P. (eds) *Handbook of attachment: Theory, research, and clinical applications*, 2nd ed. New York: Guilford Press.

Crowell, J. A. & Hauser, S. T. 2008. AAIs in a high-risk sample: Stability and relation to functioning from adolescence to 39 years. In Steele, H. & Steele, M. (eds) *Clinical applications of the Adult Attachment Interview*. New York: Guilford Press.

Crowell, J. A. & Owens, G. 1996. Current Relationship Interview and scoring system. State University of New York, Stony Brook.

Crowell, J. A., Waters, E., Treboux, D., O'Connor, E., Colon-Downs, C. & Feider, O. 1996. Discriminant validity of the Adult Attachment Interview. *Child Development*, 67, 2584–2599.

Daniel, S. I. F. 2009. The developmental roots of narrative expression in therapy: Contributions from attachment theory and research. *Psychotherapy: Theory, Research, Practice, Training*, 46, 301–316.

Del Giudice, M. 2011. Sex differences in romantic attachment: A meta-analysis. *Personality and Social Psychology Bulletin*, 37, 193–214.

Diamond, D., Stovall-McClough, C., Clarkin, J. & Levy, K. N. 2003. Patient–therapist attachment in the treatment of borderline personality disorder. *Bulletin of the Menninger Clinic*, 67, 227–259.

Fraley, R. C. & Phillips, R. L. 2009. Self-report measures of adult attachment in clinical practice. In Obegi, J. H. & Berant, E. (eds) *Attachment theory and research in clinical work with adults*. New York: Guilford Press.

Fraley, R. C., Vicary, A. M., Brumbaugh, C. C. & Roisman, G. I. 2011. Patterns of stability in adult attachment: An empirical test of two models of continuity and change. *Journal of Personality and Social Psychology*, 101, 974–992.

Fraley, R. C. & Waller, N. G. 1998. Adult attachment patterns: A test of the typological model. In Simpson, J. A. & Rholes, W. S. (eds) *Attachment theory and close relationships*. New York: Guilford Press.

Fraley, R. C., Waller, N. G. & Brennan, K. A. 2000. An item response theory analysis of self-report measures of adult attachment. *Journal of Personality and Social Psychology*, 78, 350–365.

Gabbard, G. O. 2001. A contemporary psychoanalytic model of countertransference. *Journal of Clinical Psychology*, 57, 983–991.

George, C., Kaplan, N. & Main, M. 1996. Adult Attachment Interview. Third edition. Department of Psychology, University of California at Berkeley.

George, C. & West, M. 2001. The development and preliminary validation of a new measure of adult attachment: The Adult Attachment Projective. *Attachment & Human Development*, 3, 30–61.

George, C. & West, M. 2012. *The Adult Attachment Projective Picture System. Attachment theory and assessment in adults*, New York: Guilford Press.

Grossmann, K. E. 1999. Old and new internal working models of attachment: The organization of feelings and language. *Attachment & Human Development*, 1, 253–269.

Hamilton, C. E. 2000. Continuity and discontinuity of attachment from infancy through adolescence. *Child Development*, 71, 690–694.

Haydon, K. C., Roisman, G., Marks, M. J. & Fraley, R. C. 2011. An empirically derived approach to the latent structure of the Adult Attachment Interview: Additional convergent and discriminant validity evidence. *Attachment & Human Development*, 13, 503–524.

Heinicke, C. M. & Levine, M. S. 2008. The AAI anticipates the outcome of a relation-based early intervention. In Steele, H. & Steele, M. (eds) *Clinical Applications of the Adult Attachment Interview*. New York: Guilford Press.

Hesse, E. 2008. The Adult Attachment Interview: Protocol, method of analysis, and empirical studies. In Cassidy, J. & Shaver, P. (eds) *Handbook of attachment: Theory, research, and clinical applications*, 2nd ed. New York: Guilford Press.

Hughes, J., Hardy, G. & Kendrick, D. 2000. Assessing adult attachment status with clinically-orientated interviews: A brief report. *British Journal of Medical Psychology*, 73, 279–283.

Jacobvitz, D., Curran, M. & Moller, N. 2002. Measurement of adult attachment: The place of self-report and interview methodologies. *Attachment & Human Development*, 4, 207–215.

Klohnen, E. & Bera, S. 1998. Behavioral and experiential patterns of avoidantly and securely attached women across adulthood: A 31-year longitudinal perspective. *Journal of Personality and Social Psychology*, 74, 211–223.

Kobak, R. R. & Madsen, S. D. 2008. Disruptions in attachment bonds: Implications for theory, research, and clinical intervention. In Cassidy, J. & Shaver, P. (eds) *Handbook of attachment: Theory, research, and clinical applications*, 2nd ed. New York: Guilford Press.

Lopez, F. G. 2009. Clinical correlates of adult attachment organization. In Obegi, J. H. & Berant, E. (eds) *Attachment theory and research in clinical work with adults*. New York: Guilford Press.

Lyons-Ruth, K. & Jacobvitz, D. 2008. Attachment disorganization: Genetic factors, parenting contexts, and developmental transformation from infancy to adulthood. In Cassidy, J. & Shaver, P. (eds) *Handbook of attachment: Theory, research, and clinical applications*, 2nd ed. New York: Guilford Press.

Magai, C. 2008. Attachment in middle and later life. In Cassidy, J. & Shaver, P. (eds) *Handbook of attachment: Theory, research, and clinical applications*, 2nd ed. New York: Guilford Press.

Main, M. 2000. The organized categories of infant, child, and adult attachment: Flexible vs inflexible attention under attachment-related stress. *Journal of the American Psychoanalytic Association*, 48, 1055–1096.

Main, M., Goldwyn, R. & Hesse, E. 2002. Adult Attachment Scoring and Classification Systems. Version 7.1. Department of Psychology, University of California at Berkeley.

Mallinckrodt, B., Gantt, D. L. & Coble, H. M. 1995. Attachment patterns in the psychotherapy relationship: Development of the Client Attachment to Therapist Scale. *Journal of Counseling Psychology*, 42, 307–317.

Mickelson, K. D., Kessler, R. C. & Shaver, P. R. 1997. Adult attachment in a nationally representative sample. *Journal of Personality and Social Psychology*, 73, 1092–1106.

Mikulincer, M. & Shaver, P. R. 2007. *Attachment in adulthood: Structure, dynamics, and change*. New York: Guilford Press.

Moran, G., Bailey, H. N., Gleason, K., DeOliveira, C. A. & Pederson, D. R. 2008. Exploring the mind behind unresolved attachment: Lessons from and for attachment-based interventions with infants and their traumatized mothers. In Steele, H. & Steele, M. (eds) *Clinical Applications of the Adult Attachment Interview*. New York: Guilford Press.

Owens, G., Crowell, J. A., Pan, H., Treboux, D., O'Connor, E. & Waters, E. 1995. The prototype hypothesis and the origins of attachment working models: Adult relationships with parents and romantic partners. *Monographs of the Society for Research in Child Development*, 60, 216–233.

Pietromonaco, P. R. & Barrett, L. F. 2000. The internal working models concept: What do we really know about the self in relation to others? *Review of General Psychology*, 4, 155–175.

Pilkonis, P. A. 1988. Personality prototypes among depressives: Themes of dependency and autonomy. *Journal of Personality Disorders*, 2, 144–152.

Pilkonis, P. A., Yookyung, K., Lan, Y. & Morse, J. Q. 2014. Adult Attachment Ratings (AAR): An item response theory analysis. *Journal of Personality Assessment*, 96, 417–425.

Pinquart, M., Feussner, C. & Ahnert, L. 2013. Meta-analytic evidence for stability in attachments from infancy to early adulthood. *Attachment & Human Development*, 15, 189–218.

Roisman, G. I., Collins, W. A., Sroufe, L. A. & Egeland, B. 2005. Predictors of young adults' representations of and behavior in their current romantic relationship: Prospective tests of the prototype hypothesis. *Attachment & Human Development*, 7, 105–121.

Roisman, G. I., Fraley, R. C. & Belsky, J. 2007a. A taxometric study of the Adult Attachment Interview. *Developmental Psychology*, 43, 675–686.

Roisman, G. I., Holland, A., Fortuna, K., Fraley, R. C., Clausell, E. & Clarke, A. 2007b. The Adult Attachment Interview and self-reports of attachment style: An empirical rapprochement. *Journal of Personality and Social Psychology*, 92, 678–697.

Roisman, G. I., Padron, E., Sroufe, L. A. & Egeland, B. 2002. Earned-secure attachment status in retrospect and prospect. *Child Development*, 73, 1204–1219.

Sagi, A., van Ijzendoorn, M. H., Scharf, M. & Koren-Karie, N. 1994. Stability and discriminant validity of the Adult Attachment Interview: A psychometric study in young Israeli adults. *Developmental Psychology*, 30, 771–777.

Simpson, J. A. 1990. Influence of attachment styles on romantic relationships. *Journal of Personality and Social Psychology*, 59, 971–980.

Simpson, J. A. & Belsky, J. 2008. Attachment theory within a modern evolutionary framework. In Cassidy, J. & Shaver, P. (eds) *Handbook of attachment: Theory, research, and clinical applications*, 2nd ed. New York: Guilford Press.

Slade, A. 1999. Attachment theory and research: Implications for the theory and practice of individual psychotherapy with adults. In Cassidy, J. & Shaver, P. R. (eds) *Handbook of attachment: Theory, research, and clinical applications*. New York: Guilford Press.

Slade, A. 2008. The implications of attachment theory and research for adult psychotherapy: Research and clinical perspectives. In Cassidy, J. & Shaver, P. (eds) *Handbook of attachment: Theory, research, and clinical applications*, 2nd ed. New York: Guilford Press.

Steele, H. & Steele, M. 2008. Ten clinical uses of the Adult Attachment Interview. In Steele, H. & Steele, M. (eds) *Clinical Applications of the Adult Attachment Interview*. New York: Guilford Press.

Stein, H., Jacobs, N. J., Ferguson, K. S., Allen, J. G. & Fonagy, P. 1998. What do adult attachment scales measure? *Bulletin of the Menninger Clinic*, 62, 33–82.

Talia, A., Daniel, S. I. F., Miller-Bottome, M., Miccoli, D., Brambilla, D., Safran, J. D. & Lingiardi, V. 2014. AAI predicts patients' in-session interpersonal behavior and discourse: A "move to the level of the relation" for attachment-informed psychotherapy research. *Attachment & Human Development*, 16, 192–209.

Teti, D. M., KileenI, L. A., Candelaria, M., Miller, W., Hess, C. R. & O'Connell, M. 2008. Adult attachment, parental commitment to early intervention, and developmental outcomes in an African American sample. In Steele, H. & Steele, M. (eds) *Clinical Applications of the Adult Attachment Interview*. New York: Guilford Press.

Toth, S. L., Rogosch, F. A. & Cicchetti, D. 2008. Attachment-theory-informed intervention and reflective functioning in depressed mothers. In Steele, H. & Steele, M. (eds) *Clinical Applications of the Adult Attachment Interview*. New York: Guilford Press.

Treboux, D., Crowell, J. A. & Waters, E. 2004. When "new" meets "old": Configurations of adult attachment representations and their implications for marital functioning. *Developmental Psychology*, 40, 295–314.

Tronick, E. Z. 2003. "Of course all relationships are unique": How co-creative processes generate unique mother–infant and patient–therapist relationships and change other relationships. *Psychoanalytic Inquiry*, 23, 473–491.

van Ijzendoorn, M. H. 1995. Adult attachment representations, parental responsiveness, and infant attachment: A meta-analysis on the predictive validity of the Adult Attachment Interview. *Psychological Bulletin*, 117, 387–403.

van Ijzendoorn, M. H. & Kroonenberg, P. M. 1988. Cross-cultural patterns of attachment: A meta-analysis of the strange situation. *Child Development*, 59, 147–156.

van Ijzendoorn, M. H. & Sagi-Schwartz, A. 2008. Cross-cultural patterns of attachment: Universal and contextual dimensions. In Cassidy, J. & Shaver, P. R. (eds) *Handbook of attachment: Theory, research, and clinical applications*, 2nd ed. New York: Guilford Press.

Waters, E., Hamilton, C. E. & Weinfield, N. S. 2000a. The stability of attachment security from infancy to adolescence and early adulthood: General introduction. *Child Development*, 71, 678–683.

Waters, E., Merrick, S., Treboux, D., Crowell, J. & Albersheim, L. 2000b. Attachment security in infancy and early adulthood: A twenty-year longitudinal study. *Child Development*, 71, 684–689.

Wei, M., Russell, D. W., Mallinckrodt, B. & Vogel, D. L. 2007. The Experiences in Close Relationship Scale (ECR) – Short Form: Reliability, validity, and factor structure. *Journal of Personality Assessment*, 88, 187–204.

Weinfield, N. S., Sroufe, L. A., Egeland, B. & Carlson, E. A. 2008. Individual differences in infant–caregiver attachment: Conceptual and empirical aspects of security. In Cassidy, J. & Shaver, P. (eds) *Handbook of attachment: Theory, research, and clinical applications*, 2nd ed. New York: Guilford Press.

Westen, D., Nakash, O., Thomas, C. & Bradley, R. 2006. Clinical assessment of attachment patterns and personality disorder in adolescents and adults. *Journal of Consulting & Clinical Psychology*, 74, 1065–1085.

Chapter 8

Adapting treatment 'style'

One of the primary reasons why attachment theory in general and attachment patterns in particular may prove interesting to treatment providers is that different attachment patterns can be related to distinct opportunities and challenges in treatment work (Slade, 2008, Tolmacz, 2009, Wilkinson, 2003). Theory and clinical experience suggest that it may be constructive to adjust treatment style to fit the client's attachment pattern and there is also some empirical evidence supporting this (Bernier and Dozier, 2002, Daly and Mallinckrodt, 2009). Of course, many issues and considerations other than attachment and attachment patterns are involved in the planning of a given course of treatment. However, due to the attachment system's central importance to the current life situation of many people seeking treatment, attachment will often be relevant to some extent.

This chapter will discuss how and to which degree it can prove beneficial to adjust treatment to the client's attachment pattern. This question should be seen in continuation of the previous chapter's consideration of how to assess clients' attachment patterns in treatment work, including how attachment patterns in treatment relationships are dynamic and not necessarily defined once and for all. The chapter's first section describes how clients' insecure attachment patterns constitute different challenges to the establishment of the initial treatment alliance, and how treatment providers can meet these challenges. Although it is usually wise to accommodate the client during initial contact – that is, to establish a treatment environment that complies with the client's attachment pattern – it may prove necessary to challenge the client's attachment tendencies during the course of treatment, also in treatments where attachment patterns are not the therapeutic focus. The chapter's second section discusses when this can be relevant and how to go about this in a constructive and respectful manner. Finally, a client's attachment pattern can, in some contexts, be significant for the choice of different treatment forms or strategies. This is the theme of the chapter's third and final section.

Establishing a treatment alliance

All forms of treatment – from prescribing medicine to long-term psychotherapy – depend on a constructive treatment alliance. In psychotherapy research, this alliance is often conceptualized as consisting of three components: 1) an emotional bond between treatment provider and client, that is, mutual sympathy, acknowledgment and respect, 2) a reasonable degree of agreement on which tasks or procedures the treatment involves and should involve, and 3) a reasonable degree of agreement as to what the goals and success criteria of the treatment are and should be (Horvath and Bedi, 2002). This definition is general enough to be relevant to most forms of treatment. In a general practitioner's practice, where the GP prescribes medicine to patients, the patient's intake of medicine will also depend on the patient's respect for and trust in the GP, agreement that the medicine is a reasonable treatment form and that the objective of the medication is relevant and desirable.

When establishing a treatment alliance, the initial contact and communication is crucial. In psychotherapy research, it has repeatedly been demonstrated that treatment alliances measured by the third treatment session are a significant predictor of the therapy's final outcome. It is thus possible to predict the final outcome on the basis of the alliance quite early on and with a reasonable degree of certainty (Martin et al., 2000). In other forms of treatment, where a large part of treatment consists of clients following a plan made in collaboration with the treatment provider, the entire treatment outcome may depend on one or two conversations. In all forms of treatment work, it is therefore worth considering how to establish a good contact and mutual understanding of the treatment's ends and means.

In contrast to secure attachment, which several studies have found to be associated with a general readiness and ability to form constructive treatment alliances, the different types of insecure attachment can, in each of their own ways, pose a challenge when establishing treatment alliances (Bernecker et al., 2014, Daniel, 2006, Diener and Monroe, 2011, Smith et al., 2010). In the following, the insecure patterns will therefore each be discussed with respect to which attitude and strategy is most constructive for the treatment provider to assume in the given context. Naturally there are limits to how much a treatment provider can adjust his or her usual relational and therapeutic style to adapt to a client's given insecure attachment pattern. Nevertheless, we all constantly adapt our communication and way of relating to the current relationship and context. As a treatment provider it can be relevant to become more aware of this ability to adapt and to use it more purposefully in a treatment context, while necessarily operating within the 'zone' in which one feels authentic and in which one is able to act credibly.

Avoidant attachment: respecting the need for distance

As described in Chapter 4, the avoidant pattern is characterized by a desire to maintain some degree of independence and distance to others as well as an inclination to downplay difficult emotional states, such as sadness, anxiety, and vulnerability. The avoidant pattern comes under pressure when the person finds himself or herself in a help-seeking position, which feels uncomfortable and potentially risky, since feeling weak can easily activate shame and feelings of inadequacy (Dozier et al., 2001, Muller, 2010). A client with strong avoidant features will be very ready to conclude that his or her difficulties are "nothing special" and that the proposed treatment will have nothing to offer. Clients with avoidant attachment will easily feel smothered, robbed of their autonomy, or condescended to by treatment providers. The most significant challenges in establishing the initial treatment alliance with avoidant clients will therefore be their disinclination to communicate openly and clearly about their problems and limited motivation to get involved in the treatment process.

An important part of establishing initial treatment alliances with avoidant clients will be to avoid increasing their feelings of discomfort, since this entails the risk that they will 'pull out' and give up on treatment (Daly and Mallinckrodt, 2009, Mallinckrodt, 2010). This can best be done by keeping contact relatively formal and 'businesslike' and by being active in and structuring the dialogue. By staying businesslike and formal, communication is kept on the avoidant client's 'home ground', where strong expressions of emotion or clearly explicated suffering are atypical. The initial strategy is to match the client's communication style. As described previously, the avoidant client can be relatively uninformative and telegram-like when describing difficulties. Therefore, it may prove necessary to ask a lot of questions. In some situations it can be useful to explain to the client why the answers to these questions are relevant, to prevent the feeling of being 'cross-examined'. In this way one can help the client to view himself or herself as 'co-responsible' regarding the treatment, which will likely appeal to the avoidant client, who dislikes being dependent on others.

It is worth remembering that, although the avoidant attachment pattern entails challenges for the treatment provider, it is also associated with resources that can be included to the advantage of the treatment process. The avoidant client's urge for control, which can prove problematic in a poor treatment alliance, can instead become a resource in many treatment situations. It is therefore crucial to adequately negotiate and reconcile the treatment's ends and means, so the avoidant client becomes a partner rather than an opponent. Compared to the ambivalent client, the avoidant client will often be relatively organized and mastery-oriented, which is also profitable in many treatment processes.

As the avoidant client is inclined to consciously or unconsciously expect the treatment provider to be dismissive of and condescending about 'weakness' and suffering, it will be important to disconfirm this – not through strong expressions of sympathy such as "I feel with you", but rather through communication that 'normalizes' the client's reaction patterns. For an avoidant client it can be comforting to be told that "In your situation it is perfectly normal to be afraid or find it hard to concentrate at work", or similar. Thus the relational balancing act with avoidant clients consists in respecting and perhaps even drawing on the clients' need for independence and emotional control, while at the same time avoiding leaving the clients to themselves to such a degree that it ends up intensifying the avoidant pattern, with the client concluding that "I should just pull myself together and stop whining" (Mallinckrodt et al., 2009, Slade, 2008, Wallin, 2007).

It is important that treatment providers do not simply assume that avoidant clients would benefit from expressing their feelings or that they need to be confronted with their 'denial' or similar. Although this may be true in a wider perspective, it is not necessarily right in a client's particular situation. In the process of establishing an initial treatment alliance with a client, or where the treatment format itself does not enable a more personal, continual contact, efforts to 'shake' the avoidant client from his or her preferred coping strategy will, in the best case, be without effect and, in the worst case, threaten treatment.

Ambivalent attachment: Meeting the need for emotional support

The primary challenges in treating ambivalent clients are their continuous vigilance of the treatment provider potentially letting them down as well as their chaotic communication style. The ambivalent client feels exposed and insecure and will harbour a hope and need to be 'rescued' by the treatment provider, while at the same time ultimately experiencing the treatment provider as unreliable. Therefore the ambivalent client will likely insist on continued reassurance that the treatment provider takes their problem seriously and is dedicated to solving it, just as the client can be inclined to 'dramatize' his or her communication of the experienced problem (Lopez, 2009, Wallin, 2007, Wilkinson, 2003). Clients with ambivalent attachment may put considerable pressure on their treatment providers who – with good reason – can become nervous of 'slipping up'.

As clients with ambivalent attachment have a strong need for the treatment provider's continuous communication of 'being there' and being reliable, it becomes extra important to be clear about what the client can expect of the treatment provider and the treatment, and to not promise more than you can keep. In the initial contact with ambivalent clients, it is best if treatment providers are able to be patient with the client's demands for support and attention without becoming irritated or cutting off the client, but also without amplifying the attachment-related hyperactivation further by joining in the ambivalent client's atmosphere of 'disaster' (Daly and Mallinckrodt, 2009, Slade, 2008). The ambivalent client will often have much to tell and it will often be helpful in the establishment of a constructive treatment alliance, if the treatment provider, to some degree, allows room for this and does not just insist on a narrow, predefined agenda. Giving the ambivalent client a chance to narrate will increase his or her sense of being heard and taken seriously.

In contrast to the avoidant client, who will likely feel more comfortable with a task-oriented and formal treatment provider, there is a significant risk that treatment providers who come across as too businesslike or neutral will be considered cold and unengaged by the ambivalent client. This will make the ambivalent client focus more on the relationship and on checking up on the treatment provider's stance and trustworthiness, which will happen at the expense of attention to the treatment, including perhaps to specific instructions in this connection. In the initial establishment of alliances or in treatment relationships that are necessarily short-term or impersonal, this would be a disadvantage. Much can be gained by communicating engagement and support of the client. In this case, signalling empathy and compassion is in order – for example, "I can understand it must be really hard for you to have to deal with this operation when you've also just lost your job."

Whereas some ambivalent clients will primarily meet the treatment provider with helplessness, others will be more angry and reproachful and perhaps even hold the treatment provider responsible for previous failed treatments (Wallin, 2007). Although it can be hard for treatment providers to not feel bothered by this, 'fighting back' is not constructive when establishing an alliance. Treatment providers may find it easier to tolerate this relational style if they keep in mind that it is rooted in an underlying feeling of powerlessness and fear of new disappointments. Thus, the relational balancing act with the ambivalent client consists in acknowledging the experience of suffering and the need for emotional support, without aligning so much with the sense of crisis that it intensifies the ambivalent client's feeling of insecurity and fear that the situation is deemed to end badly. It may help to meet the client's need for comfort and support without adhering too rigidly to the treatment's framework, but also without supporting unrealistic expectations that the treatment provider will be unable to fulfil (Mallinckrodt et al., 2009).

Just as the avoidant client can make some treatment providers desire to 'break through the armour' or challenge the denial of emotions, ambivalent clients may engender an inclination to 'counteract' overdramatization by simply asking them to "pull themselves together" and stop being "hysterical". This kind of message will make no sense to the ambivalent client in a strained situation – the client will likely just feel rejected, which will give rise to further activation of the attachment system. As long as a secure treatment relationship has not been established, the best way of getting the ambivalent client to 'turn down' the panic will not be by asking them to pull themselves together, but rather by making an extra effort to communicate your presence and readiness to help them.

Disorganized attachment: cautiousness and flexibility

Of the different attachment patterns, disorganized attachment probably constitutes the biggest challenge to the establishment of a constructive treatment alliance. Disorganized clients are likely to vary a lot in their way of relating, which makes demands of the treatment provider's flexibility, and they can be reticent to engage themselves due to fear that the treatment provider will prove not only inadequate, but perhaps even inappropriate or threatening. In relation to such fears, the extent of the disorganization and whether actual trauma is part of the background will make a difference. The more the client's attachment pattern is marked by a severe traumatization, the harder the treatment provider's task of establishing a secure treatment relationship will be (Liotti, 2011, Muller, 2010).

When treating a disorganized client, it is important to be extra careful and attentive to changing signals from the client, who may at one moment operate with an avoidant strategy while, at the next, switch to a more ambivalent strategy. The disorganized client can shift quite suddenly from being intensely marked by crisis to a complete denial of vulnerability and need for help. This can easily confuse and frustrate treatment providers, if they do not understand how this behaviour originates in complex internal working models reflecting the experience that others' help is both an absolute necessity and extremely risky (Lyons-Ruth and Jacobvitz, 2008, Lyons-Ruth et al., 2004). For treatment providers, it is best to act with an appropriate mixture of flexibility and stability, both adjusting the approach according to the client's current 'position' and at the same time avoiding oscillating chaotically with the client. More than other clients, clients with disorganized attachment have a strong need for treatment providers who are stably present and can 'go the distance'. This also entails a readiness to 'repair' the relationship with the client, when misunderstandings and mistakes inevitably arise.

As the disorganized client's balance is fragile, it is important not to pressure the client more than absolutely necessary. It is also important to take care of the client by downregulating the intensity if traumatic material is brought up. As described in Chapter 6, disorganized clients may suddenly 'leak' stories about losses or abuse. Some disorganized clients may very abruptly present trauma-related material to treatment providers, also in contexts where this has no relation to the treatment's focus (Wallin, 2007). Although this is unlikely to be a conscious strategy, it can appear as an attempt to 'test' the treatment provider or scare him away. Without an already established secure treatment relationship with room for, and time to consider, the client's traumatic experiences, it will not be expedient to dwell further on such stories. At the same time, of course, such stories cannot just be ignored, as this could intensify the sense of unreality that the disorganized client possibly already struggles with. Therefore, it is important to acknowledge the presence of anxiety-provoking and overwhelming experiences, while simultaneously conveying that this is not the time to discuss them. If relevant, it may be appropriate to refer the client or advise about possible treatments of these aspects elsewhere.

Similar to avoidant clients, clients with disorganized attachment react with discomfort to activation of the attachment system. However, for the disorganized clients, attachment activation is also intensely anxiety-provoking. Some disorganized clients may attempt to keep the attachment system deactivated by relying on other behavioural systems instead; for example, the 'caregiving system' which underpins caregiving behaviour, or the 'ranking system' which underpins socially competitive behaviour (Liotti, 2011). Thus, a client who is seriously ill may resist activation of his own attachment system by focusing attention on caring for close relations and perhaps even the treatment provider. Or he may be critical and competitive and devote his attention to a search for gaps in his doctor's knowledge and competences. Even though such reactions can appear undesirable or inappropriate, they serve to protect the client against overwhelming anxiety and the more complete collapse of coping strategies that attachment activation would cause. When establishing initial treatment alliances with disorganized clients, or when the treatment relationship is short-term, it is important to be careful with challenging the client's coping strategies or otherwise bringing the attachment system into focus. This requires precise regulation of the interpersonal distance, since *either* too distant and unavailable *or* too empathetic and responsive behaviour on the part of the treatment provider may contribute to activating the disorganized client's attachment system.

Constructively challenging client attachment patterns

Even if a client's attachment pattern is not in focus in a given treatment, it may often prove helpful to challenge the client's attachment-related style to some extent. This can be helpful because some of the inclinations inherent in the insecure patterns may in the long run subvert the treatment relationship and perhaps even the treatment outcome. Although the general message of the previous section was that one should meet the client where the client is – which requires some degree of 'synchronization' with the client's attachment pattern, even when it is insecure – this section describes how to gradually adjust this approach in situations where the client's insecure pattern becomes a problem for treatment.

The focus is not on treatment-related efforts towards a change of the client's attachment pattern – this will be discussed in Chapter 9. This section, however, deals with strategic challenging of and 'complementing' clients' attachment patterns in the context of treatment efforts where the focus may be on other psychological problems, on somatic illnesses and problems, or on different forms of counselling. As mentioned in Chapter 2, there are both theoretical arguments and some empirical evidence for the advantages of treatment providers gradually pulling clients in a direction that 'corrects' their insecure attachment patterns; for example, by being slightly more focused on emotions with an avoidant client or slightly more reserved with an ambivalent client (Bernier and Dozier, 2002, Daly and Mallinckrodt, 2009, Mallinckrodt, 2010, Tyrrell et al., 1999).

Challenging clients' preferred relationship pattern ideally requires a previously established good and secure contact between client and treatment provider. Furthermore, it is important to constantly be aware of the client's response and adjust intervention accordingly so that the client is challenged in some areas, but not to such an extent that it becomes threatening or frustrating. When treatment providers who work with insecurely attached clients experience an urge to challenge or 'adjust' their clients' relational style, there is always the risk that this urge is based on their own frustration of interacting with the clients rather than an actual treatment-based necessity. Thus, it will be helpful to discuss such assessments with colleagues or a supervisor. It is important to always keep the treatment's goal in mind: if one considers it relevant to challenge a client's attachment pattern, how does this serve the general aim of the treatment? And how does this correspond with the risk of the client abandoning treatment or becoming less cooperative?

All treatment work is necessarily related to ethical considerations and obligations. If treatment providers strive to 'correct' elements of a client's attachment pattern, they take on additional responsibility for, and commitment to, the client. Some of the seemingly unconstructive reaction patterns that characterize insecurely attached clients were originally established as ways of protecting themselves from emotional pain while maximizing the feeling of security. If one challenges these reaction patterns, it is important to minimize the risk of repeating the painful experience that originally caused the 'construction' of the insecure attachment patterns. It is, for example, important not to encourage the avoidant client to express his feelings more openly and then cut him off when he does so, or to work to win the disorganized client's trust and subsequently fail this trust.

Avoidant attachment: engaging and fostering emotional connection

In many treatment contexts, avoidant clients' inclination to downplay their own suffering and to refrain from communicating difficulties and discomfort to others can be quite problematic and perhaps even risky. When treating an illness such as diabetes, for example, it is exceedingly important that the client takes a number of danger signals seriously and acts pertinently to these rather than shrugging them off as 'no big deal'. The inclination to constantly 'have one foot out the door' because of the discomfort associated with needing to seek help can also be a disadvantage in many forms of treatment, where a certain engagement on the client's behalf is conducive to the final outcome. For these reasons – even though it may initially cause discomfort for the avoidant client – it may be relevant to direct and maintain the client's attention to the actual suffering or threats inherent in the situation and to insist that the client commits to the treatment.

It is often relevant to explicitly discuss a client's engagement, possibly by clarifying how the client's reluctance affects treatment (Wallin, 2007). It is important not to do this in a reproachful manner, for example, saying, "You really have to invest more in this treatment, if anything is to come from it," as this will likely come across as criticism. It would be more helpful to express understanding for the client's ambivalence or reservations against getting involved, while gently pointing out that this attitude may be disadvantageous in the long run. One might for example say, "My impression is that you struggle to believe that this treatment can help you, and that you are holding yourself back a little – is this true?" This will constitute a starting point for talking about the mixed emotions and for discussing the degree of investment necessary from the client. Obviously, the key to the client's engagement is a desire for recovery or for overcoming the difficulties that made treatment necessary in the first place. So even if the client prefers not to dwell on his problems, it can be necessary to remind him about them (Muller, 2010). In this context it may be important to thoroughly explore what *the client* experiences as a problem. It is extremely difficult to engage an avoidant client in a treatment primarily aimed at treating something that the treatment provider and others consider a problem, but which the client does not find problematic.

Avoidant clients can be especially disinclined to verbalize their own feelings or to pay attention to them in general. However, feelings contain important information – for example, about whether one's personal boundaries were overstepped, or whether one has been too hard on oneself – which is why treatment providers may in some situations wish to bring clients into better contact with their feelings (Slade, 2008). This may entail paying attention to the avoidant client's non-verbal signals. The client may not express in words that she is experiencing difficulties, but she may sigh and look despondent. The treatment provider can then inquire into what the sigh expresses. It is important to be aware that this can be very hard for the avoidant client to verbalize – he or she may not necessarily have a ready answer. Rather than insisting on clients putting their emotions into words with the risk that they may feel inadequate in this respect, treatment providers can instead offer a range of possible suggestions, which the clients can refer to and 'try on' while getting into closer contact with their feelings. Of course, it is important to avoid attributing emotions to clients that they do not feel, and to remain open and inquiring.

Another way of helping clients to become more aware of their own emotional reactions could be to describe how other people have experienced and reacted to similar situations, or even what your personal reaction or experience would be, so the clients can 'mirror' themselves in these descriptions and consider how their reactions resemble or deviate from these. One can also point out the occasional discrepancy between the avoidant client's narration and the accompanying expressions of emotion. For example, "You tell me that you are so busy at work that you are unable to sleep and forget which day it is, and then you laugh. But part of you does not find this funny and feels differently about this – is that not so?" The purpose of such interventions will be to bring the client into closer contact with his or her subjectively experienced suffering, where it is necessary to further the client's engagement in the treatment (Muller, 2010).

Ambivalent attachment: regulation and facilitating perspective

Whereas the avoidant client can be hard to engage, this will usually not be a problem where ambivalent clients are concerned. However, the ambivalent client's emotional hyperactivation and the narrative chaos, which makes it hard to make head or tail of the problems, can prove challenging in the treatment process. Research indicates that, although ambivalent clients are emotionally engaged in treatment, they may struggle to comply with the framework or boundaries of the treatment – for example, to accept timeframes or live up to the guidelines for exercises, medicine intake, etc. (Dozier, 1990, Mallinckrodt et al., 1995). In the long term, this can be subversive to many treatment efforts.

Part of a constructive challenge for the ambivalent attachment pattern will be to establish clear guidelines and agreements regarding treatment. As mentioned in relation to considerations concerning initial treatment alliances with ambivalent clients, it may prove helpful to avoid being too rigid regarding structure and guidelines at first, as this can hinder the establishment of good contact with the ambivalent client. However, once contact has been established, there is room for gradually insisting on clearer guidelines (Daly and Mallinckrodt, 2009). Of course, this could usefully be accompanied by spending time explaining to the client what the purpose of a given rule or framework is, so that the client can see its connection to the general treatment goal and does not simply feel rejected.

The ambivalent client's emotional reactivity and 'drama' can often 'derail' treatment – partly because it draws the treatment provider's as well as the client's attention toward the interpersonal and emotional aspects of the treatment relationship. In many treatment contexts this means that attention is removed from the treatment's focus. If treatment providers are to constitute a correcting influence to the 'dramatizing' tendency of ambivalent clients, it is important that they do not inadvertently give the client more attention and care when he or she engages in dramatic emotional displays. This will merely support the sense that it is necessary to complain loudly in order to be heard. Instead the effort should be to meet the client with a tempered acknowledgment of his or her strong feelings, while at the same time turning mutual attention back to clarification of or working with the treatment's actual focus. The treatment provider needs to help the client 'down-regulate' emotional reactions (Slade, 2008, Wallin, 2007).

Whereas the avoidant client may have particular difficulties with verbalizing emotional reactions, the ambivalent client struggles to create a more generalized, abstract overview or assessment of situations and relationships. The multitude of detached fragments of different narratives unconnected by an explicit common thread can create much confusion in dialogue with the treatment provider. For treatment providers it may be helpful to gradually contribute to 'structuring' the narrative; for example, by stopping the client and asking, "How does what you are telling me now relate to what you were talking about before?" (Holmes, 2001). Just as one can offer the avoidant client possible formulations of emotional reactions, one can also offer the ambivalent client possible interpretations or general assessments that he or she can consider. If these are expressed too authoritatively, there is a significant risk that the ambivalent client will simply embrace these 'undigested'. Therefore it is important to be tentative and signal that as a treatment provider you cannot know how aspects of the client's story are related, but that you have some possible, helpful ideas.

As ambivalent clients can be inclined to lean on treatment providers and let them carry the responsibility for the treatment process and outcome, it may be wise and relevant to work on increasing the clients' ability to act independently and their ownership of the process. This is especially important if one hopes to initiate a process that clients will subsequently have to continue on their own. In these cases ambivalent clients are especially at risk of, for instance, following a certain diet as long as they are in continuous contact with the treatment provider, only to give up quickly when the relationship to the treatment provider no longer holds them to it. It may be wise to point out when clients contribute positively to the treatment, explicating the difference it makes, and in other ways emphasizing the client's agency in treatment.

Disorganized attachment: organizing and offering 'safe zones'

In treatment work with disorganized clients, past traumatic incidents and the associated reactions can easily impede the treatment process because they 'swallow' the client's attention and energy and subvert the establishment of a trustful bond to the treatment provider (Korfmacher et al., 1997, Reis and Grenyer, 2004, Wallin, 2007). Few treatment forms will provide the necessary framework for actually working with the client's traumatic experiences. Even in treatments with potential space for working with traumatic experiences – especially in different forms of psychotherapy – there is a dilemma of the degree to which one should work 'through' or 'around' traumatic experiences. An example is in work with parents whose relationship to their children is threatened. In such cases it may be more constructive to work on a present-oriented action plan, rather than begin to discuss the parents' traumatic stories, which could lead to a worsening of their condition and thus also their immediate ability to serve as adequate caregivers (Moran et al., 2008). It can thus be relevant to make an effort to 'encapsulate' the traumatic experience rather than automatically assuming that it will help to put it into words. In treatment work with people who have been traumatized, one needs to be constantly alert to the risk of re-traumatization.

The disorganized client's tendency to dissociate can be problematic in many treatment contexts, because the client who dissociates can in some sense fall outside the treatment provider's 'reach' and stop taking in information (Hesse and van Ijzendoorn, 1999, Liotti, 2011). It can therefore be important to counteract this tendency by helping the client to become more 'present', draw some deep breaths, feel his or her body, etc. It is necessary to understand, however, that becoming more present is related to an increased experience of anxiety for the disorganized client. Therefore, it is important to help the client regulate this fear. One way of doing this can be to support the client in establishing 'safe zones', that is, mental 'places' where the client can seek refuge when something becomes too overwhelming. In some sense this is what disorganized clients do when they dissociate – only, in that case, it simply happens automatically without the client necessarily registering that it happens or what it was a reaction to.

With the client, you can thus help formulating images or sensations that the client connects to an experience of security, and help the client activate these images when anxiety threatens to take over. A client who struggles to focus on a current treatment because of a history of violent abuse in childhood may perhaps find peace in the image of being in a beautiful garden, and the treatment provider can help the client to clarify this image whenever the client needs 'breathing space'. In experimental attachment research, a number of studies of 'security priming' have been conducted, in which experimentally induced activation of representations of security-providing attachment figures was shown to partially counteract the unfortunate effects of insecure attachment patterns, at least momentarily (Mikulincer and Shaver, 2007). Thus, there is indication that activation of images that clients themselves connect with experienced security may contribute to 'creating coherence' and 'regulating' the client so that he or she is better able to collaborate with the treatment provider.

A challenge when treating disorganized clients is that activation of the attachment system causes the client's mentalization to collapse – the clients cease to relate reflexively to their own and others' thoughts, feelings and intentions (Jurist and Meehan, 2009, Liotti, 2011). When the client stops mentalizing, this can give rise to destructive and unhelpful interaction with the treatment provider, where the client for example instinctively acts as if the treatment provider is out to get him. An important effort to make when treating disorganized clients is therefore to support clients' mentalization. One of the means to achieve this can be to be explicit and 'transparent' about one's experience of the interaction with a client. It is important to express assumptions about the client's state of mind as 'guesses' and connect them to specific actions that gave rise to the impression. For example, "When you yell at me like that, I get the sense that you are angry or afraid, and perhaps think that I don't understand you – is that correct?" In mentalization-based therapy, which will be described in more depth in Chapter 9, a number of guidelines for how to engage in such exchanges have been developed. These guidelines may also be inspiring and applicable for treatment providers who work in other fields of practice (Bateman and Fonagy, 2003, Fonagy and Bateman, 2006).

If disorganized clients defend themselves against attachment system activation by letting a different behavioural system lead in the contact and appear aggressively competitive, inappropriately caring, or perhaps flirtatious, treatment providers may feel it necessary to curb this interaction for their own sake, for the sake of the treatment, or both. In that case it will also be important for treatment providers to take a mentalizing stance and, for example, refrain from competing with the client but rather comment on the interaction and clarify the roles and guidelines required by the treatment (Diamond et al., 2008, Liotti, 2011).

Selecting treatment form and strategy

In many contexts, the type of treatment will be predefined and the only way of taking clients' attachment patterns into account will therefore be by adjusting the treatment provider's relational 'style' as described in the previous sections. However, in some cases treatment providers or treatment institutions will have more possible treatment forms to choose from in relation to a given client. As a therapist, you may be able to offer both cognitive behavioural therapy and existential psychotherapy. In some treatment environments, clients can be referred to extra 'modules' in addition to the general treatment. In some psychiatric settings, for example, clients can also be referred to individual psychotherapy or music therapy in addition to psychopharmacological treatment and milieu therapy. Of course, there are many other considerations than attachment and attachment patterns involved when choosing a treatment form, including clients' wishes and commitment, practical considerations, etc. Nevertheless, clients' attachment patterns may be one of the factors involved in such an assessment.

Research into the degree of 'match' between clients' attachment patterns and different treatment forms is still limited, and most studies in this area focus on the effect of different forms of psychotherapy. In general, the evidence indicates that clients with secure attachment patterns are the clients who best benefit from most forms of psychotherapy (Levy et al., 2011). It is likely that this is related to a greater ability and readiness to establish a constructive treatment alliance (Bernecker et al., 2014, Diener and Monroe, 2011, Smith et al., 2010), and that this tendency can also be generalized to many other treatment forms. However, it would be absurd to conclude that because of this psychotherapy should only be offered to securely attached clients, as insecure clients will often have a greater need for help. Therefore, the question as to whether particular treatment forms are 'more suited' to clients with particular insecure attachment patterns is extremely pertinent (Daniel, 2006). The next chapter will focus on treatment where part of the goal is to change clients' insecure attachment towards being more secure. Here the focus is rather on the result of treatment, where change of attachment is not part of the goal; this could both be somatic treatment, but also psychological treatment aimed at other issues or at more delimited problems such as phobias or alcohol abuse.

Although the available evidence is sparse, there is some indication that clients with avoidant attachment patterns reach better results in cognitive behavioural therapy compared to more relationship-oriented therapy, for instance, psychodynamic therapy (McBride et al., 2006, Tasca et al., 2006). Cognitive behavioural therapy is characterized by being a highly structured treatment form focused on observable symptoms, and by being a rather 'rational' process in which clients are involved as 'co-examiners/researchers' when mapping and fighting unwanted symptoms. It makes sense that this treatment style matches avoidant attachment relatively well – it operates within the avoidant client's comfort zone and draws on some of the avoidant client's strengths. It will likely be easier for the avoidant client to engage in treatment forms that are relatively structured and 'rational' and where client and treatment provider can focus on clearly defined tasks, such as practising being in public in the treatment of agoraphobia, rather than focusing on the client–treatment provider relationship or the avoidant client's emotional life.

With regard to ambivalent attachment, a single study indicates that clients with ambivalent features gain more from relationship-oriented treatment forms that devote more time to discussing the relationship to others and feelings in this connection (Tasca et al., 2006). This point is especially relevant in relation to psychological treatment, but it also surpasses this. Whereas avoidant clients may be satisfied with being helped to help themselves, ambivalent clients will prefer and probably benefit more from a more extensive contact with a treatment provider, who can support the client actively. Left to their own devices, ambivalent clients can easily become overwhelmed by feelings of helplessness. Whereas clients with avoidant attachment are likely to be tolerant to courses of treatments where treatment providers vary, ambivalent clients will be more sensitive to such changes. Ambivalent clients seek a more personal and emotional relationship with treatment providers and can therefore easily become unsettled by and frustrated over changes along the way.

Disorganized attachment is related to the poorest prognosis in several treatment contexts (Cyranowski et al., 2002, Reis and Grenyer, 2004), which should certainly not be used as a reason for not providing treatment, but does serve as a call for realism with regard to treatment goals and for the possible relevance of devoting extra resources and time. The Italian psychiatrist Giovanni Liotti, who has worked extensively with disorganized attachment, has argued that when working with disorganized clients it may prove especially relevant to compose a team of two or more treatment providers who collaborate on treatment (Liotti, 2011), in order to better contain and endure the disorganized client's at times violent and destructive manner of behaving in treatment relationships. However, he also points out that this requires good coordination and communication between treatment providers.

References

Bateman, A. W. & Fonagy, P. 2003. The development of an attachment-based treatment program for borderline personality disorder. *Bulletin of the Menninger Clinic*, 67, 187–211.

Bernecker, S. L., Levy, K. N. & Ellison, W. D. 2014. A meta-analysis of the relation between patient adult attachment style and the working alliance. *Psychotherapy Research*, 24(1), 12–24.

Bernier, A. & Dozier, M. 2002. The client–counselor match and the corrective emotional experience: Evidence from interpersonal and attachment research. *Psychotherapy: Theory, Research, Practice, Training*, 39, 32–43.

Cyranowski, J. M., Bookwala, J., Feske, U., Houck, P., Pilkonis, P., Kostelnik, B. & Frank, E. 2002. Adult attachment profiles, interpersonal difficulties, and response to interpersonal psychotherapy in women with recurrent major depression. *Journal of Social and Clinical Psychology*, 21, 191–217.

Daly, K. D. & Mallinckrodt, B. 2009. Experienced therapists' approach to psychotherapy for adults with attachment avoidance or attachment anxiety. *Journal of Counseling Psychology*, 56, 549–563.

Daniel, S. I. F. 2006. Adult attachment patterns and individual psychotherapy: A review. *Clinical Psychology Review*, 26, 968–984.

Diamond, D., Yeomans, F. E., Clarkin, J. F., Levy, K. N. & Kernberg, O. F. 2008. The reciprocal impact of attachment and transference-focused psychotherapy with borderline patients. In Steele, H. & Steele, M. (eds) *Clinical applications of the Adult Attachment Interview*. New York: Guilford Press.

Diener, M. J. & Monroe, J. M. 2011. The relationship between adult attachment style and therapeutic alliance in individual psychotherapy: A meta-analytic review. *Psychotherapy*, 48, 237–248.

Dozier, M. 1990. Attachment organization and treatment use for adults with serious psychopathological disorders. *Development and Psychopathology*, 2, 47–60.

Dozier, M., Lomax, L., Tyrrell, C. L. & Lee, S. W. 2001. The challenge of treatment for clients with dismissing states of mind. *Attachment & Human Development*, 3, 62–76.

Fonagy, P. & Bateman, A. W. 2006. Mechanisms of change in mentalization-based treatment of BPD. *Journal of Clinical Psychology*, 62, 411–430.

Hesse, E. & van Ijzendoorn, M. H. 1999. Propensities towards absorption are related to lapses in the monitoring of reasoning or discourse during the Adult Attachment Interview. *Attachment & Human Development*, 1, 67–91.

Holmes, J. 2001. *The search for the secure base. Attachment theory and psychotherapy*. London: Brunner-Routledge.

Horvath, A. O. & Bedi, R. P. 2002. The alliance. In Norcross, J. C. (ed.) *Psychotherapy relationships that work: Therapist contributions and responsiveness to patients*. London: Oxford University Press.

Jurist, E. L. & Meehan, K. B. 2009. Attachment, mentalization, and reflective functioning. In Obegi, J. H. & Berant, E. (eds) *Attachment theory and research in clinical work with adults*. New York: Guilford Press.

Korfmacher, J., Adam, E., Ogawa, J. & Egeland, B. 1997. Adult attachment: Implications for the therapeutic process in a home visitation intervention. *Applied Developmental Science*, 1, 43–52.

Levy, K. N., Ellison, W. D., Scott, L. N. & Bernecker, S. L. 2011. Attachment style. *Journal of Clinical Psychology*, 67, 193–201.

Liotti, G. 2011. Attachment disorganization and the clinical dialogue: Theme and variations. In Solomon, J. & George, C. (eds) *Disorganized attachment and caregiving*. New York: Guilford Press.

Lopez, F. G. 2009. Clinical correlates of adult attachment organization. In Obegi, J. H. & Berant, E. (eds.) *Attachment theory and research in clinical work with adults*. New York: Guilford Press.

Lyons-Ruth, K. & Jacobvitz, D. 2008. Attachment disorganization: Genetic factors, parenting contexts, and developmental transformation from infancy to adulthood. In Cassidy, J. & Shaver, P. (eds.) *Handbook of attachment: Theory, research, and clinical applications*, 2nd ed. New York: Guilford Press.

Lyons-Ruth, K., Melnick, S., Bronfman, E., Sherry, S. & Llanas, L. 2004. Hostile–helpless relational models and disorganized attachment patterns between parents and their young children: Review of research and implications for clinical work. In Atkinson, L. & Goldberg, S. (eds) *Attachment issues in psychopathology and intervention*. London: Lawrence Erlbaum.

McBride, C., Atkinson, L., Quilty, L. C. & Bagby, R. M. 2006. Attachment as moderator of treatment outcome in major depression: A randomized control trial of interpersonal psychotherapy versus cognitive behavior therapy. *Journal of Consulting & Clinical Psychology*, 74, 1041–1054.

Mallinckrodt, B. 2010. The psychotherapy relationship as attachment: Evidence and implications. *Journal of Social and Personal Relationships*, 27, 262–270.

Mallinckrodt, B., Daly, K. & Wang, C. C. D. 2009. An attachment approach to adult psychotherapy. In Obegi, J. H. & Berant, E. (eds.) *Attachment theory and research in clinical work with adults*. New York: Guilford Press.

Mallinckrodt, B., Gantt, D. L. & Coble, H. M. 1995. Attachment patterns in the psychotherapy relationship: Development of the Client Attachment to Therapist Scale. *Journal of Counseling Psychology*, 42, 307–317.

Martin, D. J., Garske, J. P. & Davis, M. K. 2000. Relation of the therapeutic alliance with outcome and other variables: A meta-analytic review. *Journal of Consulting and Clinical Psychology*, 68, 438–450.

Mikulincer, M. & Shaver, P. R. 2007. Boosting attachment security to promote mental health, prosocial values, and inter-group tolerance. *Psychological Inquiry*, 18, 139–156.

Moran, G., Bailey, H. N., Gleason, K., DeOliveira, C. A. & Pederson, D. R. 2008. Exploring the mind behind unresolved attachment: Lessons from and for attachment-based interventions with infants and their traumatized mothers. In Steele, H. & Steele, M. (eds) *Clinical applications of the Adult Attachment Interview*. New York: Guilford Press.

Muller, R. T. 2010. *Trauma and the avoidant client. Attachment-based strategies for healing*. New York, W. W. Norton & Company.

Reis, S. & Grenyer, B. F. S. 2004. Fearful attachment, working alliance and treatment response for individuals with major depression. *Clinical Psychology and Psychotherapy*, 11, 414–424.

Slade, A. 2008. The implications of attachment theory and research for adult psychotherapy: Research and clinical perspectives. In Cassidy, J. & Shaver, P. (eds) *Handbook of attachment: Theory, research, and clinical applications*, 2nd ed. New York: Guilford Press.

Smith, A. E. M., Msetfi, R. M. & Golding, L. 2010. Client self rated adult attachment patterns and the therapeutic alliance: A systematic review. *Clinical Psychology Review*, 30, 326–337.

Tasca, G. A., Ritchie, K., Conrad, G., Balfour, L., Gayton, J., Lybanon, V. & Bissada, H. 2006. Attachment scales predict outcome in a randomized controlled trial of two group therapies for binge eating disorder: An aptitude by treatment interaction. *Psychotherapy Research*, 16, 106–121.

Tolmacz, R. 2009. Transference and attachment. In Obegi, J. H. & Berant, E. (eds) *Attachment theory and research in clinical work with adults*. New York: Guilford Press.

Tyrrell, C. L., Dozier, M., Teague, G. B. & Fallot, R. D. 1999. Effective treatment relationships for persons with serious psychiatric disorders: The importance of attachment states of mind. *Journal of Consulting and Clinical Psychology*, 67, 725–733.

Wallin, D. J. 2007. *Attachment in psychotherapy*. New York: Guilford Press.

Wilkinson, S. R. 2003. *Coping and complaining. Attachment and the language of disease*. New York: Brunner-Routledge.

Chapter 9

Attachment patterns as the focus of treatment

In most treatment work, clients' attachment patterns constitute a background factor; although they can be taken into consideration when planning treatment, they will not form the treatment focus. However, there are treatment contexts where attachment patterns are either part of, or perhaps even the essence of, what treatment attempts to change. This encompasses psychotherapeutic or milieu therapeutic work that is aimed at changing the client's way of behaving in close relationships, or alleviating mental illnesses or problems intimately connected to the client's attachment history.

Much has been written about preventive and therapeutic work aimed at supporting secure attachment in children, and a number of well-validated treatment systems have been developed for this (Berlin et al., 2008). As the focus of this book is adult attachment and adult attachment patterns, this literature will not be discussed here. Generally, however, research in this area indicates that relatively brief, focused interventions primarily aimed at changing parents' behaviour towards their child can be effective in paving the way towards secure attachment in the child (Bakermans-Kranenburg et al., 2005). These interventions do not necessarily affect the parents' attachment patterns. However, family therapy may work to change parents' attachment patterns, and this will be treated later in this chapter.

The relationship between attachment patterns and mental illness is the object of much empirical research and theoretical discussion and, since this relationship has implications for the relevance of a therapeutic effort to change clients' attachment patterns, this chapter's first section will focus on this. The second section will discuss what a change of attachment patterns entails, what is actually being changed, and what such a change requires. Finally, the chapter's third and last section deals with changing clients' attachment patterns through different specific treatment modalities: individual psychotherapy, couples and family therapy, and milieu and group therapy.

Attachment patterns and psychopathology

Already in the original formulation of attachment theory, Bowlby (1973, 1980) connected insecure and traumatic attachment experiences with the later development of mental disorders. For instance, he emphasized the relationship between the loss of a caregiver in childhood and later depression. A number of Bowlby's descriptions of associations between attachment experiences and later mental disorders have, with time, been supported by systematic research in the area (Dozier et al., 2008). Part of the early research in the area was based on hypotheses about the connection between specific disorders and specific insecure patterns; for example, between anorexia and avoidant attachment, or between borderline personality disorders and ambivalent attachment. However, with increased research a somewhat more complex picture has emerged.

Attachment patterns and specific psychological disorders

Taking attachment research's identification of qualitatively different attachment patterns in children and adults as their starting point, researchers have recently devoted much attention to the relationship between attachment patterns and psychopathology, including whether different mental disorders are systematically connected to specific attachment patterns. Theory as well as data indicate that people with mental disorders are more likely to have insecure attachment patterns than people without mental disorders (Adam, 1994, Bakermans-Kranenburg and van Ijzendoorn, 2009, Dozier et al., 2008, Mickelson et al., 1997, Riggs et al., 2007). As mentioned in Chapter 1, very few of the existing studies have followed people over a longer period of time, which would make it possible to conclude that insecure attachment is part of the background for developing mental disorders and not the other way round. Most studies in the area are cross-sectional, that is, studies where attachment patterns and the presence of mental disorders are assessed at the same point in time. This means that in principle no conclusion can be drawn about the causal connection. Insecure attachment can be part of the background for a mental disorder, but it could just as well be the current mental disorder that makes attachment appear insecure and, finally, it may be that a mutually intensifying interaction exists between mental disorder and insecure attachment.

Theoretical arguments have been put forward for internalizing disorders – that is, disorders where the person focuses inwards on difficulties and negative emotions, such as anxiety disorders and depression – being especially connected with hyperactivating/ambivalent patterns. In contrast, externalizing disorders – that is, disorders where the person reacts externally with problem behaviour such as drug abuse or antisocial tendencies – are claimed to be especially connected with deactivating/avoidant patterns (Dozier et al., 1999). An analysis of the first 10,000 AAI results reported in research supports this hypothesis to some degree (Bakermans-Kranenburg and van Ijzendoorn, 2009). Nevertheless, the results are marked by some contradictory findings, and for most psychiatric diagnoses or categories there is no unequivocal connection to specific forms of insecure attachment.

Most categories of mental disorder employed by official diagnostic systems are quite compounded and can cover a range of clinical behaviour, also with regard to interpersonal dimensions. For example, some people with a major depression will appear antagonistic and self-critical, while others will appear plaintive and 'cling' to other people (Blatt and Zuroff, 1992). Many mental disorders are also characterized by frequent comorbidity – that is, they often appear in conjunction with other mental disorders. For example, people with anorexia often suffer from depression too, and many people with personality disorders meet the criteria for several different personality disorders at once (Clark, 2007, Santos et al., 2007). It is therefore not surprising that research into the association between attachment patterns and specific diagnoses rarely arrives at simple and unequivocal results.

Although it is unlikely that there are any mental disorders from which it is possible to infer a given insecure attachment pattern solely on the basis of the diagnostic category, there are still groups where one or several patterns are over-represented. One of the most empirically substantiated connections is between dissociative disorders and disorganized attachment (Liotti, 1999, Riggs et al., 2007). Avoidant and disorganized attachment are overrepresented among clients suffering from schizophrenia (MacBeth et al., 2011, Tyrrell et al., 1999), while borderline personality disorder is more marked by ambivalent and disorganized attachment (Barone, 2003, Fonagy et al., 1996, Patrick et al., 1994). With regard to disorders that are significantly more widespread among the general population, such as anxiety or unipolar depression, the picture is more complex and, compared to more severe diagnostic categories, a higher percentage of clients suffering from these disorders also have secure attachment patterns (Dozier et al., 2008).

Attachment as a general risk factor or 'buffer'

By now it should be clear that research in the area does not support a simple or linear picture of the relationship between attachment patterns and mental disorders, but rather a picture of attachment as being one amongst many factors significant to the development of mental disorders. Longitudinal studies, where the same people are followed for a longer period of time, indicate that insecure attachment constitutes a general risk factor for a number of later mental disorders and problems, whereas secure attachment constitutes a resource or a 'buffer' protecting against later problems (Mikulincer and Shaver, 2007a, Thompson, 2008). However, neither is capable of explaining the presence or absence of mental disorders, but must be seen in connection with other risk factors and protective factors; for example, genetic factors, socioeconomic conditions, life events, other relationships, etc. Bowlby (1973) himself used the metaphor of 'branching railway lines' to describe a developmental understanding in which several tracks could lead to the same destination, and where what began as the same track could end up branching out in several tracks going in different directions. This picture corresponds well to the empirical findings in the research area today encapsulated by the heading 'developmental psychopathology' (Rutter and Sroufe, 2000).

Insecure attachment does not constitute psychopathology in either children or adults, and cannot reasonably be described as 'deviant' or 'abnormal' when considering that up to half of all people without particular clinical or socioeconomic challenges are assessed as being insecurely attached. Having said that, there are still indications that, when compared to secure attachment, insecure attachment patterns can be related to considerable suffering for the people themselves and/or their close relations, just as insecure attachment can, in some cases, stand in the way of people developing and expanding their potential in many aspects of life (Mikulincer and Shaver, 2007a). In therapeutic contexts it can therefore prove relevant to work directly or indirectly with clients' insecure attachment patterns, with the overall goal of increasing well-being, improving relationships and preventing future mental disorder (Mallinckrodt et al., 2009).

With regard to therapeutic treatment of already present mental disorder, working with attachment patterns can also play a role and, perhaps in some cases, contribute to an alleviation of suffering (Levy et al., 2006a, 2006b). Research in the area is still relatively limited. Among other things, it is unclear whether, and how, alleviation of mental disorders and symptoms such as anxiety or depression are related to changes in attachment patterns. Theoretically, it is possible to imagine that, although insecure attachment may initially be part of the background for developing an anxiety disorder, other factors will maintain the anxiety once it has developed, which is why a change in a client's attachment pattern may not in itself lead to an improvement of the symptoms of anxiety. In the same way, it is perfectly possible to achieve therapeutic improvement of different psychiatric symptoms, without this necessarily requiring therapeutic work with attachment inclinations. Thus, psychotherapeutic work does not always entail work with attachment patterns, nor will therapeutic work with attachment and attachment patterns always lead to symptom-related improvement. There is a great need for more research into change mechanisms in psychotherapy to shed further light on how, and to which degree, attachment-related and symptom-related changes are connected in different treatment forms. However, the rest of this chapter will focus on efforts to change attachment patterns as a goal in itself to increase well-being and to ensure better and more satisfying relationships.

Psychotherapeutic change of attachment patterns

The traditional theoretical image of attachment patterns as stable mental structures with firm roots in childhood calls for the question of whether changing attachment patterns through psychotherapy is indeed possible. The short answer is "Yes." However, there is reason to reflect more on this question – partly because there is reason to elaborate the empirical substantiation of this conclusion, partly because the scope of this change is not yet clear, and partly because it is worth examining which role the client–therapist relationship plays in this context.

Can attachment patterns be changed through psychotherapy?

As attachment patterns are deep-seated mental structures which have developed over a long period of time in adult clients, a number of authors are sceptical as to whether these can be changed – at least, through anything other than years of therapeutic treatment (Eagle and Wolitzky, 2009). However, empirical research indicates that attachment patterns are both more complex and more malleable than traditionally assumed. The image of attachment patterns as something 'etched' into a person from his or her second or third year of life is thus a view on the decline. The relatively few studies assessing clients' attachment patterns before and after individual psychotherapy suggest that it is possible to change clients' attachment patterns towards a more secure style, also through shorter treatment forms (Berant and Obegi, 2009, Daniel, 2006).

The empirical studies of change in attachment patterns have focused on a variety of treatment forms in relation to different client groups and have employed different methods for measuring clients' attachment patterns. Fonagy and his colleagues were the first to document an increased prevalence of secure attachment measured with the AAI after a year's intensive psychodynamic treatment of a mixed group of psychiatric patients at Cassel Hospital in London (Fonagy et al., 1995). Since then, other studies have shown a reduction of insecure attachment measured with the AAI after a year's transference-focused therapy for borderline personality disorder (Levy et al., 2006b), and after a 16-session treatment of post-traumatic stress disorder (Stovall-McClough and Cloitre, 2003). Other studies have shown a reduction of attachment-related avoidance and/or anxiety measured with questionnaires after intensive dynamic short-term treatment for interpersonal problems (Travis et al., 2001), after 16–20 sessions of interpersonal therapy or cognitive behavioural therapy for depression (McBride et al., 2006), after cognitive behavioural group therapy or psychodynamic-interpersonal group therapy for binge-eating disorder (Tasca et al., 2007), and after 3–18 weeks of inpatient group psychotherapy for a mixed patient group (Kirchmann et al., 2011).

Common to several of these studies is the absence of a 'matched' untreated control group and very high occurrences of insecure attachment prior to treatment. This means that caution is advisable with regard to the interpretation of the results (Kirchmann et al., 2011). As discussed in Chapter 7, attachment patterns are not completely stable in the general population, so some degree of change would be expected in any group followed over time. As clients participating in these studies were generally insecure prior to treatment, they could really only change in the direction of increased security, although changes between different insecure categories also occur. Without an untreated control group, it is not possible to conclude with any certainty how much of this change would have occurred naturally, and how much of this change can be ascribed to the therapy. However, in Levy and colleagues' study, transference-focused psychotherapy was compared to two other forms of therapy that did not result in a corresponding increase in the percentage of secure clients, which supports the idea that something special in the process of transference-focused therapy contributed to the change (Levy et al., 2006b). The study by Kirchmann and colleagues included an untreated control group, so in that case the change in attachment may be attributed to the treatment received.

It is important to consider how suitable the existing methods for assessment of attachment patterns are for repeated measurement as part of studies of therapeutic outcome. With regard to the AAI, it is certainly possible that when being asked the same interview questions a second time, they no longer have the same ability to 'surprise the unconscious' that according to Hesse (2008) is an important part of the function of the interview. Clients may subsequently have considered the questions further and developed new and potentially more coherent narratives with which to respond to them. The question is, then, to which degree this corresponds to actual change in attachment patterns and to which degree this is a 'training artefact' that does not reflect a comprehensive change in behaviour in close relationships (Eagle, 2006). This consideration also calls for a closer examination of what a change in attachment patterns actually entails.

What does a change in attachment patterns entail?

The current sparse data does allow for a tentative conclusion that psychotherapeutic treatment can move insecure attachment towards a greater degree of security, without this necessarily requiring long-term treatment. However, the specific details of this change are less clear. Which therapeutic elements have this effect, are some treatment forms better 'geared' towards working with clients' attachment patterns than others, and what is the 'scope' of attachment-related change?

Bowlby (1988) himself wrote about revision of the 'internal working models' as a goal for therapeutic treatment. However, he was not particularly elaborate in his description of how such a change might take place and what it requires from therapy and from the therapist. Generally, he pointed to two elements in psychotherapy that could support revision of insecure attachment patterns: 1) clients gain insight into their own automatic assumptions and behaviour, and 2) clients have new and different experiences in relation to therapists. Bowlby suggested that when clients in therapy discuss their experiences of close interpersonal relationships, it will be possible to identify recurring, maladaptive patterns and connect these to the experiences in clients' attachment histories, in which they are rooted. In this way, a client with, for example, an avoidant attachment pattern may become aware of his inclination to suppress anger and sadness, understand how this reaction originally made sense in relation to his dismissive parents, and simultaneously acknowledge how this reaction is inappropriate in the current relationship to his partner. Bowlby furthermore pointed out that clients will be inclined to relate to the therapist in correspondence with their insecure attachment patterns – what is termed 'transference' in psychodynamic therapy (McWilliams, 2004) – which enables the therapist to point this out to the client and, furthermore, to react in ways that do not confirm the client's expectations of, for example, being rejected, but rather offer new and more constructive relational possibilities. Gradually such experiences in the interaction with the therapist can lead to a revision of existing working models. The client may, for example, learn that openness about one's vulnerability does not necessarily lead to rejection and ridicule, but can bring about understanding and care.

A long-standing discussion in the psychotherapy literature is to which degree therapeutic change is a result of insight into one's own reaction patterns and to which degree change is the result of new and different relational experiences – and different forms of therapy emphasize these mechanisms differently (Stern, 1998, Stern et al., 1998). It is likely that both mechanisms are in play in relation to revision of attachment patterns, but that they affect different 'components' of the internal working models. Attachment patterns and internal working models are complex entities consisting of feelings, thoughts, motives and action strategies, which furthermore range from general tendencies to relationship-specific patterns (Cobb and Davila, 2009, Collins et al., 2004). Different therapeutic techniques aim towards changing different components of the internal working models; some of these components may generally be more available to therapeutic intervention than others, and some may take longer to change than others (Eagle and Wolitzky, 2009).

One question regarding revision of internal working models is thus which role cognitive, emotional, and behavioural changes play respectively. Bowlby himself focused on the cognitive or thought-related components and emphasized the importance of understanding one's own interpersonal patterns and their developmental background and of revising expectations based on insecure attachment relationships. Change will thus, for example, occur when an ambivalent client acknowledges that his expectations that people are unreliable is based on his experiences with a unpredictable mother, and that there is no reason to assume that this will be true of all people with whom he forms a relationship.

However, later attachment theoretical literature has increasingly focused on the importance of feelings and emotion regulation in the conceptualization of the difference between secure and insecure attachment and thus also in descriptions of what a change of internal working models entails (Mikulincer et al., 2003). More experience and emotion-oriented therapeutic work will, for example, attempt to make an avoidant client more aware of and comfortable with his own emotional reactions or help an ambivalent client regulate the panic that arises when she fears her boyfriend will leave her. Finally, therapeutic work can also intervene on a practical level where the client is 'coached' in behaving in new ways in close relationships – for example, the aforementioned ambivalent woman could be supported in not acting on her fear by checking her boyfriend's email, going through his wardrobe, and cross-examining him about his hourly movements, but instead share her anxiety and vulnerability with him and perhaps invite him to couples therapy.

As thoughts, feelings, and actions related to close interpersonal relationships are interconnected, it is very likely that a change in one or more of these components will automatically lead to changes in the others (Cobb and Davila, 2009). New ways of behaving lead to new relational experiences, which will bring about other thoughts and feelings. New ways of understanding relationships can lead to new feelings and new actions. Access to other feelings or a better regulation of emotions opens the door to new possible actions and new ways of creating meaning. To a certain extent the path you choose to follow can therefore be a question of individual 'taste' – both the therapist's and the client's. Nevertheless, therapy that is attentive to and targeted towards working with all three domains will have a better chance of consolidating changes in a client's attachment patterns, as it will always require a certain effort to 'translate', for example, a cognitive insight into its action-related implications.

Other important questions regarding change in attachment patterns concern the importance of conscious and unconscious processes as well as the relationship between changes in relationship-specific models and more generalized models. A more cognitive 'path' to change especially emphasizes the conscious, explicit revision of assumptions and expectations, but it is an open question to which degree a more rational acknowledgment – for example, that not all people are unreliable or that there is no reasonable basis for concluding that you are worth less than others – is actually capable of changing the more implicit automatic ascription of meaning that causes problems in the close relationships (Lyons-Ruth, 1998). Likewise, it is unclear to which degree work with thoughts, feelings, and actions in relation to specific attachment relationships affects the more generalized working models, as well as whether efforts to influence more generalized assumptions and action patterns really influence clients' ways of interacting in specific current and future attachment relationships (Cobb and Davila, 2009). In both cases, it is likely that there is a certain 'resistance' to changes on one level spreading further through the system, but in the end it is a question that must also be addressed through research, which in turn can contribute to guiding therapists' approach to working with attachment-related changes.

Even if clients give more coherent narratives in the AAI or answer "Yes" to more security-based statements in an attachment questionnaire after having been in therapy, it is far from certain that this corresponds to a complete 'revolution' in their internal working models (Eagle and Wolitzky, 2009). There may still be relationships or contexts where insecure strategies are prevalent, or there may be unconscious, automatized processes that remain unchanged. However, psychotherapy may of course be directed at more limited goals and not aim towards a complete change of the client's attachment, but rather towards a change in the client's 'trajectory'. This may contribute to starting processes in the client's life which in the long term will lead to more thorough attachment-related change; for example, through change in the client's close personal relationships. Changes in clients' attachment patterns do not necessarily have to occur within the boundaries of therapy – the therapy can instead facilitate a change which will not become clear until later and in other contexts.

Obviously change of attachment patterns seems more demanding and challenging when thinking in categorical rather than dimensional terms. If internal working models are believed to be singular, categorical entities founded through a lifetime of attachment relationship experiences, it can be difficult to see how 16 hours of psychotherapy would be able to change these. However, if one instead – as it is argued in Chapter 7 – considers attachment patterns as complex, multiple, and distributed on a continuum, it may be easier to see how gaining a new understanding of one's own reactions, practising new relational behavioural patterns, getting into contact with underlying feelings, or experiencing that more caring and appreciative relationships are possible, can 'shift' the balance of the entire system, so that security-based models become more accessible in a wider range of situations and relationships (Cobb and Davila, 2009, Mikulincer and Shaver, 2007b). Shifts in attachment patterns thus do not become a question of 'all or nothing', but of degrees and accessibility. At the same time, shifts in attachment patterns do not necessarily occur once and for all, at an identifiable moment in time, but rather as a continuous process that can be 'uneven' and move back and forth.

Clinical observations and some research results indicate that a process of change from an insecure to a more secure attachment pattern may imply a phase in which attachment appears more chaotic and disorganized than was the case at the treatment's start (Daniel, 2006, Diamond et al., 2003). A client with avoidant attachment who begins to express strong feelings of anger and sorrow may, for example, shift chaotically between a more deactivating and more hyperactivating position for a period of time and will thus appear to be disorganized. However, this can be a step on the way to a gradual integration of more deactivating and hyperactivating tendencies, which gradually settle somewhere 'in the middle' in a more balanced position (Crittenden and Landini, 2011).

What role does the therapeutic relationship play?

Although some forms of therapy, such as cognitive behaviour therapy, emphasize the obtaining of rational insight and implementation of new behavioural patterns, all authors concerned with change of interpersonal patterns – including attachment patterns – agree that the relationship to the therapist plays a significant role in the context. As described in Chapter 8, an important part of any treatment relationship is establishing a constructive alliance between treatment provider and client. In that context, the therapists' ability to adjust their initial contact with clients in accordance with clients' attachment patterns plays a role. When the goal of treatment is to change insecure attachment patterns, part of the therapist's task will unavoidably be to gradually adjust therapeutic contact to enable the formation and activation of more security-based internal working models (Mallinckrodt, 2010). The considerations regarding constructively challenging clients' insecure attachment patterns, which were examined in Chapter 8, are therefore especially relevant here.

As mentioned in Chapter 2, Bowlby (1988) believed the therapist's role was to serve as a secure base for clients' exploration of their own psychology and relationships to others. With regard to efforts towards changing insecure attachment patterns, this is slightly paradoxical, as insecure attachment patterns are inherently characterized by difficulties in establishing and depending on a secure base. If therapists, for example, work with a client whose attachment is marked by disorganization, they cannot simply step in and serve as a secure base – the most significant part of the therapeutic work may in fact be to establish a therapeutic relationship in which it is possible for the client to depend on the therapist (Eagle and Wolitzky, 2009).

It can thus be argued that the more clients' attachment is marked by insecurity, the greater the importance of therapeutic 'relationship work' becomes; that is, the effort to create a good and safe contact to the client, which enables a common examination of thoughts, feelings, and behavioural patterns in relation to attachment (Farber and Metzger, 2009). This does not necessarily entail a sequential process in which one first secures the relationship and then goes on with therapeutic work. In practice, these processes go hand in hand, but the conditions for the rest of the therapeutic work will improve as progress is made in the relationship work. Research indicates that the more a client's relationship to the therapist resembles a secure attachment relationship, the less 'ruptured' the therapeutic dialogue is, and the more the client is ready to examine his or her thoughts, feelings, and actions (Mallinckrodt et al., 2005). Secure attachment to the therapist is thus conducive to therapeutic work.

Ruptures in the therapeutic interaction can also be termed 'alliance ruptures' (Safran et al., 2002). A rupture in the alliance may be when a client feels misunderstood by the therapist and stays away from the next session, when a client experiences the therapeutic 'space' as insecure and stays quiet, or when a client scolds the therapist for not being interested in helping but only interested in, for example, remuneration. Alliance ruptures are situations where either the therapeutic bond or the agreement about the treatment's tasks and goals are threatened. Sometimes ruptures can be obvious to both parties and at other times they can be more obscured, for example, when the client is not able to express his or her lack of trust in the therapist. Safran and Muran (2000) distinguish between what they term 'withdrawal ruptures', where clients pull away from therapeutic contact, and 'confrontation ruptures', where clients openly express dissatisfaction. There is reason to expect that both types of alliance ruptures are frequent when working with clients with insecure attachment patterns, and that withdrawal may be particularly related to avoidant patterns while confrontation is more likely in relation to ambivalent patterns.

Central to the relationship work with insecure clients is the effort to 'repair' the alliance ruptures that will inevitably arise. In many ways, this corresponds to the role that caregivers play in the relational exchanges with infants that in time lead to establishing secure attachment bonds (Beebe et al., 2010; Marvin et al., 2002). The relationship to an infant is never characterized by complete harmony, but will often be marked by situations where child and caregivers are not 'in sync' with each other, and where the child is insecure or over- or under-stimulated. Caregivers who provide security provide it exactly by virtue of their ability to register these mismatches when they occur and to adapt their care according to the child's needs until harmony is re-established. Through this, children learn to expect that uncomfortable emotional conditions or relational 'misunderstandings' will be helped and repaired, which in time forms part of the background for children's ability to calm themselves when feeling anxious or uncomfortable (Fonagy et al., 2002). Just as it is unlikely that completely 'rupture-free' relationships between children and caregivers are possible or desirable, ruptures in a treatment alliance are not necessarily a bad thing in psychotherapy for insecurely attached clients, as long as the therapist is capable of repairing contact and preventing a collapse of therapy.

In the attachment literature it has been discussed whether a change of clients' attachment patterns requires clients to establish an actual attachment relationship to the therapist (Farber and Metzger, 2009, Obegi, 2008). The empirical studies that showed changes in clients' attachment patterns following relatively short-term therapy indicate that this is not necessarily the case. At the same time, the literature suggests that client–therapist relationships resembling secure attachment relationships are generally conducive to the therapeutic process and likely to therapy outcome as well. It may be that a more complete reorganization of clients' insecure attachment patterns requires a form of relational process where clients, in one or more specific relationships, experience attachment-related interactions that 'contradict' the insecure internal working models (Mallinckrodt, 2010). This 'work' need not necessarily take place in the therapeutic relationship. Therapy literature can at times be blind to the existence of other significant relationships in the client's life; a new romantic relationship or changes in existing relationships may, for example, play a greater role in the consolidation of attachment-related experience. Experiences in relationship to the therapist can be important in initiating such changes and, for clients lacking close relationships, the relationship to the therapist can play an especially important role.

Working with attachment in different forms of therapy

While attachment theory has long primarily influenced the developmental psychological field, recent decades have seen a tremendous growth in the interest in attachment and attachment theory in psychotherapeutic theory and practice. There is no actual 'attachment therapy' for adults – that is, an adult psychotherapy method which is solely informed by attachment theory and research (Slade, 2008). However, several therapeutic schools have, to a certain degree, integrated attachment-theoretical concepts in their work, and many more eclectic practitioners draw on attachment-theoretical thinking in their work. Some more recent therapy methods, including 'mentalization-based therapy' (Bateman and Fonagy, 2003), have solid roots in attachment theory and research.

The following three sections will focus on how different specific therapeutic methods and modalities relate to the work of changing clients' attachment patterns. This may take place within the framework of individual psychotherapy or through therapeutic work with current attachment relationships in the context of couples and family therapy. Finally, much recent work has addressed changing clients' attachment patterns through group therapy and milieu therapy.

Individual psychotherapy

In the context of individual psychotherapy, the interest in attachment and attachment patterns has been especially prominent within psychodynamic therapies, where theories about the roots of mental disorders in the relationship to childhood caregivers are already prevalent, and where the therapeutic goal is usually a more comprehensive change in personality and relationships rather than just overcoming isolated symptoms such as phobias or eating disorders (McWilliams, 2004). Bowlby was psychoanalytically trained, but partly formulated attachment theory in opposition to certain psychoanalytical ideas, just as he deviated somewhat from the therapeutic practice in which he was trained. For example, he worked with children and their parents rather than just with child clients in individual analysis. This theoretical and practical confrontation led to some animosity between attachment theory and psychoanalysis (Fonagy, 1999). However, in recent decades this has changed, with a gradual approximation occurring between psychodynamic therapy and attachment theory.

Main and colleagues' AAI method and the growing research into representational aspects of attachment have contributed to the increased interest in attachment theory and research among psychodynamic practitioners. Thus, several psychodynamic authors have suggested that the AAI can serve as a 'measure' for some of the elements of personality, which psychoanalysis and psychodynamic psychotherapies traditionally aim towards changing (Gullestad, 2003, Steele et al., 2009).

Many of the authors from psychoanalytical or psychodynamic therapy traditions, who have begun to include attachment theory and terminology in their work, focus on the unconscious or implicit aspects of the internal working models and how these are changed through new relational experiences in interaction with the therapist. This, for example, applies to Karlen Lyons-Ruth (1998, 1999), who has written about the change of 'implicit relational knowing' through the therapeutic process, and David Wallin (2007), who has written a book in which attachment theory is integrated with relational psychoanalysis. There are also schools within newer dynamic short-term therapy that integrate attachment theoretical points; for example, Diana Fosha's 'Accelerated Experiential-Dynamic Psychotherapy (AEDP)' (Fosha, 2001). Common to these forms of therapy is the idea that a client's relational problems and other symptoms are closely connected to an insecure attachment history, and that the primary source of change is the relationship to the therapist – including the more 'non-verbal' part of the interaction.

The English psychiatrist Jeremy Holmes is among those who have written most about attachment and attachment patterns in the context of psychodynamic therapy (Holmes, 1997, 1999, 2001, 2009). Holmes especially focuses on the narrative components of the interaction between client and therapist and argues that clients with different insecure attachment patterns have different narrative problems, which therapy profitably can focus on. He thus describes therapy with avoidant clients as a question of 'breaking' barren and rigid stories, therapy with ambivalent clients as a question of 'creating' a coherent organizing story, and therapy with disorganized clients as a question of establishing a narrative framework strong enough to 'contain' the traumatic experience. It is a central assumption that facilitating an 'autobiographical, narrative competence' in clients will also contribute to moving clients towards a more secure attachment pattern (Slade, 2008).

In England, the psychologist Peter Fonagy and the psychiatrist Anthony Bateman have developed the already mentioned 'mentalization-based therapy', which has become widely employed in a short span of time (Allen and Fonagy, 2006, Bateman and Fonagy, 2003, Jurist and Meehan, 2009). Mentalization-based therapy was originally developed for the treatment of serious personality disorders, but has a broader application. A central part of the background for this therapy is the theory of mentalization, which is claimed to have its foundation in secure attachment relationships (Fonagy et al., 2002). In mentalization-based therapy, the therapist strives to increase the client's capacity for mentalization by discussing thoughts and feelings relevant to the current therapeutic interaction. Emphasis is placed on an inquisitive and curious approach, where the therapist is relatively open about his or her own mentalization and 'shortcomings'. In mentalization-based treatment for borderline personality disorder, both individual and group therapy is involved.

Although the majority of the literature about attachment theory's implications for individual psychotherapy is written within psychodynamic traditions, there are also authors from other therapeutic schools who have included attachment-theoretical thinking. Attachment theory has many parallels with interpersonal theory, which is focused on how relational experiences result in interpersonal styles that can be more or less problematic (Bernier and Dozier, 2002, Ravitz et al., 2008). Interpersonal therapy aims at making clients more aware of how they behave in interpersonal interaction and how they, to some degree, maintain problematic interaction patterns through their behaviour (Florsheim and McArthur, 2009). Attachment theory has gradually become integrated in several forms of interpersonal therapy, including 'Interpersonal Psychotherapy (IPT)' (Ravitz et al., 2008, Weissman et al., 2000) and Lorna Smith Benjamin's 'Interpersonal Reconstructive Therapy (IRT)' (Benjamin, 2003). Both these forms of therapy focus on loosening the 'grip' that old insecure relationship patterns have on clients to make room for security-based ways of relating.

Although attachment theory's great focus on the consequences of childhood experiences differs from the focus on current thought patterns and symptoms that is generally found within cognitive behavioural therapy, there is a certain kinship between attachment theory and cognitive theory. Thus Bowlby (1969, 1973, 1980) referred much to the growing body of knowledge on cognitive information processing when formulating attachment theory. Attachment theory resembles cognitive theory due to its focus on cognitive 'models' that shape people's interpretations of their interaction with others – although internal working models are more complex structures than the cognitive schemas, which are the focus of much cognitive behaviour therapy (McBride and Atkinson, 2009).

Some newer developments in the field of cognitive behaviour therapy include an increased focus on emotions and emotion regulation and on the interpersonal roots of cognitive schemas, which has paved the way for a greater degree of dialogue with attachment theory and research. Thus, inspiration from attachment theory can be found in Marsha Linehan's 'Dialectical Behaviour Therapy' for borderline personality disorder (Linehan, 1993) and in Jeffrey Young's 'Schema Therapy' (Young et al., 2003). Attachment theory also forms an important part of the theoretical foundation for Paul Gilbert's 'Compassion-Focused Therapy' (Gilbert, 2009). These therapies are all considered part of the 'third wave' of cognitive behavioural therapies, in which a focus on acceptance rather than on 'disproving' cognitive errors plays an important part. Thus, a central mechanism of change is believed to be the development of an accepting understanding and compassion towards attachment-related pain – which could be described as facilitating the ability to function as a secure base and safe haven for oneself.

All in all, the tendency seems to be that interest in attachment theory and research is spreading within psychotherapy theory and practice and that attachment terminology in some respects begins to serve as a common 'language' in more integrative therapies. This also entails that theory and terminology become somewhat less precise, since the effort towards integration leads to the concepts being used in new ways to cover meanings that only partially overlap – each therapeutic school has its own interpretation of attachment theoretical concepts and points. There is a potential for fruitful mutual exchange, but also for a degree of conceptual confusion in the current therapeutic 'embrace' of attachment theory and research.

Family and couples therapy

The majority of the literature about therapeutic change in adult attachment patterns focuses on individual psychotherapy. Many of the discussions and points contained in this literature are also relevant to family and couples therapy. However, there is more at play here, since families and romantic relationships are attachment domains par excellence. Thus, it will often be possible to work with attachment patterns in the context of real, current attachment relationships. Although the evidence in this area is more limited than for individual therapy, there are theoretical reasons to assume that couples and family therapy has an even greater potential for changing attachment patterns, because it is possible to work directly on changing long-term, close relationships which, in themselves, are part of the background for the original and continued development of attachment patterns. In individual therapeutic efforts to change insecure attachment patterns, there will always be a question of 'transferability' – whether a client's newfound way of interacting in therapeutic relationships can be transferred to other relationships. In couples and family therapy, these other relationships are already in focus. However, couples and family relationships can also constitute a 'conservative' influence that contributes to maintaining and supporting clients' insecure attachment patterns in so far as the interaction continues to be marked by lack of care or other negative patterns. Partners or families participating in therapy may prevent some clients from trying out new thoughts, feelings, or other forms of interaction, with which they would be more ready to experiment in individual therapeutic contact.

As mentioned earlier, several intervention programmes aimed at furthering children's secure attachment through working with families do not involve an effort to change parents' attachment patterns. However, there are also therapy programmes that work with parents' attachment patterns and attachment history with a view to improving their relationship with their children (Berlin et al., 2008). Many authors have commented on how pregnancy and emerging parenthood entail a special 'window of opportunity' for working with attachment and revising insecure attachment patterns. Becoming a parent inevitably actualizes one's own attachment history, but can also contribute to a changed perspective on this history and create a motivation for change This is, for example, utilized in 'Child-Parent Psychotherapy (CPP)' developed by Alicia Lieberman and colleagues on the basis of Selma Fraiberg's psychoanalytical 'Infant-Parent Psychotherapy'. In this form of therapy, experiences in parent–child relationships serve as the starting point for examining and processing parents' own attachment history (Lieberman and Pawl, 1993, Toth et al., 2008). The same applies to some long-term home visitation programmes for expectant and new parents, including the 'UCLA Family Development Project' developed by Christopher Heinicke and colleagues (Heinicke and Levine, 2008) as well as Arietta Slade and colleagues' 'Minding the Baby' programme, which especially draws on mentalization theory (Sadler et al., 2008). These treatment forms are all psychodynamically informed to a significant extent.

There is also a group of authors who have worked to integrate attachment theory with systemic family therapy. A central figure in this context is the English family therapist John Byng-Hall (1991, 1999), who worked with Bowlby at the Tavistock Clinic in London. Whereas attachment theory is generally inclined to having a narrow focus on the dyad – be it child–parent relationships or romantic relationships – Byng-Hall focused on the extended family system. He was concerned with what he termed 'family scripts' – a family's common narrative about the available roles and how to behave in the given family. These scripts are also concerned with the way families relate to attachment and to attachment-related exchanges. In this view, family interventions are about re-negotiating these scripts to better support care and open communication and thus more secure attachment patterns. Related ideas can be found in 'Attachment Narrative Therapy (ANT)', as described by the English psychologist Rudi Dallos (Dallos, 2006, Dallos and Vetere, 2009).

The Canadian psychologist Susan Johnson has been a driving force in the development of a variant of 'Emotion-Focused Couple Therapy', with special emphasis on attachment and attachment patterns. According to Johnson (2009), many of the problems that couples struggle with are generally about attachment and about what she calls 'attachment injuries'. Attachment injuries may, for example, concern infidelity or having failed your partner as an attachment figure at a time they desperately needed you. Emotion-focused couple therapy works to increase awareness of negative interaction patterns and the underlying emotional motives that drive each partner's contribution. This is followed by a clarification of the contrast between the underlying emotional motives and the actual effect on the partner and the interaction – a woman, for example, desires greater intimacy with her partner whom she experiences as distant, which makes her criticize him and thus drive him even further away. When the underlying emotions are clearly expressed in the therapeutic dialogue, this paves the way for a new mutual understanding and for negotiating new ways of interacting. An important step can be to facilitate forgiveness for 'attachment injuries'.

Attachment theory and research informs many interventions in couples and family therapy (Johnson and Whiffen, 2003), and there is significant potential for working with attachment patterns in this context. An important question, of which there is limited empirical knowledge, is for whom an individual therapy would be the most promising road to a change in attachment and for whom couples or family therapy would be more effective.

Group psychotherapy and milieu therapy

A rapidly growing literature addresses how attachment affects a group psychotherapeutic context. Some of the literature about attachment and group psychotherapy deals with the way in which clients' attachment patterns influence the climate of the group and to which degree clients' attachment patterns can predict individual outcomes (Harel et al., 2011, Illing et al., 2011, Kirchmann et al., 2011, Mallinckrodt and Chen, 2004, Tasca et al., 2006). Here, results generally resemble the results from individual therapy – secure attachment is conducive to constructive contributions to the group and the group climate, and clients with secure attachment gain more from group psychotherapy, while avoidant clients appear to be harder to engage.

Just as there is no individual 'adult attachment therapy' per se, there is no official 'group attachment therapy', either. However, an increasing number of institutions work with mentalization-based therapy in groups (Karterud and Bateman, 2012) – a treatment form that draws heavily on attachment theory. Although mentalization-based therapy's primary aim is to increase client mentalization level rather than change client attachment patterns, this can, to some extent, be considered two sides of the same coin due to the close connection between secure attachment and mentalization. Mentalization-based group psychotherapy has significant potential for psychiatry, where there are seldom resources to offer individual psychotherapy on a grander scale.

A number of studies have showed a change in clients' attachment patterns after completed group psychotherapy with different client groups and treatment forms (Lawson et al., 2006, Muller and Rosenkranz, 2009, Tasca et al., 2007). There is thus reason to believe that group psychotherapy has potential in the effort to change insecure attachment patterns. Of course, the group psychotherapy context differs from individual therapy in important ways. First, contact to the therapist or therapists is significantly 'diluted', and second, the relationships to other group members play a central role as well. This provides other possibilities for working with attachment patterns, where the possibility of 'mirroring' oneself and getting feedback from other group members with different attachment-related inclinations will likely play an important role (Yalom, 1995). However, there is a need for a deeper understanding of the mechanisms that are at play in group therapeutic work with client attachment patterns, as well as of how therapists can be optimally conducive to attachment-related changes in this context (Page, 2010).

Some of the literature on attachment-related change deals with treatment on psychiatric wards or in treatment institutions that work to set up a 'therapeutic milieu', where part of the treatment package may be group therapy and another part will typically be a consistent relationship to a contact person. Here, a significant question is whether contact persons can and should be attachment figures and, if so, how this may benefit the treatment of adolescents or adults with disorganized, insecure attachment patterns (Schuengel and van Ijzendoorn, 2001). A single study has shown how both young clients' and contact persons' attachment patterns were significant for the clients' use of the contact person as a secure base at a treatment institution (Zegers et al., 2006).

Compared to both individual psychotherapy and couples and family therapy, the literature dealing with attachment theory's relevance to milieu and group psychotherapy, or with change of attachment patterns through these treatment modalities, is limited. Since milieu and group psychotherapy play a big role in many psychiatric treatment contexts where individual psychotherapy is generally only offered to a few, there is a large unclaimed potential here. However, attachment theory's focus on dyads necessitates further theoretical development to better understand how interaction in groups and networks contributes to influencing and shaping attachment patterns.

References

Adam, K. S. 1994. Suicidal behavior and attachment: A developmental model. In Sperling, M. B. & Berman, W. H. (eds) *Attachment in adults: Clinical and developmental perspectives*. New York: Guilford Press.

Allen, J. G. & Fonagy, P. (eds) 2006. *The handbook of mentalization-based treatment*. Chichester: John Wiley & Sons.

Bakermans-Kranenburg, M. J. & van Ijzendoorn, M. H. 2009. The first 10,000 Adult Attachment Interviews: Distributions of adult attachment representations in clinical and non-clinical groups. *Attachment & Human Development*, 11, 223–263.

Bakermans-Kranenburg, M. J., van Ijzendoorn, M. H. & Juffer, F. 2005. Disorganized infant attachment and preventive interventions: A review and meta-analysis. *Infant Mental Health Journal*, 26, 191–216.

Barone, L. 2003. Developmental protective and risk factors in borderline personality disorder: A study using the Adult Attachment Interview. *Attachment and Human Development*, 5, 64–77.

Bateman, A. W. & Fonagy, P. 2003. The development of an attachment-based treatment program for borderline personality disorder. *Bulletin of the Menninger Clinic*, 67, 187–211.

Beebe, B., Jaffe, J., Markese, S., Buck, K., Chen, H., Cohen, P., Bahrick, L., Andrews, H. & Feldstein, S. 2010. The origins of 12-month attachment: A microanalysis of 4-month mother–infant interaction. *Attachment & Human Development*, 12, 6–141.

Benjamin, L. S. 2003. *Interpersonal Reconstructive Therapy: Promoting Change in Nonresponders*. New York: Guilford Press.

Berant, E. & Obegi, J. H. 2009. Attachment-informed psychotherapy research with adults. In Obegi, J. H. & Berant, E. (eds) *Attachment theory and research in clinical work with adults*. New York: Guilford Press.

Berlin, L. J., Zeanah, C. H. & Lieberman, A. F. 2008. Prevention and intervention programs for supporting early attachment security. In Cassidy, J. & Shaver, P. (eds) *Handbook of attachment: Theory, research, and clinical applications*, 2nd ed. New York: Guilford Press.

Bernier, A. & Dozier, M. 2002. The client–counselor match and the corrective emotional experience: Evidence from interpersonal and attachment research. *Psychotherapy: Theory, Research, Practice, Training*, 39, 32–43.

Blatt, S. J. & Zuroff, D. C. 1992. Interpersonal relatedness and self-definition: Two prototypes for depression. *Clinical Psychology Review*, 12, 527–562.

Bowlby, J. 1969. *Attachment and Loss: Vol. 1. Attachment*. London: Pimlico.

Bowlby, J. 1973. *Attachment and Loss: Vol. 2. Separation*. London: Pimlico.

Bowlby, J. 1980. *Attachment and Loss: Vol. 3. Loss*. London: Pimlico.

Bowlby, J. 1988. *A secure base: Clinical applications of attachment theory*. London, Routledge.

Byng Hall, J. 1991. The application of attachment theory to understanding and treatment in family therapy. In Parkes, C. M. & Stevenson-Hinde, J. (eds) *Attachment across the life cycle*. New York: Tavistock/Routledge.

Byng Hall, J. 1999. Creating a coherent story in family therapy. In Roberts, G. & Holmes, J. (eds) *Healing stories: Narrative in psychiatry and psycohtherapy*. London: Oxford University Press.

Clark, L. A. 2007. Assessment and Diagnosis of Personality Disorder: Perennial Issues and an Emerging Reconceptualization. *Annual Review of Psychology*, 58, 227–257.

Cobb, R. J. & Davila, J. 2009. Internal working models and change. In Obegi, J. H. & Berant, E. (eds) *Attachment theory and research in clinical work with adults*. New York: Guilford Press.

Collins, N. L., Guichard, A. C., Ford, M. B. & Feeney, B. C. 2004. Working Models of Attachment: New Developments and Emerging Themes. In Rholes, W. S. & Simpson, J. A. (eds) *Adult attachment: Theory, research, and clinical implications*. New York: Guilford Publications, Inc.

Crittenden, P. M. & Landini, A. 2011. *Assessing adult attachment. A dynamic maturational approach to discourse analysis*. New York: W. W. Norton & Company.

Dallos, R. 2006. *Attachment narrative therapy. Integrating systemic, narrative and attachment approaches*. Maidenhead: Open University Press.

Dallos, R. & Vetere, A. 2009. *Systemic therapy and attachment narratives. Applications in a range of clinical settings*. London: Routledge.

Daniel, S. I. F. 2006. Adult attachment patterns and individual psychotherapy: A review. *Clinical Psychology Review*, 26, 968–984.

Diamond, D., Stovall-McClough, C., Clarkin, J. & Levy, K. N. 2003. Patient–therapist attachment in the treatment of borderline personality disorder. *Bulletin of the Menninger Clinic*, 67, 227–259.

Dozier, M., Stovall-McClough, C. & Albus, K. E. 2008. Attachment and psychopathology in adulthood. In Cassidy, J. & Shaver, P. (eds) *Handbook of attachment: Theory, research, and clinical applications*, 2nd ed. New York: Guilford Press.

Dozier, M., Stovall, K. C. & Albus, K. E. 1999. Attachment and psychopathology in adulthood. In Cassidy, J. & Shaver, P. R. (eds) *Handbook of attachment: Theory, research, and clinical applications*. New York: Guilford Press.

Eagle, M. N. 2006. Attachment, psychotherapy, and assessment: A commentary. *Journal of Consulting & Clinical Psychology*, 74, 1086–1097.

Eagle, M. N. & Wolitzky, D. L. 2009. Adult psychotherapy from the perspectives of attachment theory and psychoanalysis. In Obegi, J. H. & Berant, E. (eds) *Attachment theory and research in clinical work with adults*. New York: Guilford Press.

Farber, B. A. & Metzger, J. A. 2009. The therapist as secure base. In Obegi, J. H. & Berant, E. (eds) *Attachment theory and research in clinical work with adults*. New York: Guilford Press.

Florsheim, P. & McArthur, L. 2009. An interpersonal approach to attachment and change. In Obegi, J. H. & Berant, E. (eds) *Attachment theory and research in clinical work with adults*. New York: Guilford Press.

Fonagy, P. 1999. Psychoanalytic theory from the viewpoint of attachment theory and research. In Cassidy, J. & Shaver, P. R. (eds) *Handbook of attachment: Theory, research, and clinical applications*. New York: Guilford Press.

Fonagy, P., Gergely, G., Jurist, E. L. & Target, M. 2002. *Affect regulation, mentalization, and the development of the self*. New York: Other Press.

Fonagy, P., Leigh, T., Steele, M., Steele, H., Kennedy, R., Mattoon, G., Target, M. & Gerber, A. 1996. The relation of attachment status, psychiatric classification, and response to psychotherapy. *Journal of Consulting and Clinical Psychology*, 64, 22–31.

Fonagy, P., Steele, M., Steele, H., Leigh, T., Kennedy, R., Mattoon, G. & Target, M. 1995. Attachment, the reflective self, and borderline states: The predictive specificity of the Adult Attachment Interview and pathological emotional development. In Goldberg, S. & Muir, R. (eds) *Attachment theory: Social, developmental, and clinical perspectives*. Hillsdale, NJ: Analytic Press.

Fosha, D. 2001. The dyadic regulation of affect. *Journal of Clinical Psychology*, 57, 227–242.

Gilbert, P. 2009. Introducing compassion-focused therapy. *Advances in Psychiatric Treatment*, 15, 199–208.

Gullestad, S. E. 2003. The Adult Attachment Interview and psychoanalytic outcome studies. *International Journal of Psychoanalysis*, 84, 651–668.

Harel, Y., Shechtman, Z. & Cutrona, C. 2011. Individual and group process variables that affect social support in counseling groups. *Group Dynamics: Theory, Research, and Practice*, 15, 297–310.

Heinicke, C. M. & Levine, M. S. 2008. The AAI anticipates the outcome of a relation-based early intervention. In Steele, H. & Steele, M. (eds) *Clinical Applications of the Adult Attachment Interview*. New York: Guilford Press.

Hesse, E. 2008. The Adult Attachment Interview: Protocol, method of analysis, and empirical studies. In Cassidy, J. & Shaver, P. (eds) *Handbook of attachment. Theory, research, and clinical applications*, 2nd ed. New York: Guilford Press.

Holmes, J. 1997. Attachment, autonomy, intimacy: Some clinical implications of attachment theory. *British Journal of Medical Psychology*, 70, 231–248.

Holmes, J. 1999. Defensive and creative uses of narrative in psychotherapy: An attachment perspective. In Roberts, G. & Holmes, J. (eds) *Healing stories: Narrative in psychiatry and psycohtherapy*. London: Oxford University Press.

Holmes, J. 2001. *The search for the secure base. Attachment theory and psychotherapy.* London: Brunner-Routledge.

Holmes, J. 2009. From attachment research to clinical practice: Getting it together. In Obegi, J. H. & Berant, E. (eds) *Attachment theory and research in clinical work with adults.* New York: Guilford Press.

Illing, V., Tasca, G. A., Balfour, L. & Bissada, H. 2011. Attachment dimensions and group climate growth in a sample of women seeking treatment for eating disorders. *Psychiatry: Interpersonal and Biological Processes*, 74, 255–269.

Johnson, S. M. 2009. Attachment theory and emotionally focused therapy for individuals and couples: Perfect partners. In Obegi, J. H. & Berant, E. (eds) *Attachment theory and research in clinical work with adults.* New York: Guilford Press.

Johnson, S. M. & Whiffen, V. E. (eds) 2003. *Attachment processes in couple and family therapy.* New York: Guilford Press.

Jurist, E. L. & Meehan, K. B. 2009. Attachment, mentalization, and reflective functioning. In Obegi, J. H. & Berant, E. (eds) *Attachment theory and research in clinical work with adults.* New York: Guilford Press.

Karterud, S. & Bateman, A. W. 2012. Group therapy techniques. In Bateman, A. W. & Fonagy, P. (eds) *Handbook of mentalizing in mental health practice.* Washington, DC: American Psychiatric Publishing.

Kirchmann, H., Steyer, R., Mayer, A., Joraschky, P., Schreiber-Willnow, K. & Strauss, B. 2011. Effects of adult inpatient group psychotherapy on attachment characteristics: An observational study comparing routine care to an untreated comparison group. *Psychotherapy Research*, 22(1), 95–114.

Lawson, D. M., Barnes, A. D., Madkins, J. P. & François-Lamonte, B. M. 2006. Changes in male partner abuser attachment styles in group treatment. *Psychotherapy: Theory, Research, Practice, Training*, 43, 232–237.

Levy, K. N., Clarkin, J. F., Yeomans, F. E., Scott, L. N., Wasserman, R. H. & Kernberg, O. F. 2006a. The mechanisms of change in the treatment of borderline personality disorder with Transference Focused Psychotherapy. *Journal of Clinical Psychology*, 62, 481–501.

Levy, K. N., Meehan, K. B., Kelly, K. M., Reynoso, J. S., Weber, M., Clarkin, J. F. & Kernberg, O. F. 2006b. Change in attachment patterns and reflective function in a randomized control trial of transference-focused psychotherapy for borderline personality disorder. *Journal of Consulting & Clinical Psychology*, 74, 1027–1040.

Lieberman, A. F. & Pawl, J. H. 1993. Infant–parent psychotherapy. In Zeanah, C. H., Jr (ed.) *Handbook of infant mental health.* New York: Guilford Press.

Linehan, M. M. 1993. *Cognitive-behavioral treatment of borderline personality disorder* New York: Guilford Publications.

Liotti, G. 1999. Disorganization of attachment as a model for understanding dissociative psychopathology. In Solomon, J. & George, C. (eds) *Attachment disorganization.* New York: Guilford Press.

Lyons-Ruth, K. 1998. Implicit relational knowing: Its role in development and psychoanalytic treatment. *Infant Mental Health Journal*, 19, 282–289.

Lyons-Ruth, K. 1999. The two-person unconscious: Intersubjective dialogue, enactive relational representation, and the emergence of new forms of relational organization. *Psychoanalytic Inquiry*, 19, 576–617.

MacBeth, A., Gumley, A., Schwannauer, M. & Fisher, R. 2011. Attachment states of mind, mentalization, and their correlates in a first-episode psychosis sample. *Psychology and Psychotherapy: Theory, Research and Practice*, 84, 42–57.

McBride, C. & Atkinson, L. 2009. Attachment theory and cognitive-behavioral therapy. In Obegi, J. H. & Berant, E. (eds) *Attachment theory and research in clinical work with adults*. New York: Guilford Press.

McBride, C., Atkinson, L., Quilty, L. C. & Bagby, R. M. 2006. Attachment as moderator of treatment outcome in major depression: A randomized control trial of interpersonal psychotherapy versus cognitive behavior therapy. *Journal of Consulting & Clinical Psychology*, 74, 1041–1054.

McWilliams, N. 2004. *Psychoanalytic Psychotherapy: A Practitioner's Guide*. New York: Guilford Press.

Mallinckrodt, B. 2010. The psychotherapy relationship as attachment: Evidence and implications. *Journal of Social and Personal Relationships*, 27, 262–270.

Mallinckrodt, B. & Chen, E. C. 2004. Attachment and interpersonal impact perceptions of group members: A social relations model analysis of transference. *Psychotherapy Research*, 14, 210–230.

Mallinckrodt, B., Daly, K. & Wang, C.-C. D. 2009. An attachment approach to adult psychotherapy. In Obegi, J. H. & Berant, E. (eds) *Attachment theory and research in clinical work with adults*. New York: Guilford Press.

Mallinckrodt, B., Porter, M. J. & Kivlighan, D. M., Jr 2005. Client attachment to therapist, depth of in-session exploration, and object relations in brief psychotherapy. *Psychotherapy: Theory, Research, Practice, Training*, 42, 85–100.

Marvin, R. S., Cooper, G., Hoffman, K. & Powell, B. 2002. The Circle of Security project: Attachment-based intervention with caregiver–pre-school child dyads. *Attachment & Human Development*, 4, 107–124.

Mickleson, K. D., Kessler, R. C. & Shaver, P. R. 1997. Adult attachment in a nationally representative sample. *Journal of Personality and Social Psychology*, 73, 1092–1106.

Mikulincer, M. & Shaver, P. R. 2007a. *Attachment in adulthood: Structure, dynamics, and change*. New York: Guilford Press.

Mikulincer, M. & Shaver, P. R. 2007b. Boosting attachment security to promote mental health, prosocial values, and inter-group tolerance. *Psychological Inquiry*, 18, 139–156.

Mikulincer, M., Shaver, P. R. & Pereg, D. 2003. Attachment theory and affect regulation: The dynamics, development, and cognitive consequences of attachment-related strategies. *Motivation and Emotion*, 27, 77–102.

Muller, R. T. & Rosenkranz, S. E. 2009. Attachment and treatment response among adults in inpatient treatment for posttraumatic stress disorder. *Psychotherapy: Theory, Research, Practice, Training*, 46, 82–96.

Obegi, J. H. 2008. The development of the client–therapist bond through the lens of attachment theory. *Psychotherapy: Theory, Research, Practice, Training*, 45, 431–446.

Page, T. F. 2010. Applications of attachment theory to group interventions: A secure base in adulthood. In Bennett, S. & Nelson, J. K. (eds) *Adult Attachment in Clinical Social Work*. New York: Springer.

Patrick, M., Hobson, R. P., Castle, D., Howard, R. et al. 1994. Personality disorder and the mental representation of early social experience. *Development and Psychopathology*, 6, 375–388.

Ravitz, P., Maunder, R. & McBride, C. 2008. Attachment, contemporary interpersonal theory and IPT: An integration of theoretical, clinical, and empirical perspectives. *Journal of Contemporary Psychotherapy*, 38, 11–21.

Riggs, S. A., Paulson, A., Tunnell, E., Sahl, G., Atkison, H. & Ross, C. A. 2007. Attachment, personality, and psychopathology among adult inpatients: Self-reported romantic attachment style versus Adult Attachment Interview states of mind. *Development and Psychopathology*, 19, 263–291.

Rutter, M. & Sroufe, L. A. 2000. Developmental psychopathology: Concepts and challenges. *Development and Psychopathology*, 12, 265–296.

Sadler, L. S., Slade, A. & Mayes, L. C. 2008. Minding the baby: A mentalization-based parenting program. In Allen, J. G. & Fonagy, P. (eds) *Handbook of Mentalization-Based Treatment*. Chichester, UK: John Wiley.

Safran, J. D. & Muran, J. C. 2000. Resolving therapeutic alliance ruptures: Diversity and integration. *Journal of Clinical Psychology*, 56, 233–243.

Safran, J. D., Muran, J. C., Samstag, L. W. & Stevens, C. 2002. Repairing alliance ruptures. In Norcross, J. C. (ed.) *Psychotherapy relationships that work: Therapist contributions and responsiveness to patients*. London: Oxford University Press.

Santos, M., Richards, S. C. & Bleckley, K. M. 2007. Comorbidity between depression and disordered eating in adolescents. *Eating Behaviors*, 8, 440–449.

Schuengel, C. & van Ijzendoorn, M. H. 2001. Attachment in mental health institutions: A critical review of assumptions, clinical implications, and research strategies. *Attachment and Human Development*, 3, 304–323.

Slade, A. 2008. The implications of attachment theory and research for adult psychotherapy: Research and clinical perspectives. In Cassidy, J. & Shaver, P. (eds) *Handbook of attachment: Theory, research, and clinical applications*, 2nd ed. New York: Guilford Press.

Steele, H., Steele, M. & Murphy, A. 2009. Use of the Adult Attachment Interview to measure process and change in psychotherapy. *Psychotherapy Research*, 19, 633–643.

Stern, D. N. 1998. The process of therapeutic change involving implicit knowledge: Some implications of developmental observations for adult psychotherapy. *Infant Mental Health Journal*, 19, 300–308.

Stern, D. N., Sander, L. W., Nahum, J. P., Harrison, A. M., Lyons-Ruth, K., Morgan, A. C., Bruschweiler Stern, N. & Tronick, E. Z. 1998. Non-interpretive mechanisms in psychoanalytic therapy: The 'something more' than interpretation. *International Journal of Psycho Analysis*, 79, 903–921.

Stovall-McClough, K. C. & Cloitre, M. 2003. Reorganization of unresolved childhood traumatic memories following exposure therapy. *Annals of the New York Academy of Sciences*, 1008, 297–299.

Tasca, G. A., Balfour, L., Ritchie, K. & Bissada, H. 2007. Change in attachment anxiety is associated with improved depression among women with binge eating disorder. *Psychotherapy: Theory, Research, Practice, Training*, 44, 423–433.

Tasca, G. A., Ritchie, K., Conrad, G., Balfour, L., Gayton, J., Lybanon, V. & Bissada, H. 2006. Attachment scales predict outcome in a randomized controlled trial of two group therapies for binge eating disorder: An aptitude by treatment interaction. *Psychotherapy Research*, 16, 106–121.

Thompson, R. A. 2008. Early attachment and later development: Familar questions, new answers. In Cassidy, J. & Shaver, P. (eds) *Handbook of attachment: Theory, research, and clinical applications*, 2nd ed. New York: Guilford Press.

Toth, S. L., Rogosch, F. A. & Cicchetti, D. 2008. Attachment-theory-informed intervention and reflective functioning in depressed mothers. In Steele, H. & Steele, M. (eds) *Clinical applications of the Adult Attachment Interview*. New York: Guilford Press.

Travis, L. A., Bliwise, N. G., Binder, J. L. & Horne Moyer, H. L. 2001. Changes in clients' attachment styles over the course of time-limited dynamic psychotherapy. *Psychotherapy: Theory, Research, Practice, Training*, 38, 149–159.

Tyrrell, C. L., Dozier, M., Teague, G. B. & Fallot, R. D. 1999. Effective treatment relationships for persons with serious psychiatric disorders: The importance of attachment states of mind. *Journal of Consulting and Clinical Psychology*, 67, 725–733.

Wallin, D. J. 2007. *Attachment in psychotherapy*. New York: Guilford Press.

Weissman, M. M., Markowitz, J. C. & Klerman, G. L. 2000. *Comprehensive guide to interpersonal psychotherapy*. New York: Basic Books.

Yalom, I. D. 1995. *The theory and practice of group psychotherapy*, 4th ed. New York: Basic Books.

Young, J. E., Klosko, J. S. & Weishaar, M. E. 2003. *Schema therapy: A practitioner's guide*. New York: Guilford Press.

Zegers, M. A. M., Schuengel, C., van Ijzendoorn, M. H. & Janssens, J. M. A. M. 2006. Attachment representations of institutionalized adolescents and their professional caregivers: Predicting the development of therapeutic relationships. *American Journal of Orthopsychiatry*, 76, 325–334.

Final considerations

The intention with this book has been to describe adult attachment patterns and their relevance for working with adults in different treatment contexts. Taking attachment into consideration is obvious for most treatment providers who work with children, but the theory of adult attachment is not yet widely known in treatment circles. However, as this book hopefully has demonstrated, there is good reason to disseminate knowledge of newer developments in attachment theory and research across a broad range of adult treatment contexts. Attachment theory is an empirically well-substantiated theory, which can supplement and in some cases correct the psychological theories already drawn upon in different forms of treatment.

These years, attachment theory is spreading across psychology and related fields of practice, and for good reason. However, the popularity of attachment theory is sometimes related to a tendency towards stretching it beyond its area of validity and reducing too many aspects of interpersonal relationships into a question of attachment and attachment patterns. Therefore, this book has made a sustained effort to clarify how far the domain of attachment reaches, and where the theory's explanatory power ceases. The aim has been to draw a nuanced picture of what existing theory and research in the area can contribute, including where the limits are of our knowledge at present. Attachment theory does not hold all the answers and, even though attachment is unquestionably an important dimension of human life, there are also other significant areas of life to which attachment theory and research cannot contribute.

A communicative dilemma in this book has been between rendering attachment research intelligible and accessible – not just for psychologists, who may be well versed in the topic already – and at the same time communicating the significant complexity and nuances that increasingly characterize the field. This dilemma has most clearly become manifest in the tension between the categorical understanding of attachment patterns, which eases communication, and a more complex and multidimensional understanding of attachment patterns, which corresponds better to the accumulated empirical evidence. Hopefully, this book has succeeded in communicating both some simplified main features as well as a sense of the area's complexity.

The research area of adult attachment patterns and their treatment implications is in rapid development, and even academic researchers with easy access to the literature may struggle to keep up. Because attachment theory has always been committed to empirical evidence, the study of attachment cannot be accomplished by a canonization of Bowlby's works as theoretical 'dogma', and much of the early attachment literature has since been corrected or expanded. This is both good and creditable, but also troublesome for practitioners who seek the attachment-theoretical position to a given question. This book has strived to aid practitioners in gaining an overview of the field's current knowledge. At the same time, it is important to emphasize that much of what is written in the previous chapters will likely be updated by new research and new practical approaches to working with adult clients and their attachment patterns.

Unfortunately, attachment nomenclature may sometimes be used in a derogative or pathologizing way among people who have acquired this 'language'. In parts of the attachment literature there is a tendency to idealize secure attachment and overly problematize insecure patterns. The ambition of this book has been to communicate understanding and respect, which are necessary conditions for all good treatment work. It is easier to show understanding and respect, even for 'difficult' clients, when leaning on the attachment-theoretical point that all ways of interacting in close relationships – also the ones that are inappropriate or difficult to participate in – have their origin in meaningful reactions to particular relational environments.

Appendix
The Patient Attachment Coding System (PACS)

The PACS (Talia and Miller-Bottome, 2013) is applied to verbatim psychotherapy transcripts or audio recordings, and may be used to classify clients' attachment in one of four main attachment classifications (secure, avoidant, preoccupied, or disorganized), based on any single session of treatment. Coding with the PACS produces both dimensional and categorical data concerning clients' attachment, and this instrument can thus be profitably used in clinical research and assessment. An initial validation study has shown that the classification of clients' in-session discourse with the PACS correlates highly (kappa = .91) with their AAI classification, and that the ratings and classifications yielded by the PACS have high inter-rater reliability (Talia et al., 2014).

While toddlers maintain proximity with their caregivers using physical behaviours, adults regulate emotional proximity mainly using language. The PACS classifies clients' attachment based on discrete linguistic structures and patterns that serve to regulate emotional proximity. The PACS emerged from a qualitative analysis of sessions from a group of clients, who had been independently assessed with the AAI. This analysis showed that clients from each attachment category revealed particular discursive behaviours that seemed to regulate emotional proximity with the therapist in systematically different ways. For example, emotional proximity tends to increase when one asks for help or openly expresses distress – characteristic of secure clients' discourse. In contrast, by minimizing any disclosure of distress or complaining endlessly while ignoring offers of help and support – characteristics of avoidant and preoccupied clients respectively – emotional proximity can be avoided or resisted.

The markers yielded by this analysis were then grouped according to their probable attachment-related function, and matched to three scales devised in analogy with the Strange Situation: *Contact Seeking, Avoidance*, and *Resistance*. The Contact Seeking scale contains discursive behaviours that tend to increase emotional proximity and the likelihood of receiving support from the therapist. The Avoidance scale contains discursive behaviours that tend to decrease emotional proximity. The Resistance scale contains discursive behaviours that tend to thwart the therapist's capacity to provide help and take the place of expression of independent thought or agency. Subsequent analyses led to the addition of a fourth scale, *Exploring*, which contains discursive behaviours that demonstrate autonomy and positive self-efficacy in relation to the therapist, while remaining open to affective connection.

The training for coding with the PACS usually lasts around 30 hours, and may take place in a week or less. A rater is considered reliable when able to code correctly 8 or more sessions in a set of 10. For trained coders, coding a session with the PACS takes approximately one hour. The following is the sequence of steps taken in coding and classifying a transcript:

1   The coder reads the transcript all the way through and notes for the occurrence of any number of markers of attachment behaviour evident in the discourse. Each marker is listed and carefully described in a 40-page rating manual (Talia and Miller-Bottome, 2013). A given marker can be assigned to a single word, a part of a phrase, a phrase, or a passage, as long as the portion of the text meets the criteria specified in the manual.
2   To give a rating to the 12 subscales (*Help, Gratitude, Disclosure, Direct Avoidance, Downplaying, Releasing, Direct Resistance, Involving, Merging, Self-Asserting, Affective Sharing, Autonomous Reflection*), the coder counts the occurrence and intensity of the markers that are specific to each. Each subscale is rated from 1 to 7 in 0.5 increments.
3   The coder rates the four main scales based on the score given to the 12 subscales, which are grouped in threes under the four main scales.
4   Finally, based on the configuration of scores on the four main scales, a classification of either secure, avoidant, preoccupied, or disorganized is given.

In the PACS, *secure* clients are characterized by high scores on the Contact Seeking scale and/or the Exploring scale as they tend to openly express distress, ask for help, show gratitude, and autonomously reflect upon and explore their experience. *Avoidant* clients are characterized by high scores on the Avoidance scale, as they decrease emotional proximity to the therapist by minimizing any disclosure, conveying self-sufficiency by downplaying their distress, and releasing the therapist from providing help. Avoidant clients are further subdivided in a Detached subtype (characterized by high ratings of Downplaying) and a Helpless subtype (characterized by high ratings of Releasing). *Preoccupied* clients are characterized by high scores on the Resistance scale, as they tend to obstruct in various ways the therapist's attempts to intervene. They enlist the therapist's involvement in their point of view, and convey their experience through vague, confounding speech that prevents the expression of independent reflection or agency. Preoccupied clients are further subdivided in a Passive subtype (characterized by a high rating on the Merging scale and substantially low ratings on the Contact Seeking scale) and an Ambivalent type (characterized by a high rating on Involving and Contact Seeking). A *Disorganized* classification is assigned when the client presents with a simultaneous presence of both avoidant and preoccupied markers.

Table A.1 shows the four main scales of the PACS along with brief descriptions of the related subscales. A necessarily concise description of two of the discursive markers associated with each of the subscales is provided, together with an example of the marker taken from an actual psychotherapy session transcript (bold text indicates which passage of the excerpt receives the coding). For more information on the PACS, contact Alessandro Talia: Alessandro.talia@psy.ku.dk

References

Talia, A., Daniel, S. I. F., Miller-Bottome, M., Miccoli, D., Brambilla, D., Safran, J. D. & Lingiardi, V. 2014. AAI predicts patients' in-session interpersonal behavior and discourse: A 'move to the level of the relation' for attachment-informed psychotherapy research. *Attachment & Human Development*, 16, 192–209.
Talia, A. & Miller-Bottome, M. 2013. *The Patient Attachment Coding System: Scoring manual.* Department of Psychology, University of Copenhagen.

Table A.I The Patient Attachment Coding System.

	Subscales	Example of subscale markers	Excerpt of the marker from a transcript
Contact Seeking	*Help*: patient asks for help, directly eliciting closeness	Patient makes a request regarding the therapeutic tasks in terms of his or her needs	P: **Yeah can we talk through a plan. 'Cause this is what I need I think I need a plan.**
		Patient talks explicitly about his or her need for help	P: I keep having this problem at work where I fight with my colleagues all the time. **I really need help.**
	Gratitude: patient shows appreciation for therapist and treatment, which works to maintain closeness	Patient expresses appreciation for the ongoing activities and the objectives set out in therapy	P: **I really like the idea that we're gonna try to understand this**, 'cause it's what blocks me when I'm with other people.
		Patient praises a specific intervention made by the therapist	P: **You know, all last week I have been thinking about what you told me about how I cut off my feelings of anger with him. It was so helpful.**
	Disclosure: patient expresses distress in various ways, implicitly inviting closeness	Patient reports actual distressing emotions (such as anger, sadness, fear) experienced in the here and now	P: And he goes, he tells me this thing, I don't remember, like – that I have to accept him the way he is. He always reasons like that ... **I'm so angry about it.**
		Patient criticizes a significant other, naming flaws that affect the patient emotionally	P: **My father is just self-absorbed. He never asks about me or how I'm doing. It feels like he doesn't even care.**
Avoidance	*Direct Avoidance*: patient directly responds to the therapist's interventions and discourages closeness	After a therapeutic intervention, the patient responds very briefly and then becomes silent for at least several seconds	T: well right, so, so you feel like you need your own space ... you're not ready for the feelings that come with it? P: **yeah [............... 15 sec]**
		The therapist inquires about patient's past or present distressing feelings and in response the patient claims not to be able to answer, or that he or she is not actually distressed	T: What were you feeling when she said that? P: **I don't know ... probably – not anything.**
	Downplaying: patient downplays any implied distress, minimizing any cue for help or support	The patient laughs or chuckles directly after referring to or recounting a negative or emotionally distressing experience	P: – – um – – yeah, I had a horrible trip with my parents **(chuckles)**.
		The patient tries to downplay any negative experience by claiming that what has been expressed is normal or not uncommon	P: Yeah I felt bad when she left, **but it happens to everyone. Just how life goes I guess.**

Releasing: patient conveys self-sufficiency, pre-empting any offers of support and connection	*Patient disqualifies a negative feeling or a disclosure by stating that a) he or she does not have the right to complain, b) that there is no use in complaining, c) he or she has no authority to judge*	P: I don't know. I don't know what to do – – – **I shouldn't even complain, I have all these good things going for me, so …**
	The patient describes or makes reference to a negative experience, then quickly attributes it to a general and/or external cause	P: Last week I met this girl, I sent her a message online, but she never responded. **It's just social media these days. It's so shallow and unreliable.**
Direct Resistance: patient overrides the therapist's activity and responds in ways that are unrelated to the therapist's interventions	*After a therapeutic intervention, the patient stays focused on his or her distress without responding to the therapist's intervention in any way*	T: That's why I think, well I don't know if you feel proud of yourself but I am proud you're dealing with it. You know? Facing it. P: **I don't know what happened, I have no idea what – what is happening inside of me so badly.**
	After a therapeutic intervention, the patient makes an insubstantial contradiction to what the therapist said and without pausing changes topic or perspective	T: It seems like you really worry about what people will think of you. P: **It's not that I worry. It's concern. Concern is the issue. Like my roommate. She is always concerning herself with what she will cook, who to invite, how …**
Involving: patient persuades the therapist into joining and recognizing his or her point of view alone	*Patient quotes someone as having the same opinion that he or she has, 'building the case' for his or her point of view/experience*	P: I mean he has problems with aggression. **Even his mother says that.**
	Patient expresses his or her point of view by speaking as though he or she is talking to another person not present in the room, 'acting' out a feeling by making an unlicensed exclamation	P: And then she just took off without saying anything. Not even a thank you. **I can't! So – selfish! Why do I always have to be the one who supports you?**
Merging: patient conveys his thoughts and feelings, leaving no room for challenge	*Patient discusses an experience by quoting a purportedly past occurrence of thinking to him- or herself*	P: I was like **"maybe I still like him maybe I don't but like that's not a good reason not to be friends. And not to explain to someone"**.
	Patient makes vague statements or references characterized by incomplete, ungrammatical sentences, non-sequiturs, jargon, or other meaningless phrases, making it unclear to the therapist as to what or whom he is speaking about	P: But even then, I have limits, **but that's – that's my only place of you know – self-the self-liberation you know, with, so. But other than that I guess I just am, like she said. And so that is the one that is absolutely essential. You know, that stifles, well in my case, and it stifles – creativity – – which is also necessary.**

Resistance

Table A.1 The Patient Attachment Coding System. (Continued)

Subscales	Example of subscale markers	Excerpt of the marker from a transcript
Self-Asserting: patient definitively states his or her plans and points of view as an independent, self-efficacious agent	The patient states what concrete action he or she will take to cope with an ongoing, internal or interpersonal issue	P: And I didn't get a chance to check in with her before she left. I'll call her tonight. Yes, that's what I'll do.
	Patient states an intention or desire that seems to arise in the here and now regarding a specific interpersonal or internal problem	P: I don't want to burden him with my problems, I want to – I don't want things to change between us. I can take care of these things, it's hard, yeah, but that's what I want.
Affective Sharing: patient discloses positive experiences as an offering to include the therapist in his or her own well-being	The patient describes the positive value of a significant relationship and its contributions to the patient's sense of emotional security	P: It's really like a healthy relationship, we nurture each other but we are not on top of each other. Like we have our own separate lives, but we both bring things into the relationship, um that makes it stronger. I just – I can always go to him and he's just – there. No matter what
	Patient reports an instance of safe haven behaviour, i.e. a behaviour that aims to establish emotional closeness with a significant other in order to relieve distress	P: Yeah I was very upset about it I felt like I had really messed up. But I talked about it with my girlfriend right after and she was so understanding and reassured me a lot. Yeah, so that really made me feel better, like it wasn't just me.
Autonomous Reflective Processes: patient explores his or her own experience, assuming independence from the therapist and authority over the representation of reality	Patient actively constructs his or her own formulation of a significant interpersonal or internal problem, making new conjectures and attributions in the moment	P: I saw him as behaving in an uncaring way. But actually, as I'm thinking about it now, I was very angry with him at the time – because of the way he treated my mother. So perhaps that's why I sort of – viewed him that way.
	The patient discusses his or her own perspective on the dynamics and/or challenges within the therapeutic relationship	P: These last couple weeks I've felt some distance between us, even though I know we've finally established a space where you can give me real feedback on this. I feel like you're wanting me to share and I'm pulling back.

Exploring

Index

Made in the USA
Middletown, DE
12 October 2022

12614511R00106